The
Mystic
Healers

The Mystic Healers

PARIS FLAMMONDE

STEIN AND DAY/*Publishers*/New York

First published in 1974
Copyright ©1974 by Paris Flammonde
Library of Congress Catalog Card No. 73-91856
All rights reserved
Printed in the United States of America
Stein and Day/*Publishers*/Scarborough House, Briarcliff Manor, N.Y. 10510
ISBN 0-8128-1680-3

to
Irwin and Lucille
our miracle healer and his beautiful muse

Acknowledgments

The author wishes to express his appreciation to Mr. Jerry Mangan for his assistance in arranging certain interviews and participating in one; to Dr. Eden Gray for contributing both her astute advice and considerable research material; and to Mr. Hugh Lynn Cayce, president of the Association for Research and Enlightenment, for his corrections of points relating to his father, Edgar Cayce.

Other individuals and organizations deserving his gratitude are: Mr. John Nebel, Anne Pacurar Lombardo, Reverend William V. Rauscher, Sister Mary Justa Smith, Ph.D., and Judith R. Skutch. Dr. Lawrence LeShan, Dr. Andrija Puharich, and countless others have answered his queries or made suggestions. William J. Monaghan of the American Medical Association, and representatives of the American Cancer Society, the Human Dimensions Institute at Buffalo, New York, and the Unity School of Christianity have been most helpful. The Oral Roberts Foundation, the Kathryn Kuhlman Foundation, the Don Stewart Evangelistic Association, the Leroy Jenkins Evangelistic Association, Inc., the United Lodge of Theosophists (New York), Mr. Paul R. Hartman of the Osborn Foundation, and the Billy Hargis Foundation have all supplied data and source works.

Futher, thanks are extended to Mrs. Thomas Sugrue for permission to quote from her late husband's book, *There Is A River*; to Gil Porter and Sherbourne Press for permission to quote from *Faith Healing: God or Fraud?*

Mrs. Elizabeth Kane, chief librarian, Miss Ann Kane, Mrs. Eleanor Nauman, Mrs. Margaret Stabenow, and Mrs. Marie Catudal, associate librarians, all of the Monroe County Library, Stroudsburg, Pennsylvania, as well as many anonymous librarians and other employees at the Forty-second Street Library in New York and its annexes, have been helpful in many ways, which the author here acknowledges.

All has been made much easier and pleasanter than it might have been by the cooperation of his editors, Michaela Hamilton and Brock Baker.

Finally, as always, for more than can be mentioned, he concludes his note of gratitude to Marcia, because of whom more things are possible.

Paris Flammonde
1974

Contents

Heroes are created by popular demand, sometimes out of the scantiest materials. . . .

—Gerald White Johnson
American Heroes and Hero-Worship

A religion which promises either recovery from sickness or the secure preservation of health is certain to have an enormous number of adherents.

—W. H. G. Holmes
Memories of the Supernatural in
East and West

I
Mystical Medicine

The clearing in the forest halfway up the side of the jagged Andes is bright with the glow of the full autumn moon. Floating in the center of the circle of light from the sky, poured from a satellite man will not walk for more than ten millenia, is a prone and motionless figure. From the shadows made by the wall of giant trees even darker silhouettes begin to move in an accelerating swirl. Each head, caught in the mirrored light from space, is masked in carvings of diabolotry. Drumbeats quicken. The human carousel becomes more and more frenetic. . . .

Huge stone doors open with a grating sound, splitting apart the altar of Ishtar, old when even Babylonia was new. A tall figure, radiant in flowing robes, emerges into the white heat of the desert sun. From the golden cradle he thrusts heavenward the deformed body of the infant prince. The chant of slow, ascending notes begins . . .

"When Jesus saw him lying there, and knew that he had been in this state a long time, He said to him, 'Dost thou want to get well?'

"The sick man answered him. 'Sir, I have no one to put me into the [healing] pool . . . while I am coming, another steps down before me.'

"Jesus said to him, 'Rise, take up thy pallet and walk.'

"And at once the man was cured."

"Merlin! Merlin!"

"Sir knight?" inquired the wizened wizard, his head tilting to peer between the concentrically fractured columns of piled manuscripts which appeared to support the gloom-hidden ceiling of his tower retreat.

"This cut upon my hand, which good Gawain gave me in our recent joust, is yet unwell," replied Sir Guy.

"You should have let me treat it at the time," countered the bearded sage, with his usual lack of courtly manners. "Put this salve upon it nightly, thrice, and I will work a thing, or two, whilst thou dost sleep. It will be as ever in a week."

"Your Royal Majesty," continued the simply dressed physician to Marie Antoinette, who had no difficulty understanding his German-accented French, having herself been born an Austrian princess, "the stone is first treated so that it may absorb the magnetic energy, that is, the *gravitas universales*. Then, by holding it against the afflicted portion of the body. . . ."

"Ladies and gentlemen. Step in a little closer. You, sir, would you permit the lovely lady through? This is a unique opportunity nobody should miss, and I will not be tarrying another day. The Kansas twister season gets earlier every year. Now, friends, I offer you a potion to revitalize all men of failing powers and cure varieties of ills that curse the sweeter sex. Why, did I not shun the tossing forth of famous names, I might relate what the recent President Rutherford Birchard Hayes revealed to me of how it . . . but, no, that is a privileged medical confidence.

"Chinese Khan Elixir! That is what I have here. The boon, the balm, the panacea for all pain. Restorer of well-being and bringer of everlasting health. My friends, I guarantee that—ah, yes, two bottles, madam. And you, sir, four. . . ."

"Professors, doctors, gentlemen, welcome to the largest and most progressive city in the world. In fact, I feel safe in saying, all of Britain greets you. As you well know, the subject I will speak on is one familiar to everyone here assembled. Puységur, Charcot, Braid, Ellis, Freud, among a select few, have made major contributions in the field, and now that the Great War is over we may return to our work on hysterical paralysis. The approach and purpose of my new technique is to find the keystone without which the aggravated imagination can no longer support the conviction. . . ."

"Of course it's only aspirin, R. J., but that doesn't stop it from being one of the three top 'pain-killers' on the market. Besides, it doesn't do very much real harm. Since the Orson Welles gag with the Martians, radio is *the* medium. I say we go for another million big ones this year in spots and, maybe, our own show. How about a series about a kindly old doctor who never prescribes anything else?"

"No, Mrs. Hypochondriac, you are much wiser not to take any chances. Remember, these aren't the old horse-and-buggy days. We're going to have men on the moon before this decade's over. Science knows what it's doing. I definitely recommend a hysterectomy. Now, I could get you booked into the hospital within. . . ."

"God is a killer," cries the man on the platform. "He kills the sinners. And he saves! And he heals! Who out there among you has suffered the torments of the unbeliever? Blind, crippled, corrupted with cancer—all of those terrible defects of the flesh have been cured by the Holy Spirit through these hands." The evangelist shouts, shooting his fingers upward as if grabbing for the hand of God (or a hold on the deserted Skylab circling the earth). "Come," he calls, as the lines form and the believers rush forward. "Come and be cured, in the name of Jesus."

The likelihood of longevity is usually measured in terms of health. Anticipation of a lengthy life is an unconscious preparation for immortality. Only a very wise or greatly suffering man would sacrifice the world he knows for one he can only speculate about.

On this greed for eternity has been founded all manner of medicine. Mystic therapy is to be found not only along the margins of medicine, but within the gleaming laboratories and hospitals of the orthodox practitioner.

You lay your cash and conviction on any of a number of altars of assurance; you pay your person and you take your choice.

From the rattling beads of the shaman to the sometimes indiscriminate scalpel of the highest paid of professions, the patient's needs and hopes vary little. Frequently the practices differ only in terms of the costumes, mechanics, and environment. Whatever the technique, from tattooing and crude suturing of claw wounds to rhinoplasty and organ transplants, the fundamental requirement for a successful outcome is *faith*.

There are two kinds of occultism found in healing. The first applies to the purveying of potions and practices founded upon a reasonable degree of fact and logic and encountered in standard hospitals, clinics, and offices of men who have paid for the privilege of affixing one, or more, sets of initials after their names; it presumes to call itself a "science". Such therapy is mysterious only to the patient and may be learned by any individual of common intelligence.

The second order contends that its methods are incomprehensible to both the patient and the practitioner—at least beyond the assurance that they derive from some aspect of the supernatural. This healing is "magical," that is, it is the product of priestly personalities who claim to command impalpable powers lying beyond the abilities of the unanointed.

Therapies rejected by the adherents of the first approach are by virtue of such exclusion members of the second: they constitute the subject of this book.

Regrettably, the demonstrated incompetence, indifference, and avarice of many of those who comprise the personnel of orthodox modern medicine have driven many individuals with conventionally "curable" diseases to other varieties of practitioners. These "wonder-workers" also attract those whom the medical community has forsaken: patients with supposedly incurable afflictions, or with congenital defects.

Not by the hundreds do they come, nor the thousands. Since the dawn of history millions of the sick have crowded to the tent, the auditorium, the chapel, and the shrine. When there is no hope, only miracles suffice. And, most amazingly, they sometimes occur. The "anointed of God," or the "channel to the cosmic energy," or that ridiculous machine spouting colored water actually works! Miraculously, someone seems to have been healed.

There can be no question that many practitioners are either self-deluded or charlatans. Nevertheless, "faith healers" *do* appear to perform extraordinary feats. Several "scientific" explanations for these phenomena are possible: hypnotic power, the reversal of an hysterical condition, spontaneous remission, or the absence of the asserted condition in the first place. But disproving ninety-nine "cures" claimed by a medium or tent evangelist does not disprove the hundredth.

Charismatic healing has been lengthily chronicled, from the dawn of history, through Biblical times, up to the present. Today its influence is perhaps at its height. Not only is it furnishing new therapeutic procedures to a world whose faith in the capacity of orthodox medicine to cure all its ills has been severely shaken, but it is revitalizing that belief in the miraculous, the supernatural, a higher plane of existence, which shrinking membership in orthodox Western congregations suggests is sorely needed, if spirituality in any form is to maintain its hold.

My many years of study have resulted in numerous conclusions and convictions with respect to countless areas of esoterica. Yet this lengthy research notwithstanding, I continue to be amazed at the ubiquitous ignorance regarding a great variety of phenomena, as well as the misuse and false definitions of much of the vocabulary relating thereto, even by alleged experts.

However, ultimately, the evaluation of the specific acts, persons, and subjects hereafter described will be left to the judgment of the reader. Regardless of one's predisposition or conclusions, in the chapters which follow, you will meet the most important of THE MYSTIC HEALERS.

II
The Origin of the "Graveside Manner"

Healing in one form or another is found in most of the myths—Sumerian, Assyro-Babylonian, Egyptian, Judaic, Greek, Roman, Christian—from which ancient and modern religions have arisen, but few examples of deistic doctoring can compare with the efforts of Isis, related in *The Book of the Dead*. After the great god Osiris had been assaulted and dismembered into fourteen separate pieces which were scattered across the earth, Isis went forth, collected all but one (Oxyrhybchic had devoured the immortal phallus and was forever cursed by the Queen of Heaven), reconstituted the body, and restored it to eternal life.

One might have thought this feat of raising the dead was the ultimate form of esoteric therapy. However, in the Old Testament, Ezekiel successfully instructed a valley of bleached bones to come back to life and form an "exceedingly great army."

Another example in the ancient texts is Elisha's raising of supposedly dead children by laying the length of his body upon them. So great were the powers attributed to him that following his own demise the touch of his bones reputedly restored still another corpse to life.

In fact revivification is quite common in the annals of theological and mystical lore. Some instances are well known, such as Jesus and Lazarus; others are less familiar and vary in character, e.g. the report of the alchemist and magician Edward Kelly, associate of John Dee and adviser to Elizabeth I, who called forth the *spirit* of one dead.

All these examples contain the fundamental elements upon

which modern esoteric healing is based—belief or suggestibility on the part of those who are raised up. In fact miraculous *cures* are even more common in the ancient texts.

The New Testament, for example, records countless instances of charismatic healing, not only the several accounts of miracles worked by Christ, but of those of the apostles and others. "They shall lay hands on the sick and they shall recover," reads a passage in St. Mark.

St. Paul, "the fourteenth apostle," was a healer of the ill, as were countless others who preceded him (cf., Matthew, Mark, Luke, John, Acts, Corinthians, etc.).

A legion of subsequent figures (the vast majority popularized and canonized by the Roman Catholic Church) have been credited with such phenomena. St. Patrick was said to have brought the blind to see; St. Bernard also allegedly performed that miracle and also made the lame to walk, the dumb to speak, and the deaf to hear. The saints Hildegarde, Katherine, Margaret, Odilia, and numerous others ministered such marvels as the curing of the martyrs Damianus and Cosmas, the restoration of the Emperor Justinian to well-being, and the freeing of lepers from their dread disease.

However, few people are aware of the lengthy and widespread history of this healing power among secular monarchs and chieftains from the distant past to the recent times.

The emperors Hadrian, Constantine, and Vespasian dispelled the ills of many with their touch (the last produced many of his most remarkable results by the application of his large toe). The monarchs Olaf of Norway, Philip I of France, and England's saintly Edward the Confessor appear to have been among the initial regal healers of their lands. The thirteenth-century English king and his Capetian contemporary Louis IX, another sovereign widely recognized as both royal and religious, constitute excellent bridges between the two sorts of thaumaturgic personalities.

Shortly after this period (1327) Edward III assumed the throne of England to rule and heal his subjects. Although monarchs of the two succeeding royal houses, Lancaster and York, appear to have made but minor contributions to the art of arcane medicine, by the time the first Tudor king, Henry VII, ascended to power (1485) miraculous cures at court had been elevated to a ritual. A century and a half later the ill-fated Charles I (he was to be beheaded in 1649) maintained a sort of patient schedule, offering those who wished to be cured the option of Michaelmas or Easter, with extra days for particularly pathetic cases. According to the contemporary historian Sir James Balfour, the Scottish monarch "heallit 100 persons of the cruelles or kingis eivell [scrofula], young and olde."

Lieges of German lineage, including members of the Hapsburg family, were said to have the power of "laying on of hands."

Socially less exalted was the innkeeper of Royen (Silicia), who was widely reported to have returned more than a thousand individuals to health within a single year. A century earlier a Londoner of shadowy repute named Streeper, and a peasant known as Leveret, had displayed the miraculous gift.

Before the advent of psychoanalysis or even the introduction of the pseudoscientific elements of magnetism, ethericism, effluvia, and the like, esoteric medicine might be generally di-, vided into two major departments: the purely religious and the nonreligious, or alchemical. Miracles might be attributed to either an individual or a location associated with a holy person. Such shrines, at least in Europe, are almost invariably Roman Catholic, and are usually of fairly recent origin, but there are intriguing exceptions: among the most fascinating is the pagan shrine of the Gallic goddess Sequana.

This remarkable archaeological and medical find located twenty-five miles from Dijon, France, and fairly near the source of the Seine, is thought to have been established at least three centuries before the birth of Christ. It consists of a temple and the shrine itself, which survived both the Roman occupation of the land and the Christian fervor which succeeded to it, until it was demolished for an unknown reason by followers of St. Martin in the fourth century A.D.

The original excavation, done shortly after World War II, also revealed a *sacrarium*, featuring a hallowed font carved from stone, near a natural spring still bubbling forth its cool, clean water. Small carvings and sculptures of crippled, deformed, or otherwise diseased individuals were also found—obviously "ex-votos," figurines of supplication and thanksgiving to the goddess Sequana for health sought and received. In addition, others from the Roman and Christian era were found in abundance.

In the late 1950s, two French physicians, Dr. Robert Bernard and Dr. Pierre Vassal, conducted an exhaustive examination of these figurines.[1] Among these ex-votos, most of which explicitly depicted the particular complaint of its contributor, the researchers found a catalogue of medical problems. These included leprosy, blindness, simple mental retardation, cretinism, and incision in the skull, single and double hernias, gout, rheumatism, goiter, and probably infantile paralysis.

The selection of the site and the facilities indicate that the curative technique available was primarily hydrotherapy. Its measure of success—spiritual or practical—would seem to be reflected in the shrine's longevity. The sick kept making the pilgrimage, buoyed up only by the reports of those who had preceded them.

Ironically the same waters that fed those ancient pools flow on, and fewer than five miles beyond the Temple of Sequana is the popular Roman Catholic healing shrine of Billy-des-Fontaines.

Although many healers and most shrines during these centuries were Catholic, there were exceptions. For example, the Jansenist movement of the seventeenth and eighteenth centuries attributed the gift of touch to more than one of its supporters, one of whom, Deacon Paris, (see Carre de Montgeron's *La Vérité des miracles du Diacre Paris*) after his interment in the churchyard of Saint-Medard, became a major attraction to sufferers of paralysis, blindness, deafness, and many other afflictions. While a degree of hysteria is characteristic of most thaumaturgic medicine, in the case of Paris's tomb freneticism was so common and intense as to cause the petitioners to become known as "Convulsionists."

---

[1] *Revue Archéologique de l'Est*, Vol. IX, No. 4. Oct.-Dec. 1958.

Despite the contention of historians that cures did occur, the Church's disapproval of the entire Jansenist doctrine led to the explanation of these restorations to health as the work of the Devil. Obviously equating the power of the Prince of Darkness to heal with that of the Prince of Peace poses complex theological problems which were never answered.

III

The "Scientification" of Mystical Healing

Franz Anton Mesmer, born May 23, 1733, at Iznang, near Konstanz, Baden, Germany, stands in relationship to heterodox medicine much as Freud does to psychoanalysis. He brought an entirely new approach to the field and influenced it enormously, and he remains, notwithstanding schisms within schisms within schisms, the turning point. He initiated the "scientific" element in mystical medicine.

Having embarked on the study of theology at Dillingen and Ingolstadt, this bright, curious student soon was awarded a doctorate in philosophy. Moving on to Vienna, he transferred his attention to the law and completed his education in that discipline. Then, already possessing two doctorates, his interest was captured by medicine, to which he began to devote his efforts. He completed this task with an astrological thesis—*The Influence of the Planets on the Human Body*—and the acquisition of his degree as a physician in 1766.

It was probably in the same year that Mesmer met the healing priest of Bludenz, in Vorarlberg, Father Gassner, who certainly reinforced certain theories already brewing in the young man's mind. Fundamentally, he strongly suspected that the cosmos was permeated by indescribable currents which, while wholly invisible to the "normal" senses, registered upon the essence of the human body and psyche. Mesmer suggested, more than argued, that this unknowable flow, being a universal element, might carry the basic ingredient for human health and, further, that such a desirable and inherently *natural* condition might be achievable by direct contact with the colorless, taste-

21

less, odorless, intangible elixir of space. Modestly, he had not named this constituent of the totality of things after himself—that would be the prerogative of others; he designated it "magnetism."

Many times the German theorist demonstrated his "magnetic" therapy (later recognized as response-inducing suggestion) before dozens of physicians and bodies of "scientific" men, with varying degrees of success. But in the Age of Enlightenment, which *gloried* in its escape from the preceding period of barbarous superstition, his efforts made little initial impression.

Because he posed a problem as difficult to explain as electricity, the ancestor of modern hypnotism had to be dismissed by the "rationalists." Where was the etheric fluid? What was its nature? When was it applicable? How did it function? These questions have found no satisfactory answer to this day, or, more accurately, none of the allegedly more scientifically *refined* queries regarding the phenomenon have been resolved. Little wonder its mystery led to its general rejection two centuries ago.

Nonetheless, Mesmer may with considerable justification be viewed as the first deliberate, systematic, and *somewhat* organized psychotherapist, despite his lifetime of discovering more puzzles than solutions. However, if he bumbled about a good deal in the maze of his scientific intuition, he was not in any sense a man of limited scope. As a friend of the Mozarts, *père et fils*, he provided a small garden theater situated on the grounds of his Salzburg home for the 1773 debut of the fourteen-year-old's first opera, *Bastien and Bastienne*. The warm relationship continued for the remainder of the musical genius's life.

Mesmer also appears to have known Haydn, Beethoven, and Gluck, and played several musical instruments quite well himself.

It was by virtue of his prominent position in Europe's most elegant city that Mesmer was drawn, by circumstance and his innate curiosity, into the pages of history.

Upon being apprised of the improvement in health of a visiting socialite following the application of a simple magnet to the afflicted area—a technique the arcane effectiveness of which had not been doubted since the Middle Ages—he determined to investigate the device's true medical properties. This was not an unexpected course for Mesmer to take in light of his genuine thirst for knowledge, his general fascination with the mysteries lying beyond the curtain of man's ignorance, and his intimation of movement in this direction with his earlier treatise, *De planetarum influx,* which had weighed the effect of the solar planetary system on the human being and described the element he had defined as *gravitas universales.*

Soon Mesmer concluded that two magnets were better than one, and many more effective than a few. After taking to wearing some of the amazing metal as an amulet, he attempted to convey its assumed curative properties to everything in sight, including other elements. From these "experiments" was derived the famous therapeutic tub of "charged" water, tentacled with numerous wires—what today would be regarded as a giant battery. Ultimately, his enthusiastic conviction that he was on to something led him to try and magnetize everything under the sun— except the universe itself, which, of course, he knew was already so blessed.

Suddenly the skepticism of his colleagues no longer mattered, for the Viennese physician woke up just about a year following his magnetic adventure and found himself famous. He was nationally, then multinationally, then continentally, acclaimed as the healer of virtually all identifiable medical disorders—paralysis, gout, liver malfunction, and the like—as well as several more ordinary complaints, such as menstrual discomfort.

Other doctors sought his secret, and he rapidly gained disciples who averred that their results reflected the miraculous ones of the master. He was professionally accepted; his reputation assured. The Augsburg Academy reported, "What Dr. Mesmer has achieved in the way of curing the most diverse maladies leads us to suppose that he has discovered one of nature's mysterious motive energies," and the Bavarian Academy of the Sciences established him as an honored member, announcing, "It is understandable that the activities of so outstanding a personality, who has won fame by special and incontrovertible experiments and whose erudition and discoveries are as unexpected as they are useful, must add luster to our institution."

However, at that moment of triumph a doubter arose, one who realized what the practitioner, his imitators, and admirers, had not—that it was *the man*, not the magnets performing the medical miracles. This doubting Thomas would cause the eclectic intellectual to discard his "philosopher's stone" and all its allied trappings; he would cause the celebrated scholar to be cast out, by those who had so recently sung his praises; he would nearly destroy the man. Yet he also would alter the course of physical medicine, and open the doors to mental therapy, psychology, misguided religions, parapsychology, and numerous other fields. The name of this remarkable iconoclast was—Franz Anton Mesmer, himself.

Mesmer had come to recognize that his good works were his, not medicine's, nor magic's. It was during this period, in 1776, that he encountered Father Gassner, a Catholic priest who practiced charismatic healing after the fashion related in the Bible, i.e. the laying-on-of-hands. How much the magnetist was influenced by the cleric and his approach cannot be determined. It is most likely that it was the confluence of two minds, where ideas flowing from different sources found a common level and commingled. Whatever the process, a letter dated that year declared, "Dr. Mesmer performs most of his cures today, not by the use of the magnet, but merely by directing or indirectly touching the diseased part," which makes it quite clear that the wonder-worker believed in the power of his *magnetic* ministrations for not more than a year.

Yet knowing how unacceptably mad it would sound were he to proclaim that he, and he alone, through some strength he did not even faintly comprehend, healed the sick of many afflictions by no more effort than a word or a gesture, Mesmer faltered before the abyss of the unknown and the self-destroying task of truth. He did not disabuse his colleagues and the public of the myth of magnetism. In an astute bit of pitch-switching, he stopped speaking of physical magnets and palmed in *animal* magnetism: an indefinable, omnipresent quality present in all creatures, and of great curative power—for those who knew the secret of its use. And in this extraordinary compound of inductive brilliance, specific ignorance, essential confusion, slight charlatanry, and other ingredients, "mesmerism"—the ability to introduce and implant suggestion of a mild intensity to near total subjugation—was born.

The physician's newly refined thesis was that health was a condition of being in rhythm with the natural universe, and that a disruption of that harmony created many ills, especially ones disturbing the nervous system. His therapy emphasized either tranquilizing the subject or intensifying the hysteric state until, like a fever, it "broke" and the afflicted individual returned to normal. His successes were many, yet, even as they peaked, underground tremors of professional discontent began to be felt, while on the surface all seemed to be progressing smoothly.

Mesmer had established his own hospital, which prospered, even though he often treated patients for no fee. (Of course, irrespective of the therapy or its quality, this practice has rarely endeared a physician of any kind to the medical profession, let alone a controversial one.)

Maria Theresia Paradies, a talented young pianist whose blind eyes had been examined by the most prominent doctors in and out of the Austrian court, came to Mesmer's hospital. What actually occurred is still in doubt, but two versions have descended to us: first, that Mesmer cured her nearly completely, but temporarily; second, that her sightlessness was uninterrupted by his efforts.

In favor of the latter argument are comments of the disenchanted doctors of the time, plus the fact that Paradies was certainly blind soon after she was forcibly removed from Mesmer's care and treatment by her parents, under pressure from the medical community, the law, and even the Austrian throne itself.

Supporting Mesmer are the physician's own notes and protestations, his hundreds of earlier cures, and a substantial and highly persuasive letter written by the girl's father testifying to her having been made to see and describing in some detail the joys and sorrows she suffered as a result of visual revelation.

All the material available strongly indicates that Maria Theresia was an hysteric whose condition was alleviated by the first Viennese psychotherapist, only to be thrust back into blackness by the traumatic experiences of being emotionally and physically torn from the man who had redesigned her existence. Such a remission would not only have been likely, but probable, assuming the patient had been partially or wholly cured of hysteric blindness, considering the near-certainty of transference in such a case, and then its sudden violation.

Following the scandal of the Paradies affair, Mesmer left Austria, and after a brief period of wandering finally settled in Paris in February 1778. Here the scientific academies rejected him, acting in concert with the medical establishment of Vienna. Despite the ungracious reception of his colleagues, the public, the aristocracy, and even the court—save the king himself —flocked to the German *Wundermann*. He constantly petitioned the scientific societies to observe and evaluate his discoveries but was always rebuffed, denied even the opportunity to display his skills, while ladies-in-waiting to Marie Antoinette, princes, dukes, duchesses, and others of great position, including the Marquis de Lafayette, buoyed him with enthusiastic support. Finally, based upon his popularity, not his genius, a minister to the throne condescended to offer him a sinecure, but there was a reservation. Mesmer rejected an annual stipend of twenty thousand livres rather than produce several disciples as skilled as he in his art.

Having been in the city little more than six months, he departed, moving east once more. But on this occasion his loss was bemoaned and decried by major figures of the realm, and his supporters offered to provide enough money for Mesmer to initiate his own academy. In a short space of time one-third of a million livres had been raised by subscription, and *Herr Doktor* returned to Paris in triumph.

Five years of enormous public popularity and professional jealousy ensued, until, in March 1784, a special commission composed of members of the Academy of Medicine and the Academy of Science was convened to evaluate and submit a conclusion with respect to magnetism. The body was a distinguished one, consisting of, among others, Lavoisier, regarded by some as the creator of modern chemistry, the astronomer Bailly (both of whom would fall before the deadly instrument *not* named for an attending colleague, the physician Guillotin), and Benjamin Franklin. The group finally judged magnetic treatment "effective," although it often subjected patients to severe reactions, including convulsions (thus being a precursor of shock therapy). They also recognized that "there is undoubtedly some power at work, a power that influences men's actions and dominates them. This power is the property of the magnetizer himself." Unfortunately, these comments were merely a preamble to the ultimate conclusion that there was no such thing as "animal magnetism," and, being nonexistent, it could hardly cure anyone. In addition the report suggested, and a private analysis prepared for Louis XVI specifically stipulated, that the technique was not only useless, but perhaps actually harmful. Thus, in August 1784, an assembly of highly intelligent scientists embalmed in ignorance and shortsightedness, and, with the pallbearing minds of pomposity, buried for another century the brilliantly extracted essence of an idea that was to alter Western society. But the interment buried a seed, not a corpse, for in that very year the pupil who would refine and partially understand what the master had only mined and quasi-conjured with was at work. By the end of 1784, Count Maxime de Puységur established the authenticity of deliberately and artificially induced trance, i.e., mesmerism, or "hypnotism," and established the high road to modern psychology.

IV
The Evolution of Intangible Medicine

Theoretician or technician? Who makes the more important contribution: he who senses the existence of a phenomenon and seeks it out, although he does not understand the nature of that which he intuits, or he who analyzes the discovery, comprehends it, at least in part, and develops its application? As the latter can only achieve his accomplishment as a result of his predecessor's perception, however unresolved it may be, the answer is probably apparent. Yet it was Mesmer's pupil, Count de Puységur, who isolated and established a control technique for practical hypnosis. In 1784 he printed *Raport des cures opérées à Bayonne par le magnétisme animal.* The wealthy aristocrat, although possessed of no serious scientific education, was an admitted, even ardent, follower of Mesmer and his methods. Nonetheless, while a perceptive dabbler, his efforts were confined mostly to the treatment of peasants who lived about his country estate—but sufficient success accompanied his practice to gain him a reputation.

It was a divergence from the approach of the master which was to gain him his fame, however. While dealing with a patient Puységur accidentally stumbled upon a state of somnambulism and proceeded to determine that it—rather than the usual hysterical Mesmeric response—was objectively and intentionally achievable. Having induced trance, he established that the state was such as to allow the subject most normal sense perceptions and, in addition, that the patient might be conditioned to obey instructions not natural to the unhypnotized individual.

28

Puységur's next step was to work out the concept of implanting an order in the mind of the somnambulistic subject with the intention of having it executed after he "awoke." To wit: Mesmer instinctively realized that there was something in the psyche of man to which he involuntarily reacted; Puységur defined the manner by which this phenomenon could be directed, and gave the world functional hypnosis. As with the spheric shape of the earth, a tiny handful of men had been aware of the effect of what came to be known as hypnosis for millennia, and even of some of its implications, but one man had to make it a factor in objective knowledge.

The Seybert Commission, established in 1825 by the Royal Academy of Medicine in France, finally gave the entire question a fairer hearing. It took six years to arrive at a conclusion on the theories and practice of magnetism, and it was considered a relative victory for the practitioners. From this point onward various other hurdles were surmounted: "animal magnetism," with its ebb and flow of mystical fluid, was discarded; "cosmic electricity," which substituted currents for the invisible elixir, followed it into oblivion; "etherology" and other more spiritual versions of the "universal essence" thesis fell by the wayside. But all were leading to the behavioristic isolation of the phenomenon to be actually named "hypnotism" by the English physician Braid, whose major contribution to the field was his demonstration that the trance state could be produced directly or indirectly, and that the induction process did not necessarily require specific suggestion.

In the tradition of most practices which become popular, hypnotism soon began to fragment into "schools" employing slightly tempered techniques and professing barely distinguishable differences in theory. Among the better known were Liébeault's, in Nancy, which, in turn, influenced Bernheim and the German Albert Moll. Elsewhere, in France, Charcot was initiating the "Paris school" and would number among his followers Binet and Fáré. Countless individuals made contributions of varying degrees of importance to the evolution of suggestion as a therapeutic technique, in addition to the aforementioned: Drs.

Charpignon, Teste, Kluge, Wollfahrt, Kerner, as well as other notables including La Fontaine, Kant, Goethe, Richter, Hegel, the barons Reichenbach and Du Potet, and Bishop Lacordaire.

The physician Bernheim writes of a patient, suffering from paralysis of the tongue, being prepared for corrective surgery, who was cured when a thermometer was placed in his mouth—he believed that it was the instrument which was intended to relieve his condition. The professor of medicine has recorded a case of aphonia where a young girl was given speech when he stroked her larynx slightly as he prepared for treatment, saying, as he did so, "You will speak aloud." Yet, as did Paracelsus, Bernheim credited faith with the greatest suggestive power and tells of the following instance:

> The Princess of Schwartzenburg had suffered for eight years from paraplegia for which the most celebrated doctors in Germany and France had been consulted. In 1821 the Prince of Hohenlohe, who had been a priest since 1815, brought a peasant to the princess, who had convinced the young prince of the power of prayer in curing disease. The mechanical apparatus, which had been used by Dr. Heine for several months to overcome the contracture of the limbs, was removed. The prince asked the paralytic to join her faith both to his and the peasant's.
>
> "Do you believe that you are already helped?"
>
> "Oh, yes, I believe most sincerely!"
>
> "Well, rise and walk."
>
> At these words the princess rose and walked around the room several times, and tried going up and downstairs. The next day she went to church and from this time on she had the use of her limbs.

In the late nineteenth century—during the whole of which a variety of suggestive therapies were accomplishing numerous kinds of success—T. J. Hudson, a noted scholar of the paranormal, divided heterodox healing into a half-dozen principal categories. As they reflect the thinking of the time and are quite applicable today, it seems productive to quote them verbatim: [1]

1. *Prayer and religious faith,* as exemplified in the cures performed at Lourdes and at other holy shrines. To this class also belong the cures effected by prayer alone, the system being properly known in this country as the Faith Cure and the Prayer Cure. [In our time the designation *spiritual* healing is also applied, and these are the methods common to the famous evangelical practitioners, as well as some one-to-one relationship workers.]

2. *The Mind Cures,* a professed method of healing which rests upon the supposition that all diseased states of the body are due to abnormal conditions of the mind, and that the latter (and thus the former) can be cured by the direct action of the mind of the healer upon the mind of the patient. [Certain of the contemporary "mental therapies," e.g., Scientology, Concept Therapy, Humanetics, and the like, partake of some portion of this thesis.]

3. *Christian Science.* This method of healing rests upon the assumption of the unreality of matter. This assumed as a major premise, it follows that our bodies are unreal, and, consequently, there is no such thing as disease, the latter existing only in the mind, which is the only real thing in existence. [Today, besides the Christian Scientists, some other metaphysical and quasi-theosophical cults depend on aspects of this argument.]

4. *Spiritism* [now more commonly known as *spiritualism*], which is a system of healing based on the supposed interposition of spirits of the dead, operating directly, or indirectly through a medium, upon the patient. [Still standard spiritualistic procedure, although there is a growing shifting of emphasis among the more sophisticated sensitives, particularly in England.]

5. *Mesmerism.* This includes all the systems of healing founded on the supposition that there exists in man a

---

[1] Thomas Jay Hudson, *The Law of Psychic Phenomena*, p. 156.

fluid which can be projected upon another, at the will of the operator, with the effect of healing disease by the therapeutic action of the fluid upon the diseased organ. [Presently, such theses are pretty much restricted to very esoteric sects, especially those which are aura-oriented, or, occasionally, Eastern-influenced mysticisms.]

6. *Suggestive Hypnotism.* [Modern usage, in any medical sense, would be either as a substitute for chemical anesthetic, or as in hypnotherapy, and several forms of individual and group "analysis."] This method of healing rests upon the law that persons in the hypnotic condition are constantly controllable by the power of suggestion, and that by this means pain is suppressed, function modified, fever calmed, secretion and excretion encouraged, etc., and thus nature, the healer, is permitted to do the work of restoration.

Hudson made many pertinent points in his writings on suggestibility. One has application to all forms of miracle healing: "The subjective mind of an individual is as amenable to control by the suggestions of his own objective mind as it is by the suggestion of another." An amplification of that insight especially applies to religious or spiritual healing: "The faith required for therapeutic purposes is a purely subjective faith, and it is attainable upon the cessation of active opposition on the part of the objective mind." [2]

It is not without interest that Hudson, who was enormously receptive, perhaps even credulous, with respect to an amazing assortment of psychic phenomena, viewing the birth and rise of a new "metaphysical" religion, should have observed:

Christian Science, so-called, furnishes a very striking example of the principle involved in the proposition that the requisite subjective faith may be acquired without the concurrence of objective belief, and even in defiance of

[2] *The Law of Psychic Phenomena,* p. 156.

objective reason. The system is based upon the assumption that matter has no real existence; consequently we have no bodies, and hence no disease of the body is possible. It is not known whether the worthy lady founder of the school ever stopped to reduce her foundation principles to the form of a syllogism. It is presumed not, for otherwise their intense, monumental, and aggressive absurdity would have become as apparent to her as it is to others. Let us see how they look in the form of a syllogism:

Matter has no existence. Our bodies are composed of matter. Therefore our bodies have no existence.

It follows, of course, that disease cannot exist in a non-existent body.

That the above embraces the basis of the system called Christian science [sic] no one who has read the works of its founder will deny. Of course, no serious argument can be adduced against such a self-evident absurdity. [3]

Yet, despite its abandoning all the best of Paracelsus, Mesmer, Puységur, and those who derived from them, while retaining that which was wholly vulnerable to ridicule and logical annihilation, the new wave rolled on. Reason had nothing to do with it. It was founded on blind, irreducible *faith*. Faith is a syllogistic circle, being based solely upon itself. You either have it—or you don't.

[3] Ibid., pp. 156-157.

V

Mary Baker Eddy: The Healer Who Could Not Heal

It is generally assumed that major historical healers are attracted by a call from On High, or, even more frequently believe themselves directly anointed by the finger of God, and are possessed of the power to correct the natural malfunctions with which some unfortunates are born, heal the afflicted, and cure all diseases known to man—although often not to physicians. For the most part, such types are the ones who rise to national, occasionally even international, prominence as messengers of physical—and, of course, psychical—salvation. Yet this is not always the case.

In *Twelfth Night* (Act II, scene iv), Shakespeare observed that "some men are born great, some achieve greatness, and some have greatness thrust upon them." Among American presidents, for instance, some might accept Jefferson, Franklin D. Roosevelt, and Lincoln as examples of each category respectively. But it is more difficult to cite an important religious figure who fits the final category. Among prominent healers, it verges on the impossible. Among religious leaders involved in healing, only one individual is available—Mary Baker Eddy.

Only one religious group of any importance in modern times has been literally based upon the concept of preventive and therapeutic medicine of the mind and spirit, that being the odd concoction of Mary Baker Glover Eddy's called "Christian Science." Despite his contempt for what he saw as an unattractive, barely educated female of few funds, questionable sincerity, and limited intelligence, the devout iconoclast Sam Clemens

34

described her as "the most daring . . . masterful woman [to appear] on earth in centuries."

Few people got to know her well after she began to take "the call" seriously and came to regard herself as one of history's anointed. She personally foreordained that it would "take centuries" before "the marvel of [her] life could be known in a millionth of its details." Therefore, objective source material is difficult to unearth, perhaps impossible. The Christian Science church, being synonymous with its dictatorial founder, beatified and canonized her while she lived, and if the process of deification was suspended until she had time to get to heaven, one may note it must have been instantaneous 'spiritportation.'

The first and officially accepted hagiography was composed by a sycophant, Sibyl Wilbur, and bore not merely the imprimatur of the high priestess, but heavy evidence of her guiding hand, as well. In this panegyric Eddy is *love*, and all who contest her being *love* are, themselves, hate; she is virtue, and all who . . . etc.

Counterpointing this promotional piece was a volume by Georgine Milmine which may most easily be described as in total opposition. However, as to worth—in contradistinction to evaluation—Milmine's analysis is the product of investigation and verification, and is doubtlessly far superior in objectivity and accuracy. Somewhat less cutting, but also immeasurably more objective are later biographies, including *Mrs. Eddy*, by Edward F. Dakin. Both of the last two were bought up in great quantities by the church and are not easy to procure.

Mary Baker Eddy was born in Bow, near Concord, New Hampshire on July 16, 1821, a fragile, neurasthenic, seventh child of two narrow-minded, strong-willed Down Easters. Childhood did nothing to improve her less than attractive face and form, or her delicate health, which expressed itself—both in reality and in an early talent for manufactured maladies—in high excitability, hysterical fits, and even apparent convulsive attacks and claimed hallucinations, all before adolescence. Although a few years of such behavior caused her parents to accept a suggestion from the family doctor not to take her performances too seriously, she was able to parlay her "delicacy" into a preadulthood of laziness and self-indulgence. As is not unusual with certain hysteric types, particularly ones tending toward pathological egocentricity or monomania, her social deficiencies did not interfere with the evolution of an incredible intransigence, an absolutely immovable will, upon which she constructed a life, a following, a church, and an irrational religion which yet persists, despite lacking virtually every temperamental, educational, physical, humane, intellectual, and spiritual attribute one would have assumed essential.

The most normal and happy period of her life was during her very brief marriage, lasting the last half of her twenty-second year, to a skilled workman named Washington Glover. Penniless after her husband's premature death she gave birth to a son, George Washington, and then proceeded to become an ever less welcome but increasingly autocratic ward, first of her father and then of her sister, for nearly a decade. Yet, notwithstanding her abandonment of her child to anyone who would board him, her presence was trying in the extreme. She suffered real or alleged physical and psychological indispositions constantly, not the least of her purportedly therapeutic demands being the installation of a hammock (or, perhaps, from a mental point of view, a cradle) in the basement, in which she insisted she be rocked out of her muscular aches and psychic disharmonies for hours at a time. Soon her ill health—quite probably enormously amplified by her extraordinary idleness and probably psychotic egocentricity—deteriorated severely, reaching a point of incapacitation making little movement possible. By the time she was thirty she appeared to have become, or achieved the state of being, a permanent cripple.

Few commentators appear to question that functional paralysis existed, but there is considerable disagreement as to how much was actually due to organic disorder and what derived from pure hysteria. Whatever the syndromic diagnostic distribution, this remarkable creature enticed and trapped a rather handsome, full-bearded itinerant dentist, of dubious credentials, and they were wed on June 21, 1853.

Nothing changed.

The woman who would be the first in modern times to create a successful religious sect merely transferred the yoke of parasitism from her natural family to her acquired one, and "Dr." Daniel Patterson pulled them slowly, uneventfully through another ten years, ultimately finding escape only by being captured by the Confederate Army during the Civil War. Destitute again, the prisoner-of-war widow descended once again upon her sister, Abigail Tilton. It took little time for her health to fray and unravel, and the forty-year-old matron once more withdrew into the bed and condition of chronic invalidism.

Physicians forsook her case, herb doctors and medicine men failed to elicit improvement, spiritualism was unable to effect a change, hydrotherapy worsened her condition, not even our old friend mesmerism could revitalize the patient. She seemed prepared to accept her fate.

Finally the spreading reputation of Phineas Parkhurst Quimby reached her and, absolutely convinced he was her last and only hope, she scrounged together the fare and summoned the great will to make the trip to Maine where he practiced.

Barely strong enough to climb the first flight of stairs, she collapsed and was carried into the waiting room and dissolved, physically and mentally, into a chair. Quimby emerged, consulted with her, and began his treatment. Within less than a month the incurable cripple was in nearly full health, and before returning home ascended the almost two hundred steps to the cupola of the city hall to survey the city.

How? Why? By general agreement—allowing for personal interpretation—that *is* what occurred. A miracle? A strong mind encountering a stronger mind? Spontaneous remission? Mesmer might have used his phrase "a will-to-health" to explain it. Whatever it was, Mary Baker Glover took the results thankfully, and the technique ravenously. True, she redesigned it a bit, but Christian Science was the work of P. P. Quimby seen through the small end of a psychological telescope. She did little more than elaborate upon his basic thesis, evolving it into a total contradiction of what was known and demonstrable about the universe her Ultimate Healer had presumably created. Her cure was accomplished by a practitioner who said that man may appear sick sometimes when there is no actual disorder. She presented a "system" which rejected the concept of illness completely, granting only that a disruption of the cosmic spiritual harmony introduced nonhealth, always curable by praying one's way back into the universal rhythm again.

Line by line, page by page, idea by idea, technique by technique, this complex personality of singular commonness and an almost indefinable intensity, glued together by an unassailable ego, drained every iota of practice, theory, and thesis from the man from Maine. With his basic materials Mary Baker Eddy manufactured her *pronouncements* to the world—Christian Science.

As the years and editions of her masterwork *Science and Health* came and went, the image of Quimby receded further and further from the forefront of her memory, but the factual contribution of Mrs. Glover's therapist and mentor cannot be denied—especially when it was enunciated by the messiah herself.

A newspaper interview, published in Lynn, Massachusetts, in March 1871, posed nine questions to her. The sixth was: "Has this [Christian Science] theory ever been advertised or practiced before you introduced it or by any other individual?"

"Never advertised and *practiced by only one individual who healed me, Dr. Quimby,* of Portland, Maine, an old gentleman *who made it a research for twenty-five years,* starting from the standpoint of magnetism, thence going forward and leaving that behind. I discovered the art in a moment's time, and *he acknowledged it to me;* he died shortly after, and since then, eight years, I have been founding and demonstrating the science [emphasis added]."

Yet, in one edition of *Science and Health* she states that the revelation came upon her in 1866.

In another instance, in a letter to Quimby, datelined Warren, Maine, and written in April 1864, she wrote: "I [told a patient] *I was not done with my pupilage* [with Quimby] yet, and recommended her to visit you [emphasis added]." [1]

In the first edition of *Science and Health* she wrote, "We made our first discovery that science mentally applied would heal the sick, in 1864." This record, while a bit more self-serving than some of her earlier ones, was not altered until the third edition, issued six years later. Even as late as 1887, in the *Christian Science Journal* of June, she was making acknowledgments which would conflict with her later versions of her entry into the art of spiritual therapy, e.g., "I was under . . . treatment of Dr. Quimby from 1862 until his death in 1866." And "it took about ten years of hard work for me to reach the standard of my first edition of *Science and Health* published in 1875." That is, by her own testimony, she was regaining her own health by studying the Maine healer's theories and work, before she was capable of beginning the writing upon which she was to base her thaumaturgic religion.

Even the examination of dates is not actually essential to recognize Quimby as the subsequently unacknowledged herald of the new cult. It is an unusual religion that knows its own father.

In 1931 Jeane Phillips pointed out that there were "about two thousand references in the Quimby manuscript" to be found in the subsequent writings of Mary Baker Eddy. Examples include:

1. *Quimby:* "As man contains all the elements of this material world or life, he is a miniature world in himself." (Quimby Ms.)

Eddy: ". . . man epitomizes the universe . . . the body of the Soul embraces the universe . . ." (*Science and Health*, 1st ed. Boston, 1875, p. 229.)

Eddy: He [man] reflects Infinity, and includes in this

[1] Jeane Phillips, *Mary Baker Eddy Early Writings Compared with Quimby Manuscript*, p. 153.

reflection the entire universe of God's creating." *(Science,* 19th ed. p. 150.)

Eddy: "Mind and its thoughts comprise the whole of God, the universe, and man. *(Science,* 3rd ed. Vol. 1, p. 11.)

2. *Quimby:* "To cure an error intelligently is to know how to produce it . . . if your wisdom had been perfect it would have revealed the disorder or error." *(Mary Baker Eddy Early Writings,* p. 167.)

Eddy: "A knowledge of error and its operations must precede that understanding of Truth which destroys error." *(Science,* 1930 ed.)

3. *Quimby:* ". . . what we call man is not man, but a shadow." *(Early Writings,* p. 276.)

Eddy: ". . . you are not a man or woman . . . man is the reflex shadow of the Soul . . ." *(Science of Man,* Lynn, Massachusetts. 1876 p. 3.)

Yet, before she dismissed her Baptist, she suggested he was only sexist inches away from being the Second Coming (this time around she fully intended the Messiah to be a woman). Shortly after her health was restored, she wrote of him:

"I can see dimly . . . the great principals which underlie Dr. [sic] Quimby's faith and work." And, in her more Alice-creating-Wonderland mood: "The truth which he opposes to the error of giving intelligence to matter and placing pain where it never placed itself, if received understandingly, changes the currents of the system to their normal action . . . the body which is full of light is no longer in [sic] disease." Or: Quimby "speaks as never man before spoke and heals as never man healed since Christ." [2] Her devotion to the finally discovered cause was all-consuming; the monomaniacal drive had found a vehicle to fuel.

On the practical side, as has been the case with many who have thought they had the key to the cosmos, she was constantly assailed by difficulties, usually self-inflicted. Ill, she had been impossible; well and an oracle, she was wholly intolerable. Her husband had given her an annual stipend on the condition they never meet again and her sister soon sent her packing forever. Since any and all industry was beneath her, she scanned the horizon for a new host to which she could financially and residentially attach herself, and, over the ensuing and admittedly difficult years, she found a considerable number, almost invariably individuals or families hardly above subsistence level themselves—for the better-off expect professional house guests to be attractive or amusing, and although truly singular, she possessed neither of these charms, nor any others as far as anyone has been able to discover.

This corrosive manner caused all of her tenancies to be brief, and for years she was asked to leave or was literally cast out of one place after another, perhaps numbering in the scores—but always persisting, always persevering, always writing the *new* gospel. Her fortitude and psychic strength appear to have been formidable, especially for a woman of middle age in the postwar years of the nineteenth century. She knew the Word, but even her tremendous egocentricity did not blind her to the fact that she personally lacked every characteristic needed to be a healer. She finally realized that the only solution was to acquire a disciple who would perform the actual therapy. The few prospects she encountered proved unsuitable for the task, and as a last resort she placed a small advertisement in a newspaper offering to teach "any person ... to commence healing on a principle of science with ... unparalleled success in the most difficult cases," but to no effect.

Still destiny will not be denied and almost two years afterwards, in 1870, she found her Peter. His name was Richard Kennedy; he was a factory laborer of twenty-one. She would instruct him in the art of healing, he would support her, and they would split his professional fees.

And so began Christian Science with a financial agreement between the messiah and the first disciple, reinforcing a great American tradition particularly prevalent among healers—a dollar for deliverance, a little cash for Christ. "Dr." Kennedy hung up a shingle in Lynn, Massachusetts, in July 1870, initiated Phineas Parkhurst Quimby's therapy, achieved immediate success, and the movement was begun. For Mary, who could hardly permit another to be credited with her "genius," it was time to emerge and spread the Word to the world beyond young Kennedy.

Cure the population of its ills and harvest a vast green crop of currency was the philosophy—and she was deadly serious about both. To her they were inseparable endeavors. From the shadows entered "Mrs. M. Glover, Teacher of Moral Science," who offered a dozen-class course for $100—a tuition soon to be tripled. Further stipulations were also integrated in the contract: a tithe of all annual earnings from practice should be returned to the mentor, and that a forfeit of $1,000 would be made by any student taking the course but not engaging in practice (to compensate for the lost annual ten per cent, we may assume).

Her course in mystic medicine was titled *Scientific Treatise on Mortality, as taught by Mrs. Mary Baker Glover,* a text totally lifted from the *Questions and Answers* by Quimby, which she had transcribed during her period as his patient and supporter. Yet not unexpectedly her admiration and admitted indebtedness to him diminished rapidly as her own business prospered. She was possessed of gratitude in small measure and vindictiveness in large. Her mentor was the recipient of the first and her initial disciple who, however involuntarily, had led her out of the wilderness, was the object of the latter.

As her classes grew, her funds mounted, and her influence spread, her arrogance and egocentricity evolved accordingly, as did her strength, vitality, and even a reclamation of some of the youthfulness she had never really incorporated in her being. Doubtless it was the last that suddenly turned her preoccupation with her young protégé to antagonism, then hostility, and, finally, hatred. Within a matter of months her aberrant interest in Kennedy had caused her to go from mistrusting him, to accusing him of dishonesty, to proclaiming him a corruptor of the faith. Assaulted thus, the healer settled his financial accounts with the unbalanced woman and set up an independent practice. Unfortunately for him, she was not to leave it at that, and continued to attack him verbally and in print, even to the extent of denouncing him as a demoniacal influence in an early edition of "The Word," *Science and Health.*

This *third* book of the Bible, for Christian Scientists, was originally printed with the funds of two acolytes in 1875, and was almost 500 pages long. Today it is unobtainable, for immediately upon publication better-educated consultants and wiser minds began editing out the more insanely, inanely extravagant distortions of fact and philosophic conjecture, and each succeeding version revealed the surgical literary hand cutting away the grotesqueries of the founder's illiterate "metaphysics." But that was long ago, and the endless reinterpretations and modifications have reduced an intriguing cabalistic conundrum to a mundane, colorless gospel—a few of the ideas remain but the fire is wholly extinguished.

The thesis into which Mary Baker's "scissors-job" evolved is so philosophically incoherent and generally illogical it is impossible to explain precisely what it is. Contradictions and arcane doubletalk whirl past dicta and *ex cathedra* pronouncements, but her "system" is one of the few *new* religions of the Western world. As much as it is possible to say, these are her contentions.

God is all and God is good, therefore all is good. Man is not only part of the all, and therefore good, but exists in the image of God who is both all and good, and therefore he is doubly good. As all is good, both being merely other expressions for God, nothing evil can actually exist in the universe. Illness is obviously painful and a reflection of bodily or mental corruption, and therefore evil, which cannot exist in the real, or spiritual, cosmos. Yet, it is apparent in men. How? Because, since his beginnings, man has *imagined* illness to exist, he has collectively absorbed the concept of sickness as inevitable and individually manifests endless varieties of these false ideas. He thinks he is ill and he is ill; he knows he is well and he is cured.

The physical doesn't exist. All is spirit, and the body is as illusory as its infirmities. In Mary Baker Eddy's original, now modified argument, if man could clearly recognize and accept that he only *thinks* he has form, he would not age or die, for these are mere extensions of the misconceptions of physical imperfection. As man is one with the good and the all, he is an aspect of God who is eternal and in whom no flaw can exist, and should prevail forever.

God is all, all is mind, mind is good, good is real, reality is health, health is harmony, harmony is cosmos, the cosmos is infinite, infinity is God, God is all, all is ... and the endless, overlapping carousels spin on.

Originally Christian Science explicitly offered a cure for absolutely any disease or affliction, condemning as evil inventions of illness all forms of orthodox medicine. Brain tumors, cancer, tuberculosis, leprosy, down through common colds, headaches, and hangnails were subject to the exorcism of the skilled (and accredited) practitioners. However, the blood of the cult has thinned, and today surgery and other forms of medicine are permitted by most adherents. It could hardly be otherwise since Mother Mary herself had employed these earthly demons on a number of occasions, and as a matter of fact, at the age of seventy, engaged as her adopted son and principal disciple a genuine medical physician, one Dr. Ebenezer J. Foster.

The history of Mary Baker Eddy (who married her third husband at the age of fifty-five) is a lengthy one. The culmination was her dissolution of the formal church structure and retirement to an Olympic retreat, which was also the largest edifice in Boston at that time. There she lived until she died at the age of eighty-nine.

She alone of the great figures of the tradition of magical healing *did not personally* participate in the practice of mental or spiritual therapy. Nonetheless, numerically speaking, it may be safely assumed that she was responsible for more cures than most of her predecessors and successors combined. She was a phenomenon, a giantess among the great figures in the field, and no one individual since her death has come close to her in stature.

VI

Magic Potions and
Mechanical Marvels

Elisha Perkins, born January 16, 1741, at Norwich, Connecticut—discounting Mesmer's "bath"—may well be credited with the introduction of the Machine Age of magical medicine. Perkins believed radiant emission from the magnetic practitioner had to be considered, and in the patient at least a natural state of receptivity. But he noted that true and full therapeutic contact was rarely effected in magnetic healing. Either the two forces for cure did not meet at all, or the healer's energy failed to achieve a sufficiently intense interrelationship with the subject's state of attraction to it. To bridge this gap between the practitioner and the patient he invented "tractors," a pair of metal sticks by which the magnetic or etheric impulse was supposed to be conveyed and intensified.

"Doctor" by courtesy . . . Perkins [was] . . . six feet tall, handsome, of commanding personality and full of that intangible something which women call charm and men call magnetism, he became in a few years one of the most popular and successful doctors in Connecticut . . . [he made an impression] with the sense of benefit and well-being which his forceful presence and kindly ways imparted to his patients, especially when he had occasion to *lay his hands upon them* in the course of making examinations or feeling pulses. This effect he thought to be due to some occult magnetic influence—obviously directly derived from his German predecessor, rather than Puységur and the mentalist schools which followed after him —and he persuaded himself that by combining together certain metals a more efficient magnetic or electro-therapeutic agent might be secured than by mere human touch [emphasis added].[1]

Perkins participated in the establishment of the Connecticut Medical Society, but "on May 17, 1796, the society passed a vote" describing his employment of animal magnetism and metallic instruments to touch and stroke the ill as "delusive quackery." One year later "Dr. Elisha Perkins was formally expelled from the society for his practices." [2]

This pioneer in the mechanization of thaumaturgy conceived and manufactured his "tractors" in the privacy and secrecy of his Plainfield, Connecticut, home, never divulging their composition or the principle upon which they allegedly functioned. Like a legion of his equally perspicacious successors, he would not sell the devices, but only lease them. Introduced to the public in 1796, it was the "first medical item patented under the United States Constitution." [3]

The healer died on September 6, 1799, at the age of fifty-nine, apparently unable to cure himself of what is reported—admittedly by his supporters—to have been exhaustion or yellow fever contracted in his efforts to help victims of a plague which struck New York that year.

"Perkinism" was perpetuated and its scope broadened by the inventor's son, Benjamin Douglas, who transplanted it to London and founded an institute in 1804 near Soho Square.

For an amusing contemporary satiric comment on the device and its creator, one may turn to a lengthy verse by "Christopher Caustic." Some of the more pointed and pertinent reflections of the period's negative response are found in several stanzas:

1 James Gregory Mumford, A Narrative of Medicine in America, p. 286. See also Joseph T. Smith, An Historical Sketch of Dr. Elisha Perkins, Inventor of the Metallic Retractors, reprinted in Maryland Medical Journal, May 1910.

2 Norwalk (Connecticut) Courier, November 5, 1909.

3 James Harvey Young, The Toadstool Millionaires, 1961.

Behold! A rising INSTITUTION
To spread Perkinean delusion;
Supported by a set of sturdymen,
Dukes, quakers, doctors, lords, and clergymen.

The learned physicians pine and hunger
The while a spruce young patent-monger
Contrives to wheedle simple ninnies
And tractorize away our guineas.

Now suffer Tractoring rogues to cure
Such sordid shoals of paltry poor,
Of whom it truly may be said,
That they were ten times better dead.

Say Perkinism should be levell'd;
'Tis Galvanism worse bedevill'd:
Indeed they both are but a schism,
From old exploded Mesmerism.

It need hardly be noted that potions predated the industrial age of mystical medicine by millennia, and even in the New World they anteceded Perkins by immeasurable ages. The Indians, who were already in residence, used them, as did the first white settlers. Not merely the fact, but the commercialization, of the potion panaceas erupted nearly a century before Perkins applied for his patent. Nicholas Boone, of Boston, inserted the first paid advertising for a patent-type medicine in a local newspaper in 1708. It was called Daffy's *Elixir Salutis*.

A century and a half of cure-all liquids, ointments, and tablets, measuring in the thousands of tons was consumed, but not until the middle of the nineteenth century did the classic "medicine man" begin to really hit his stride, and by the *fin de siècle* the available patent medicines numbered in the hundreds, perhaps thousands, and were available, not merely from the itiner-

---

[4] Christopher Caustic (pseud. of T. G. Fessenden), *Terrible Tractoration!!*, p.p. 103-104, 122, 123.

ant huckster, but over the counters of countless chemist and pharmacy shops. At the beginning of the great boom, "Bateman's Pectoral Drops" and "Hooper's Female Pills" were among the most commercially successful. They were joined by Samuel H. P. Lee's "Bilious Pills" in popularity, followed by "Scott's Emulsion" and "Lydia E. Pinkham's Vegetable Compound."

Today, it is impossible to estimate the number of "medical" products that have been offered to the American public from basement-bottled and kitchen-labeled elixirs to panaceas produced by the tank-carload in enormous, glistening pharmaceutical plants, but it most likely exceeds a million. It is perfectly reasonable to assume that over ninety per cent of these alleged medicines range from harmless through undesirable to deadly.

Most are said to correct a variety of disorders, thousands have claimed to cure cancer and other serious or fatal diseases. Since few can do half—or any—of what they promise, they are dangerous because they lead the patient to bypass proper medical examination and treatment for his or her complaint, while others are highly toxic in themselves and have debilitated or killed countless perfectly healthy victims. Whether dreadful because of omission or commission, they are usually worse than no therapy at all, or, as "Christopher Caustic" observed of such subjects almost two hundred years ago, it may frequently be said "that they were ten times better dead."

Or, to paraphrase the *British Weekly* (Dec. 21, 1911), an individual who diagnoses his own afflictions and prescribes for them has a fool for a physician and, frequently, a corpse for a patient.

Many interesting works on these patent medicines are available, e.g., *The Toadstool Millionaires* and *Medical Messiahs* by James Harvey Young, *The Great American Fraud* by Samuel Hopkins, and *100,000,000 Guinea Pigs* by Arthur Kallet.

Yet, while the patent medicine craze was always to be quantitatively more prevalent than the various cogs in the machinery of mechanical medicine, the latter was inevitably more intriguing. For pure fascination a bottle of red liquid or a jar of green salve can hardly compare with a therapeutic device flashing lights of various colors, or even a couple of anodes and a high-frequency whine crowning a patient's pate, which explains why the wizards of oddery continued to flourish.

In 1893 Dr. Hercules Sanche introduced the "Electropoise," an empty cylinder he was gracious enough to sell for $10 a unit. But while this invention failed to deliver the current its name suggested, the deceptionist's follow-up, the "Oxydonor," was even less capable of introducing a rejuvenating supply of life-invigorating gas. Yet, one must grant that this was no mere hollow tube. It was a half-hollow tube containing a small shaft of carbon. It is superfluous to remark that many people copied the general idea and, after the fashion of Sanche, restrained their humanistic impulse to give the devices away gratis for the benefit of the afflicted. For his part, the "inventor" of the "Oxydonor" parted with his miracle-makers for a mere $35 each—certainly a small enough contribution for an instrument which cured "all forms of disease."

Yet this great scientist had not exhausted either his imagination or his supply of victims. Later he offered the breathless and brainless public "Diaduction"—the ultimate element in the evolution of mechanized Christian Science. It healed everything known or unknown to man, correcting ailments that "ain't even been invented." It was a fundamental aspect of nature and its existence had been discovered and employed by this mystic of the *fin de siècle*.

Sanche, as observed, was widely imitated in his time and the years that followed, but, one by one, his greatest admirers were struck down by the attacks of the American Medical Association, the postal authorities, and more formal branches of law enforcement. Eventually, he himself succumbed to the tortoiselike corrosion of justice, although, according to Stewart H. Holbrook,[5] an authority on such pitchmen, he was still grinding out some gimmickry as late as the end of the 1950s.

Concurrent with the man who devised devices to cure all the

[5] Stewart H. Holbrook, *The Golden Age of Quackery.*

temporary and terminal ills of man, there functioned one of the small handful of men (and a couple of women) who crowd the topmost tier of charlatanry in the field of fraudulent mystical medicine. His name was Harry M. Hoxsey.

Hoxsey's career was long, labyrinthine, and ruthless. Later in his life he was to attribute the cancer cure he peddled to the pharmaceutical genius of his grandfather who had discovered it in 1840, but before this revised history was issued he claimed that it had been the result of his father's experiments which reached their fruition in 1908. In any event, after leaving elementary school he took his nimble wits and total lack of social empathy into business. In 1922 (after which date he claimed to have improved his inherited prescription) he began to operate in the field of "cancer cure," announcing his ability to heal that, and other serious illnesses, with his ointment.

By 1928 he was accused of causing the death of a "patient" and charged with practicing medicine without a license. Pleading guilty to the minor charge, he paid a hundred-dollar fine, and continued his deadly endeavors.[6]

Leading a career that was one part promotion, one part "practice," and one part a running battle with the law, even thirty years later he was still extremely successful, with an estimated eight thousand patients filling his coffers with a yearly $1,500,000 as recently as 1954.

Hoxsey had interminable allies—dupes and colleagues, among them being Gerald B. Winrod, a Nazi-oriented, Bible-thumping fundamentalist who gained a Republican senatorial nomination (during those heydays of the old-fashioned isolationism) in Kansas in 1938. Yet, despite his flurry of political glory, the revivalist politician was indicted and tried for sedition during World War II. The judge died while the proceedings were in progress, and they were dissolved and not reinstituted. In the years following, Winrod's *Defender*, an anti-Semitic, anti-black, and pro-faith-healing and pro-flying-saucers publication, gained numerous readers in literal and metonymic "middle

America." He also merchandised "Glyoxylide," another of the countless alleged cancer cures, this one originally the product of Dr. William Frederick Koch of Detroit. Amid one of his ally Hoxsey's perpetual court contests, it was revealed that Winrod's glowing praise of the former's "cancer" treatments in the *Defender* derived more from the payment to him of $80,000 than from his convictions regarding the defendant's religious and/or medical qualifications.

Not unexpectedly, not all quacks are unschooled in the Hippocratic arts; sometimes an accredited physician falls prey to one of the more prominent diseases contracted by his profession—avarice. One such, called "the dean of twentieth-century charlatans" by the *Journal of the American Medical Association,* was Dr. Albert Abrams, who was graduated from the historic University of Heidelberg, with a medical degree, and did additional work in Berlin, Vienna, London, and Paris, after which he was appointed chief of the medical clinic at Cooper Medical College, in San Francisco.

Soon Abrams had published *Spondylotherapy: Spinal Concussion* (1910) and *New Concepts of Diagnosis and Treatment* (1916), while also finding time to teach his innovative technique for $200 a course. As he was beginning to be scored by his establishmentarian colleagues, he proceeded to found his own professional fraternity, the American Association for Medico-Physical Research. Yet the key to his growing business was "Electronic Reactions," a thesis that asserted that it was the electron, not the long-known cell, upon which matter was based, and the rhythm of which must be kept in proper fluctuation. To its friends it was simply and acronymically called ERA.

Updated machines were invented, a publication was launched, and Abrams elaborated his brilliant and wholly nonsensical "medicosophy." A "single drop of blood" was, in effect, the whole of any given person and from it all diagnoses could be derived. Illness of any order could be transmuted into golden health merely by inducing the body to "conform to the vibratory rate of the disease." He saw afflictions as being spread across an abstract spectroscopic graph, which only he, and his disciples, could decipher. Curiously, fragmentarily, he may have intuited *cloning*, but the idea never really emerged from his extraordinary extrapolations of alchemy. However, his brilliance could hardly be contested. He wove amazing medical fancies and was overwhelmed by a public surging to take up his banner and lay down their common sense and hard-earned dollars.

The doctor made no house calls. It was unnecessary. The patient simply sent along a drop of blood on a card, or even a holograph would suffice. The specimen was then inserted into the diagnoser, which was wired to a "proxy patient." Nearly immediately the imperfection in the absent subject's frequency was determined and health was on its way.

In addition, the physician was a humanitarian. He did not keep his instruments to himself, but had several thousand manufactured and leased them at high cost to practitioners (the influence of Elisha Perkins still persisted), who cleared tens of thousands of dollars a year with ERA and its magic machines.

Then, at the height of his incredible success, and just as the forces of opposition were slowly beginning to merge their efforts to bring him down, Dr. Abrams died and brought to a conclusion one of the most efficient and notorious quackeries of modern times—for master charlatans never seem to leave successors capable of carrying on the fragile, complex fraud of which such careers are composed. This must have been somewhat dispiriting for those most closely allied with ERA, for Abrams left this world a multimillionaire.

F. C. Ellis was another of the educated operators. A graduate of the University of Wisconsin, he conceived and introduced the "Micro-Dynameter." Appearing before a congressional committee in the late 1930s, he described his invention as "a simple instrument" which could diagnose, via measuring the electrical current generated by a human body, all of the ills of man. It took more than a quarter of a century for logic and law to establish that the "Micro-Dynameter" was "not safe for use even in the hands of a licensed practitioner. A device whose labeling claims it to be an aid in diagnosing as many diseases as this one, when in fact it is not, is unsafe for use no matter who uses it." [7]

"Radio Therapeutic Instrument" was the title applied to the mini-mechanical concoction created and promoted by Dr. Ruth B. Drown following the Second World War. It consisted of a box, decorated with a pair of wires (the return trips to Mesmer are never-ending in this field) meant to be connected to the patient. As with others, particularly Abrams, its purpose was to diagnose, from blips of blood applied to a swatch of blotting paper, the indisposition of a subject. Soon, it followed Abrams (and, of course, spiritualism) further down the path by broadening the operation to include "absent diagnosing and healing."

One patient, sent by Drown to an associate who used her equipment, Dr. Findley D. John, found the daily forty-mile round trip for treatment beyond her energies. Instantly she was assured that she might "just as well stay home and we can treat you by radio waves. That's what's wonderful about the Drown machine; it's just as effective when the patient is miles away ..." [8]

After a year and a half of treatment by various of Drown's confreres, the patient was unimproved, and it was suggested by the practitioners that she have a mastectomy since she did not seem to be "getting hold of the trouble with our treatment." [9]

Suits followed. The federal government descended upon the fraudulent apparatus, the therapy, and, ultimately, Ruth B. Drown, convicting her of violating the Food, Drug, and Cosmetic Act. She was fined all of $100.

On November 17, 1952, the patient died of cancer.

The charlatan was still threatening the health of the stupid, ignorant, or unwary a decade later, but this time was indicted on a charge of grand theft. She died before she could be brought to trial.[10]

[7] *United States of America* vs. *Ellis Research Laboratories, Inc.* 300 Fed. (2nd) 550 (1962). Reprinted in James Harvey Young, *The Medical Messiahs*, p. 259.

[8] James Harvey Young, *The Medical Messiahs*, pp. 240–241, reprinting Food and Drug Administration file on Drown Therapeutic Instrument, Interstate Office Seizure No. 60–642K. FDA Records, Washington, D.C.

[9] Ibid.

[10] Ibid., pp. 257-258.

In 1957 the FDA obtained an injunction which slowed the expansion of Hoxseyism to a crawl, but one could always ferret out treatment if one wanted it—much as with any other poison. Only a few years ago the American Cancer Society issued a list of "Unproven Methods of Cancer Treatment" with more than twenty-five questionable techniques noted.

VII
The Brinkley Myth
and the Cayce Legend

John R. Brinkley was born in Tennessee or Arkansas or Kentucky or California or Texas, but Gerald Carson,[1] in all probability the most knowledgeable authority on this unusual individual, opts for Jackson County, in North Carolina, on July 8, 1885. Like a few of his kind, he had credentials, but even at his height they were of exceedingly dubious quality. He appears to have spent a couple of years in Bennett Medical College, but it seems to have been something less than a formal temple of Hippocrates. Later in life, Brinkley was to assert that he spent two years studying at the National University of Arts and Science in St. Louis, but that institution's records failed to support this contention, although it was a parchment-peddling operation which dispensed diplomas to anyone who dropped a few hundred dollars in the bursar's pocket. Subsequently, even that feeble front was shredded when the state examiner who certified the document which averred Brinkley's attendance conceded that the future quack had not matriculated at all, was personally unknown to him when he issued the paper, and that, additionally, it had been prepared a half-dozen years after the date it carried.

The young man obtained another accreditation during that period of his life. It was granted by a similar medical mill, the Eclectic Medical University of Kansas City, which charged the usual several hundred dollars for an ornate piece of paper assuring the reader that a full course of scientific study had been completed by individuals who had never even visited its offices.

[1] Gerald Carson, *The Roguish World of Dr. Brinkley*

Yet, in February 1916, medical license number 5845 was issued to Brinkley by the state of Kansas. Understandings of reciprocity between it and various other states, including Texas, Missouri, Tennessee, and Connecticut, afforded him the legal right to practice in those states as well. It was just as dangerous to go to an unknown doctor sixty-five years ago as it is today.

Soon this "physician" was employed by a large meatpacking firm, where his duties were occasional and minor, although he was later to claim that this association had made it possible for him to develop a high level of expertise regarding animals, especially with respect to their glands, and even more particularly with the sexually rejuvenating powers of those of male goats.

Then came the war, and, like the rest of the country, the burgeoning pitchman had to make his sacrifice. He was able to slip his way into the medical branch with a rank of first lieutenant. Afterwards he was to describe the stressful ordeal through which he went as he nearly single-handedly maintained or repaired the health, or soothed the dying, of a couple of thousand soldiers at a fort in the southwestern United States. There is general agreement that Brinkley's memory of his service to his country was slightly exaggerated—perhaps by about one hundred three per cent.

The version he told concluded on a pathetic note. As he recalled it, the enormous burden, impossible working conditions, and lack of supplies and facilities finally reduced him to a patient himself and gained him a certificate of disability. The official accounts vary slightly, recording the actual length of his duty as barely a month, followed by an additional month at a base hospital due to his insistence that he was physically incapable of duty.

Now he made his way to Milford, Kansas, where he established a general practice until he encountered a farmer who complained that he wasn't quite the man he once had been. Brinkley remarked on the prowess of some of the goats he had observed during his stay with the meatpacking firm. Allegedly this elicited an inquiry from the patient as to whether such ability might be transferable from the animal to him. The doctor explained that one could not trade organs about from one level of life to another, but soon he realized that he was assuming a very primitive and parochial view—facts were clouding his viewing of a future fortune. He made the mental adjustment, an ethical one was probably not necessary, and began his true career—as the quintessence of quacks. In simple terms, he soon went on to proclaim to the world—especially older or emotionally insecure men and younger and physically unsatisfied women—that he could totally recharge the potency and performance of virtually any male by the introduction of a young buck's glands.

"So far as I know, I was the first man that ever did this operation of taking the goat testicle and putting it in the man's testicle, yes, sir," Brinkley is quoted as having said.[2]

His initial experiment was succeeded by one which allegedly had the patient on whom the operation was performed improve to such an extent that townspeople asserted that he "had become a regular billy goat, twice as good as any other man" in town.

The money began to roll in, especially as the fees were graduated from a few hundred dollars to, eventually, upwards of $2,000. Additionally, almost at once, the operation began to assume entirely new therapeutic proportions. Not only did it restore sexual potency, but it cured all afflictions of the procreative organs, insanity, high blood pressure, any kind of paralysis, plus the entire remaining catalogue of earthly ills. Yet, skillfully undercutting the competition who could in no way be related to him in technique or theory, Brinkley warned against Christian Science and other of the mental sciences and cautioned his followers against the variety of electro-, magnetic-, and other such prefixed medical machinery.

In 1918, founded on an inheritance by Mrs. Brinkley, the goat gland business went into new and higher gear as the doctor constructed and opened a small, but impressive hospital of his own, with room for sixteen patients, a modest operating "ampitheater," a nurses' wing, offices, a dining hall and kitchen. Its

[2] Ibid., p. 34

name was altered from time to time, but a clever swindle makes the same amount of money whatever it's called, particularly when directed by a sexual deficiency specialist with the title Chief Surgeon and an assortment of initials after his name, including M.D., C.M., Ph.D., Sc.D., and fellowships and memberships in a wide range of professional and fraternal organizations. Brinkley's addition of "member of the National Geographic Society"—merely indicating that he subscribed to that fine journal—was whimsical in a way that could only have been accidental with him. Humor was not John R. Brinkley's forte. In fact, a most contrasting character flaw distinguished him—violence.

The Brinkley Hospital of that period boasted a medical staff, apart from nurses, of three—"Dr." Brinkley, his wife Minnie T., and "Dr." H. D. Osborn, recorded as a graduate of an extremely doubtful "Kansas City College of Medicine and Surgery," run by one Date A. Alexander. Notwithstanding another purported degree or two claimed by Alexander, neither were registered to function in the state. Still, Osborn sat on the board of directors with Brinkley, and spent a decade doing most of the surgical work—with even fewer qualifications than many contemporary practitioners.

All did not always go smoothly, however. Brinkley was an exceptionally clever and persuasive individual, but apparently his temper was as potentially lethal as his partner's scalpel. It is reliably reported that on one occasion he threatened to slice open the throats of some of his staff, and had to be sedated with a plank of wood. According to Carson, his research revealed that the friendly physician had almost removed Osborn's thumb with dental surgery, and may have actually bitten off his associate's ear. One can only imagine that the financial rewards were more than sufficient to justify becoming the Van Gogh of the Kansas medical world. Even the patients were not ignored by the chief surgeon when he was imbibing. It is recorded that he once chased one along the halls, slashing at him with a butcher knife, which made his slashing of a townsman's automobile tires seem almost the fun of a good-humored wag.

Convicted of bootlegging in 1920, he received a light fine and a suspended sentence. Shortly thereafter he threatened a neighbor with a pistol. But Brinkley didn't let these minor occurrences disturb his reaping of the long green of the great plains.

Never one to miss the coming thing, the charlatan constructed a radio station, had it licensed, and took the call letters KFKB. Yet, while he knew it was an instrument of great value, he was uncertain as to its most profitable application. To think about this, and because he wished to broaden his reputation and scope of personal knowledge, he decided upon a round-the-world trip, which began in the autumn of 1923 with the Brinkleys' embarking for the Orient.

Returning to Milford about six months later, he was both more determined than ever to convince the skeptics that impotency was the most dreadful fate to befall man and clear in his mind as to how his powerful—1,000-watt—station could be best used. On the other hand, the competition for the susceptible was growing no smaller. Carson writes that at that time it was "estimated that ... there were approximately seven hundred fifty surgeons, mentalists, necromancers and religious healers peddling gland treatments of one sort or another to the senior citizens of the United States." [3] Of course, that can hardly compare with the number of medical, religio-medical, and medico-mental frauds swarming across the country today.

In conjunction with his hospital and blooming radio promotion, Brinkley merchandised other products. He manufactured and sold "Sexalin" through a network of pharmacists he established across the country; he wrote, or attached his name to, a series of books, among which were counted *The Brinkley Operation* (1922), *Shadows and Sunshine* (1923), and *Compound Operation* (1926). Still, the enterprising promotor realized that as his practice and fame or notoriety grew, so did his need for more substantial medical accreditation. With the AMA barring him from receiving any recognition from respectable institutions in the United States, he decided that he would redirect his academic efforts toward Europe, especially Italy. After checking

[3] Carson, *Dr. Brinkley*, p. 58.

out Rome, Florence, and several other possibilities, to find that in fact there were none, his attention turned to the University of Pavia where, he later claimed, he took the doctoral examination and was awarded a degree in surgery in 1925. So armed, he hastened to England and seduced the British Medical Association to accept him and accord him permission to practice in Great Britain and the considerable portion of the globe under its jurisdiction.

Unfortunately for Brinkley, the mills of justice do not always grind exceeding slow, for a couple of years later he was informed by the Italian consul that his degree had been annulled, and almost immediately thereafter the British Medical Association erased his name from its rolls. Despite the various setbacks, for anyone else Brinkley's career, up to that date, had been striking and profitable, yet, according to some, he had but begun.

Along the path of his pseudomedical meanderings the Kansas quack had managed to suture together many aspects of his theory with the catgut of fundamentalistic religion. His perpetual activity, natural talent for publicity, many delighted patients, books, radio station, a hospital of his very own, world travels, and remarkable personality had laid the foundation for even greater things, although even by the conclusion of the first quarter of the century he was to be reckoned with in the South Central states, and through the outlet of innumerable pharmacies across the Midwest. But it wasn't until the autumn of 1926 that he struck his national stride, spurred by an admiring article in the old *New York Evening Journal*. It proclaimed his evangelical goat-glandism in headlines, garnished the story with intriguing subtitles, featured a photograph of the first child to have been the product of the results of the exotic operation, and, in general, hurtled Brinkley into the big time. Within little more than a year the Kansas clinic was pulling in a couple of hundred thousand dollars annually, and his claimed rate of success was well over 90 per cent.

Additionally, KFKB had really begun to sow widely and reap greatly with a programing combination of revivalism, country music and singers, health advice emphasizing sex and rejuvenation, and the issuing of prescriptions to thousands who wrote into the station delineating their ailments. This prescription programing pitch flourished for more than a dozen years and collected millions of dollars for the doctor and his unofficial pharmacy syndicate, each member of which contributed to him a considerable portion of its profits on his patent products. Gerald Carson, using five hundred as a figure representing cooperating druggists (although, as he notes, the quack's personal biographer recorded that the number was three times that many) suggests that each, on the basis of a meager four sales a day, deposited that number of dollars in the doctor's coffers. This extrapolates into nearly $750,000 a year.[4]

In the course of a long career, John R. Brinkley owned a clinic, radio station, palatial estate, a series of yachts each requiring a crew of twenty, one airplane after another, and a second radio station—KXER, as powerful as any ever to blanket this country with its signal, and he had tremendous political power. Running against Alfred M. Landon for governor, he came in third, but received 250,000 votes, only 35,000 fewer than the future Republican presidential nominee. In his first and earlier race as a write-in candidate it was widely conceded that he would have won had his name been on the ballot. Is there any doubt that John R. Brinkley is far and away the most impressive medical magician this country has produced?

However, erratic, improbable, as he was, like other members of that legion—regardless of their legitimacy or duplicity in the eyes of individuals or the public—who march to a different drummer, he was unique. As was the case with such compeers, he was a manner of living unto himself, and when, beset for decades by suits and legal assaults, he died in 1942, he left as a worthy member of the clan of ultimate charlatans.

Edgar Cayce was born in 1877 in Illinois. He began school at the age of seven, during which years his father ran a general store. He did not care for the classroom and admittedly preferred

[4] Ibid., p. 103.

daydreaming. While admonitory regarding Edgar's failings at learning, his father was pleased when he requested a Bible three years later.

Religion of the traditional order was natural to him and he later said that by the age of twelve he had read "the Book" once for every year of his life. Yet his schoolwork had not improved at all. "He was dull. No doubt about it," recounted his father, with respect to the same period of Edgar's life. "When he was twelve years old he was still in the third reader. That was the spring of 1889." [5]

One evening, after spending some time with his son, attempting to impress upon him the fundamentals of spelling, Leslie Cayce agreed to a brief recess. The boy dropped his head on the book and napped. Upon awakening a few minutes later he is said to have been able to give a complete recitation of any word on any page in the book. He appears to have revealed total clairvoyance combined with an eidetic memory, a characteristic allegedly retained during his remaining school years, through which he raced.

Despite his new success in class, Edgar was almost wholly preoccupied with exhaustively scrutinizing and rereading various portions of the Bible, and it was to this endeavor that most of his spare moments were dedicated.

The rewards of his devotion were manifold. One May afternoon, relaxing in a woodland retreat where he had fashioned a lean-to, he was immersed in a passage from the story of Manoah when a vision of a woman appeared to him and told him that his prayers were being answered. "Tell me what you would like most of all, so that I may give it to you." [6]

"Most of all I would like to be helpful to others, and especially to children when they are sick," replied Cayce.

The apparition vanished.

When he was fifteen years old his father promised to take him to the county seat, Hopkinsville, for the celebration of

---

[5] Thomas Sugrue, *There Is A River*, p. 18.

[6] Sugrue, *River*, p. 45.

Grover Cleveland's 1892 restoration to the presidency (his successful running mate was Adlai E. Stevenson, a native of the area), but during afternoon play on the preceding day he was struck in the spine with a ball. Upon returning home he instructed his mother to put a poultice of his own recipe at the base of his skull and said he would be fine the next morning. She did, and he was.

Cayce left school the next year and went to work in the fields. For Edgar the next few years were relatively uneventful. A highly symbolic dream representing the initiation and consummation of his marital life, the return of his visionary lady, the riding of a dangerous, unbroken mule, and a conversation about the Bible when he was eighteen with the great evangelist Dwight L. Moody, who gave him strong encouragement, were the only notable experiences.

He worked in a bookstore, during which time he met Gertrude Evans, his future wife. The wages he earned made any immediate plans for a wedding impossible. He moved to a Louisville bookstore, improved his situation, and then returned to work in insurance with his father. His marriage prospects were now measurably improved.

His position required that he travel about to adjacent communities, and it was around this time he began to suffer from recurrent headaches. On the occasion of an especially severe attack—while forty miles from home—he visited a physician who gave him some medicine, which he took in his hotel room. His next awareness was of being home in his own bed, with a pair of doctors gazing down at him. He had succumbed to temporary amnesia, and having been discovered wandering about half-conscious in the other town by a family friend, had been brought home. When he attempted to speak, he could manage only a croaking effect. Soon his voice was almost entirely gone and he was the seemingly permanent victim of aphonia, being able to converse only in the barest whisper. Otherwise his health was normal.

The near-lack of speech did not preclude the need for working, and he became an apprentice to a photographer.

At one point a stage hypnotist appeared, amidst great publicity, at the local theater, and, although uninvolved in the burgeoning therapeutic aspect of the phenomenon, when told of Cayce's inexplicable condition offered to cure it for a few hundred dollars. Cayce responded to induction and spoke naturally when in trance, but, despite post-hypnotic suggestion, reverted to his aphonia when reawakened. Repetition of the experiment yielded no better results. The performer explained that the failure was caused by Cayce's not going deeper into the hypnotic state than a light sleep, and abandoned the project.

Although unable to be any more effective than his predecessor, a psychologist who practiced hypnotism speculated that the patient might be able to pass the "block" if he were instructed, at that point, to assume "control" himself. An effort along these lines was attempted by Al C. Layne, a local dabbler in the art, on March 31, 1901.

In the fashion he had employed since he took naps on books to absorb their contents, Edgar put himself to sleep, with Layne doing little more than overseeing the process. Unexpectedly, the sleeping figure began to mumble. Layne requested Leslie Cayce to transcribe his son's words.

"In the normal state," Edgar went on, "this body is unable to speak, due to a partial paralysis of the inferior muscles of the vocal cords, produced by nerve strain. This is a psychological condition producing a physical effect. This may be removed by increasing the circulation to the affected parts by suggestion while in this unconscious condition."

"The circulation to the affected parts will now increase," Layne said, "and the condition will be removed." [7]

In less than half an hour Edgar awoke—wholly cured.

In conjunction with his dozing clairvoyance and his effective poultice prescription, this most recent exhibition of unnatural power led to the consideration that Cayce might be able to do for others what he had just done for himself. His healing career had begun.

[7] Ibid., p. 45.

On the following day he took on his first patient, his aide Al Layne, who suffered from a stomach disorder. Going into a trance, Cayce diagnosed the condition and specified the diet, exercises, and medication to correct it, employing medical, biological, and pharmaceutical words and phrases of which he had never heard and of which—in his conscious state—he had no understanding. This pattern was to continue for the remainder of his thousands of trance diagnoses, although his readings would become increasingly detailed, complex, and medically sophisticated as the years passed. Furthermore, from that point on Cayce's states were self-induced, although exact notes had to be taken of his analyses and prescriptions while he was in trance, because he recalled nothing he had said during those periods. Still, every few weeks his vocal power began to diminish and he had to repeat the therapy he had discovered with Layne. This and other reasons caused him to be inclined to discard the strange activity that was also interfering with his full-time duties as a professional photographer to which he had advanced.

Therefore, when in May 1902, he was offered a new job, in a bookshop located some distance away, he accepted, taking up residence in one of the town's pleasanter boarding houses. Among his fellow guests was an eye, ear, nose, and throat physician who knew some of his Hopkinsville kin. Yet, for all his optimism, within two weeks his power of speech suffered a severe decline and he was forced to return for a treatment with his Svengali, and accept his suggestion that they maintain regular contact as a precautionary measure. This arrangement also caused the readings—which he had wished to abandon—to be reinstituted.

Soon he began doing much absent diagnosing and advising, and started to accept fees for his efforts.

He was married to Gertrude in June of the following year. But Layne, for whom the new bride had never had an excess of affection, persisted in his presence and persuasiveness over Edgar's readings, even to the point of revealing to the local doctors that he visited Layne frequently to consult him about patients. When questioned as to Cayce's medical qualifications, he revealed his friend's inexplicable power, not unexpectedly causing an immediate desire on the physicians' part to witness a demonstration of the singular gift. From that point on Layne, who soon departed for a medical school to both acquire knowledge and justify the title "Doctor," which he had been employing, no longer had Edgar and a "medical" relationship with him to himself. Cayce formed an irregular affiliation with a Dr. John Blackburn, who, when the seer went into a deathlike state of unconsciousness, impenetrable by other physicians, helped restore him to normal through the communication used in his usual trance.

C. H. Dietrich, of Hopkinsville, had a daughter, Anne, whose mental growth appeared to have been arrested following a severe attack of grippe at the age of two years. Specialists agreed that her brain had been irreversibly affected. As the time approached when, normally, she would have been preparing to go to school, her father submitted her case to Edgar Cayce. He went into his usual light diagnostic trance and revealed that immediately before her illness Anne had fallen and struck the base of her spine. This accident had caused her to be especially vulnerable to the grippe and its ensuing repercussions. The "sleeping doctor" prescribed the proper treatment and within a week Dietrich reported a marked improvement. Two months later the revitalized girl began classes with her chronological contemporaries.

On one occasion, Cayce prescribed "codiron" for an ailing lady. No pharmacist could be found who knew what it was and a second reading was necessary. During it the name of the Chicago manufacturer of the medication was elicited and the "codiron" ordered by post. In some confusion the firm forwarded the bottle, since it was not yet on the market and had been named but a few days before the request had been received.

When his son, Hugh Lynn, had his eyes so seared by a flash-powder explosion that doctors wanted to operate, Cayce directed bandage-bathing with tannic acid solution in a darkened room for two weeks. The physicians fortunately agreed to assist in the ministrations, and a complete recovery followed.

By 1910 Cayce had probably given more than a thousand

readings, had been written about in articles, and was becoming very well known, both as a healer and as a curiosity. His rate of accuracy and medical success was reported to be nearly perfect.

Finally he was persuaded to go into partnership with a money-conscious doctor named Ketchum—although he stipulated stringent conditions for the alliance. It was successful and initiated the establishment of a clinic, although of a rather eclectic description as it incorporated homeopathy, osteopathy, standard medical procedures, and any other therapeutic technique which might emerge from the readings. Then in 1911, under the observation and with the aid of several physicians, and after many and lengthy diagnoses and medications, Edgar saved his wife from dying of tuberculosis. Shortly thereafter, Ketchum moved from Hopkinsville and the partnership was dissolved.

The years passed and the recorded readings poured forth. On various occasions he formed transient arrangements with various medical men, but the clairvoyant trances, usually beginning with "Yes, now we have the body of . . . ," regardless of where the patient actually was, did not change. In 1915 he met David Kahn, by whom he would be assisted for the remainder of his life.

In the early 1920s, encouraged by a businessman named Arthur Lammers, Cayce began to test his reading on subjects other than health, specifically "metaphysical" ones, including astrology, reincarnation, religious interpretation, prophecy—that is to say, he began what were to be called "Life Readings," which, at first, concentrated to a considerable degree on reincarnation.

After much discussion and evaluation, several businessmen from Chicago, New York, and other cities, who had benefited from the clairvoyant's readings proposed underwriting a foundation in Virginia Beach to support—on a full-time, properly housed and staffed basis—the work of Edgar Cayce. This eventually became the Association for Research and Enlightenment, which maintained complete records of all of the seer's activities and readings during the remainder of his life, and to this day continues to analyze and catalogue his prophetic and "occult" readings, as well as investigate other extraordinary phenomena.

Paracelsus, Mesmer, Puységur, Braid, Quimby, Eddy, Hoxsey, Abrams, Brinkley—serious investigators and quacks, stumbling about, or harvesting the yield, in the vineyards of therapy —all were exceptional in some sense, to a greater or lesser degree, but they, and their discoveries and work, were subject to explanation. To date Cayce and many of his readings have not been. Like the Comte de St. Germain, Cagliostro, and a rare few, he can be summarily dismissed, or he can be classified as an individual with a fundamentally natural, but momentarily undecipherable, power. Nonetheless there are countless written records of what he said in trance, and confining oneself to nothing but the diagnoses and prescriptions, and practices advised based upon them, one arrives at a statistical impasse. One success would have been unlikely for so medically uneducated a man; hundreds defy an explanation and equate to odds too large and too compounded by interminable vagaries to even hazard a figure.

Simple, modest, not particularly ambitious, Cayce was a curiosity during his life. In January 1945 he died and became for history what may forever remain a true mystery.

VIII
Oral Roberts and
Asa Alonso Allen

If Edgar Cayce remains a mystery, a figure of a more arcane past, Oral Roberts, and, to a slightly less degree, Asa Alonso Allen emerged after the Second World War to open the floodgates of a new and curiously mundane type of healing. Itinerant ministers of little-known sects—usually Pentecostal (see *Glossary*)—had cross-hatched the middle Southwest with their paths of wondrous cures for a long time, but they were outside the pattern of standard American religion, even of the more somber Protestant churches. But with the arrival of Roberts, Allen, and their successors, "faith healing" began to assume much broader dimensions, laying the foundation for the modern revival of the charismatic gifts throughout the greater portion of spirituality in this country.

"I believe that the laying on of hands is one of the highest expressions of the Christian faith . . . that is one reason why I lay my hands upon the people when I minister to them . . . my hands serve as a point of contact for releasing my faith for the healing . . . ,"[1] explains Reverend Roberts. "Because of the call of Christ to heal the sick and cast out devils, I am constantly traveling . . ."[2]

The evangelist views the unusualness of his life as having preceded his birth. This he bases upon a promise his mother is said to have made to God that in return for the recovery of a neighbor's dying child she would donate the product of her

[1] Oral Roberts, *If You Need Healing Do These Things*, p. 21.
[2] Ibid., p. v.

pregnancy to Him and His service. Additionally, the fundamentalist's grandfather had been a Methodist steward and his father was a Pentecostal preacher. Upon his birth in 1918, he was named Granville Oral, although it did not prevent his suffering from severe stammering during his childhood. Compounding his physically expressed handicap was the minimal subsistence level imposed upon the family of a circuit rider of the gospel.

He was still only a boy when he abandoned home and Ada, Oklahoma, for Atoka, another small community in the state, where he lodged a while with a judge and read a little law, worked in a grocer's on Saturdays, maintained a newspaper route, attended school, was a top student, was elected president of his class, and played on the first-string basketball team.

It was during a game that he collapsed on the court, fainted, and began hemorrhaging. He was immediately returned to Ada and his home, "heading back to poverty, back to a religion I had never accepted, back to my parents' discipline, and it tore me up inside." [3] Although contrary to the practice of most Pentecostals, as with many fundamentalist groups, his father summoned a physician, who diagnosed his condition as tuberculosis in both lungs. It was in the mid-thirties, he was only sixteen years old, and the affliction was regarded as extremely serious. In addition, the prognosis was not enhanced by the fact that a sister had died before her majority of the disease and his grandmother had succumbed to it as well.

The family moved to Stratford, Oklahoma, where Reverend Roberts was able to secure a permanent church and divest himself of the requirement to travel the ways of a gospel drummer. But the boy continued to fail, losing forty pounds in the succeeding five months.

While away from home the invalid had reverted to the church of his grandfather and, along with Oral's family, the local Methodist minister constantly prayed for the restoration of his health. Nonetheless, time eroded the patient's faith and he arrived at the point where all forms of religion were repugnant to him. He did

[3] Oral Roberts, *The Call*, p. 28.

not want consolation, he was "not interested in dying and going to Heaven or dying and going to hell." [4] He wanted to live and be well.

Then a revivalist came to town, with his great tent, posters, and promises of wonders. Finally relenting in his attitude, Oral permitted his brother and parents to bundle him into their automobile and carry him to the meeting.

Some of the records of this episode in Reverend Roberts's life, specifically relating to his psychic state and the visit to the itinerant evangelist, differ in detail from one another. One account describes Roberts's approach to the convocation in almost opposite terms to those spiritual doubts expressed above. In that version the youth was overflowing with intense faith. Also, in the same recollection, the revival tent was jammed and he was forced to queue up for hours, until well past midnight, before he reached the preacher—unidentified in virtually every rendition of the event—while, in another, no mention is made of the rather memorable and doubtless uncomfortable delay.[5] Regardless, ultimately he did find himself in the presence of the miracle-worker, who laid hands upon him and murmured a brief prayer. Instantly, the pain flooded from him and was replaced by a sense of the glory of the Holy Spirit, and he bounded up and raced about the sawdust trail crying aloud, "I am healed! I am healed!" [6]

Shortly thereafter the results were confirmed by an examination at the Sugg Clinic, in Ada, Oklahoma.

Eight weeks later Oral Roberts began his fundamentalist preaching—but not his healing. That aspect of his ministry was not inaugurated for another dozen years. In 1947, married, with two children, he was the pastor of a small Pentecostal Holiness Church in the narrow, dusty community of Enid, Oklahoma, when one day, "from within me God spoke to my heart and said, 'Don't be like the others, be like Jesus.' " [7]

Following profound consideration, the young preacher con-

[4] Ibid., p. 32.
[5] Roberts, *If You Need Healing*, p. 23.
[6] Roberts, *The Call*, p. 34.
[7] Roberts, *The Call*, p. 42.

cluded that this was a direction that he go forth and heal. Yet, not wanting to be precipitous, he decided to submit to his several hundred parishioners a plan he had devised to "test" the authenticity of "the call." First, he required himself to attract no fewer than a thousand people to the auditorium he had selected; second, he would regard an initial service collection of less than an amount sufficient to cover the rent for the hall as a disqualification, and, finally, he deemed it essential that God clearly demonstrate that he had truly been chosen "as an instrument to bring healing to the people." [8] The results: an attendance of over twelve hundred people, three dollars and three cents more than the lease price for the quarters, and an instant cure—in the middle of his sermon—of the "withered hand" of an old woman. A line began to form and "healing after healing occurred."

Oral Roberts's career as an evangelical healer was under way. Eventually his ministry would have offices in six foreign countries, distributing more than 100,000,000 pieces of literature annually, with various texts translated into nearly 200 languages. The central office in Tulsa would one day be staffed by 600 persons, and a remarkable multimillion-dollar university would be established on about five acres of beautiful land in the heart of the United States.

The conception and creation of the Oral Roberts spiritual and, later, educational empire is a phenomenal tale, but its entire foundation is the promulgation of the legend of the evangelist's ability to cure the sick. Despite the much modified television and public relations image he has presented since he was accepted as a Methodist minister in 1968, after more than a score of years in the Pentecostal movement, it is the promise of his miracles which originally attracted his great, if widely scattered, parish, and it is the same promise of the most mystical of the charismatic gifts of the Bible that keeps him internationally famous today.

The caption of a photograph in one of Reverend Roberts's early books shows him and a man, identified as George Morreau, standing beside a metal construction; it reads: "I was sitting in

8 Ibid., p. 43.

my wheelchair ... then Brother Roberts prayed for me in the name of Jesus of Nazareth. Suddenly I was on my feet praising God." [9] His illness is not specified.

Beneath another picture of the revivalist laying hands on the heads of two women, the text observes that "thousands testify to receiving healing in the crusades." [10] Another carries the legend that the minister "loves to pray for [sick] children because they have an instant response to the prayer of faith." [11]

Yet, apart from a few casual allusions to travel or his university plans, most of the 92-page paperback is an anthology of thaumaturgic anecdotes from the Bible and Roberts's rephrasing, and simplistic interpretation, of them.

Several of the fundamentalist's booklets are largely collections of parables and somewhat related explanations of them, but nearly all are concentrated on charismatic healing. In one the reverend describes an almost wholly crippled California woman, with a spinal block, paralysis, and insensibility along her side. He relates that she had been returned from the hospital to die.[12] Roberts's crusade came into the community and a friend persuaded her to allow herself to be transported by chair to it and into the quarters provided for seriously incapacitated invalids. As the account is related, upon seeing the evangelist approach she immediately realized the necessity of physical contact and prayed that hands would be placed on her, and that " 'his hand shall be as Thy hand and I will be healed.' " [13] Reverend Roberts recalls that there had been cures and failures that night, but as he touched her, "in the flash of a second the healing power of God swept through her body [which] ... began to tingle with life. The numbness and paralysis left her side ... and she jumped out of her chair and stood with her hands upraised, praising and magnifying God."

---

[9] Roberts, *If You Need Healing Do These Things*, p. 61.
[10] Ibid., p. 65.
[11] Ibid.
[12] Roberts, *Deliverance from Fear and from Sickness*, p. 62.
[13] Ibid., p. 63.

...she went outside [the room] and began to run around the tent, which was a quarter of a mile around... instantly and completely healed... [at home that night] she removed her hose and... screamed at the top of her voice. The leg which had been shriveled and paralyzed was restored perfectly whole and was the exact size of the other leg. [14]

Reverend Roberts, in the same book, tells of curing a totally blind girl, of Norfolk, Virginia, who had never seen at all, "not even [her] mother's face." He put his hand upon her eyes and "commanded the blindness to go in the name of Jesus of Nazareth... the presence of God came into my hand and I jerked it back... the power of God came upon her, she... screamed... 'I can see! I can see!' " [15]

Representative instances recorded by the evangelist are numerous, including the complete cure of Willie Phelps, of Roanoke, Virginia, who, from the age of six years, suffered from one leg's being two and a half inches shorter than the other. He was required to use crutches and wear a special orthopedic shoe. As is not uncommon in these anecdotes, the crowd at the meeting to which he was brought was so great entry could not be achieved. Fortunately, as the minister was departing the auditorium, he observed the boy and touched him wearily on the brow with his forefinger. Willie was instantly and completely healed.[16]

A twelve-year-old girl, suffering from rheumatic fever, who lived in Vancouver, British Columbia, was cured by what her mother was certain "was a miracle."

Elsewhere, Reverend Roberts tells of his mother's being confined to a hospital for two separate problems. Orthodox physicians corrected one of them, but the second persisted, and as it failed to improve—although she had been a dedicated Christian for half a century—she became irascible and embit-

---

[14] Ibid., pp. 64-65.
[15] Ibid., pp. 66-67.
[16] Ibid., pp. 73-74.

tered. The pain prevailed and Mrs. Roberts's faith began to fail. Then, during a visit her son thought: *There are demons in this room*, not in my mother, but in this room!

> ... I knew that my mother did not have any demons, but I also knew they were in the room . . . wherever there is sickness there are demons . . . I walked over that room praying . . . when I did this, victory came, victory came and the room was cleansed. [17]

Yet, the cure had not been actually effected, only the conditions for the phenomenon prepared. The cleric then proceeded to explain to his mother that her remaining affliction had transformed her into a spiritually negative egocentricity. Upon recognizing, accepting, and relieving herself of this psychological corruption, she was made well.

Throughout his writings Oral Roberts tells of healing a considerable variety of disorders, including cancer, tuberculosis, goiter, paralysis, congenital deformity, spinal incapacitations, headaches, as well as countless other illnesses. Also he diagnoses and prescribes for many emotional and psychological problems, especially justified and needless fears and guilts, insecurity, indulgences in any or all of the seven vices, and how to restore a recidivistic "cure."

The evangelist asserts that one of his books was solicited by "more than one million families." [18] Certainly, tens, if not hundreds, of thousands of free copies have been distributed. The great demand for it encouraged him to compose a sequel [19] which undoubtedly has swept like a blizzard of Oral manna across the land. Both of these works are practical books, in a sense. The earlier is mostly devoted to explanations of how one can direct spiritual fervor to achieve material ends, especially outright cash, by a technique he calls "seed-faith," a contemporary bread-

---

[17] Oral Roberts, *Your Healing Problems and How to Solve Them*, pp. 14-15.

[18] Oral Roberts, *Miracle of Seed-Faith*.

[19] Oral Roberts, *The Miracle Book*.

upon-the-waters approach. Of course, it also speaks of miraculous healing. The sequel, which is almost two hundred pages long, elaborates on the theses propounded in its predecessor, and emphasizes the revivalist's truly remarkable success in establishing his Oral Roberts University, an institution recently accorded full regional academic accreditation.

The school is represented by far better planning and architecture than many contemporary competitors, evolved, as it is, in easy conformation to the approximately five acres it covers, and while its campus may be a bit "modern" for some aesthetic tastes—reminding one of a miniature world's fair or international exposition—the complex is fresh, clean, integral to the attractive landscape, and is eminently effective in conveying the atmosphere of open, healthy living. It boasts Mabee Center, a large and splendid auditorium, resident dormitories, a retirement compound for older persons, and—as if to erase any doubt as to its position as an American college—its basketball team, the Titans (an interestingly pagan name for athletic representatives of so hyper-Christian an institution), was accepted as a member of the National Collegiate Athletic Association (NCAA) in 1971 and set the conference record for high scoring (105.1 average) and rebounding (60.2 average) in 1972, winning their final playoff in Madison Square Garden, New York City.

The later book is also filled with parables and anecdotes of Reverend Roberts's cures and miracles.

The great evangelist has a television program which appears weekly throughout the nation, and is patterned much after the Lawrence Welk or King Sisters format, embroidered with religion. He often features major "celebrities" like singers Johnny Cash and Pat Boone. Still, while a general prayer for the healing of the ill is included, the miracle-worker Oral Roberts has been replaced by a conservative preacher of the gospel.

On the other hand, the magazine distributed by the Oral Roberts Evangelistic Association, Inc., is replete with stories and testimonies of those who have been relieved of the most terrible of man's diseases. Among many such pieces, the February issue of *Abundant Life* featured the article "God Healed Me of Deadly

Cancer," but the text makes it quite clear that it was Clem Dizon's encounter with the revivalist that brought the cure to pass. Every copy of the magazine is rife with testimonies of redemptions from virtually every known illness, either through direct contact with Reverend Roberts, or by writing to the center, or calling the special prayer number.

Modified as the broader public image doubtless is, at the core of the complex is the Oral Roberts phenomenon; the thaumaturgist, the gifted charismatist, the simple-seeming man with the apparent faith-healing hands abides. A curious contradiction: on one side, as with many lesser practitioners he merchandises religious products in the standard mail-order fashion, e.g. cassetted sermons at $4 each, or a small library of a dozen for a 25 per cent saving; on the other, much material is given away. The incoming mail comes in tidal mountains, with many months being credited with 500,000 letters. Few are without contributions of from $1 to $5.

Yet, all things considered, it is highly probable that he is the only one of his kind who will persist historically, for he is the sole itinerant tent preacher to become a genuinely internationally known healer with a mantle of ecclesiastical respectability. He alone raised a temple of impressive buildings and an Edenesque five-acre campus, constituting a major university peopled by cherubic-faced American youths from the Norman Rockwell myth, to the praise of the God of things as he saw Him and to Granville Oral Roberts as—at least some of him—is.

Asa Alonso Allen's career is reminiscent of Oral Roberts's in many ways. Both were born in the mid-Southwest, both fluctuated between Methodism and Pentecostalism, both established colleges and, then, communities around them, both possessed considerable oratorical powers, and both achieved major economic success, for when the latter began to lay less public stress on the palliative aspects of his services, the former assumed the mantle as probably the foremost of American evangelical healers.

A product of the sweeping, flatland Bible belt, Allen was converted to the pulpit by the powerful preaching of an itinerant female revivalist whose name he never revealed. First a Methodist, he saw the greater light of Pentecostalism soon and accepted it as his way, a way that endowed him with the gift of curing the ill body and raising the impaired soul.

This was not the end of his spiritual development. Shortly thereafter he allied himself with the Assemblies of God, and his calling carried him far—too far, in at least one direction, apparently, for by the mid-fifties, within the framework of a mutually accepted understanding, he parted with the sect. Seemingly having discovered that his way was not the way of all the children of the Divine, nor even of most of the men and churches who taught the Word, he was forced into creating an appropriate vehicle for his ministry, the vast proportion of which was, of course, healing.

Interestingly, the new project did not seem to have derived from the visionary instruction or a moment's enlightenment of purpose, but from a cool pragmatic decision that this was the way he, A. A. Allen, could serve the Lord, his congregation, and his own spiritual and mundane needs.

A man of dynamic character, Allen continued to attract larger and larger crowds under enormous "canvas cathedrals." The use of the great tents was both a nostalgic holdover from the glorious days of Billy Sunday and a means of hugely increasing the potential attendance in the countless communities where there were no structures, let alone houses of worship, which could accommodate more than a few hundred people. Still, as the collapse of these vast fabricated temples was not at all unknown, an auditorium, if available, was always preferred.

Unlike the majority of his evangelical colleagues, Allen encouraged and attracted passing parishioners of all races and religious denominations, and was among the very first to end the seating segregation in his Southern ministry. As a matter of fact, he was capable of raising a crowd to a frenzy with nearly the hypnotic power of the great black preachers, and so appealed to those who admired that approach to the Lord and to their white brothers of Holy Rollery and other fundamentalist groups.

Such diverse and large-scale activities require a base of operations. There must be advance men to go forth and arrange for the public sponsorship of the minor local clergy, the publicity and advertising preceding the revivalist's arrival, the performance rehearsals of the choirs and bands, the books to be kept, as well as numerous other essential business activities—all quite apart from the healer's preparation of his mind for the preaching of the gospel and his spirit for the delivery of God's touch to heal the infirm. From a purely mechanical point of view, the greatest evangelical operations are not unlike those of a miniaturized Ringling Brothers Circus.

Fully realizing the need for a headquarters, Allen conceived and created it. Accumulating more than a thousand acres in Cochise County, Arizona, he developed a liquorless, tobaccoless, God- and Allen-serving community of basic Bibledom and called it Miracle Valley.

The small town consisted almost entirely of employees and persons in some manner related to A. A. Allen Revivals, Inc., or students attending the Bible College he established there. As with most successful ministers of this kind, physical plant evolved into a large-scale enterprise. Tens of millions of pieces of literature were being dispatched throughout the country and overseas, annually. The combination of radio and television stations being supplied with Allen broadcasts numbered over a hundred, while his own recording company had produced half that many disks of his preaching and of the performances of his religious musical groups. More than a third of a million copies of the coated-stock, multicolored *Miracle Magazine* were being distributed monthly. And, throughout the country, there were constant preparations for the healer to make numerous personal appearances to complement his semiannual two-week-long Miracle Valley revival meetings. To implement this perpetual whirlwind schedule Allen had his private plane poised on an airstrip near his splendid custom-built dodecagonal house. Although the personal incomes of the evangelist and his several associates remain, as is the custom, undisclosed, a few years before he rose to his less earthly rewards, a decade short of his Biblical allotment, his organization grossed nearly $4,000,000.[20]

"On June 15, 1970, in the vast Miracle Valley tabernacle, the man in the open casket was being crowned," or as written elsewhere, "It *was* Saint-making time." [21]

"An honor guard of four preachers, changed every ten minutes, stood proudly north, south, east, and west of the casket as the seemingly endless line of people . . . paraded by . . .'"

"Asa Alonso Allen was dead," at fifty-nine years, "but he wasn't dead to the three thousand in the tabernacle . . . and he wasn't dead to God." [22]

"Now the formal ceremony reached its initial crescendo with a blazing message of affirmation and ecstasy by Dr. Roy Gray, dean of the Miracle Valley Bible College."

But, at that moment, Brother Don Stewart noticed that "in the audience a man . . . had evidently fainted and already two ushers had him on a stretcher." [23] He "felt that someone . . . had to pray for the man . . . Brother Allen would be the first person to agree," and he moved from the services to the man's side. Kneeling beside the figure the young evangelist, in laying hands on the form, recognized him as one of the deceased's disciples.

" 'I rebuke the spirit of death,' I prayed," recalls Reverend Stewart. "The room was gripped in a vise of tight silence. Not even the crucial sound of breath or a heartbeat pulsed from Brother Hunter. 'Heal him, Lord! Raise him from this bed of anguish and agony. I call for his healing in the name of Jesus.' . . . Brother Hunter opened his eyes. Color suddenly flashed back into his face . . . 'I'm fine,' he said. Brother Hunter and I walked back into the church. I'd been gone some five minutes. Dr. Gray was concluding . . ." [24]

Friend and counselor Reverend Raymond Hoekstra memor-

[20] *The New York Times*, August 13, 1972.
[21] Don Stewart, with Walter Wagner, *The Man from Miracle Valley*, p. 1.
[22] Ibid., p. 4.
[23] Ibid., p. 5.
[24] Ibid., p. 5.

ialized the departed revivalist, at one point alluding to him as "the Spike Jones [25] of the pulpit . . . the James Cagney of the sawdust trail."

Reverend H. Kent Rogers, associated with the late minister for a decade and a half, coevangelist, and president of the Allen Revivals, which toured the country after the fashion of any multiple segment tent show, also contributed to the eulogies.

Twenty-five individuals, including Brother Stewart and the immediate family of the mourned, accompanied the body to the Miracle Valley cemetery, where the second most famous healing evangelist of his time was laid to rest. The subsequently erected tombstone read: "God's Man of Faith and Power. A. A. Allen. 1911–1970." [26]

Yet, interestingly, it was not any of Reverend Allen's companions from the old wars with the devil and society who was ordained by him to be his successor. Not Dr. Gray, whom he appointed dean of his Bible College; not Reverend Hoekstra, fraternal adviser of many years; not Reverend Rogers, president of his widespread operation and companion since 1954; no, none of these, nor any other old comrade one might have anticipated for various reasons. Reverend Asa Alonso Allen had designated as the new leader of Miracle Valley "a thirty-year-old ex-sinner who once had all but given himself to Satan"—Don Stewart. [27]

Again the great "healing" evangelist who had stunned audiences by opening fire-breathing sermons with the lightning cry: "God is a killer!" [28] had done the unexpected. Not to the sages and graybeards had he delivered his vast organization, he had bequeathed it to youth.

---

[25] A well-known leader of an essentially comic popular orchestra which satirized "standard" ballads during the 1950s.

[26] Stewart and Wagner, *The Man from Miracle Valley*, p. 6.

[27] Ibid., p. 25.

[28] Ibid., p. 135.

IX

Don Stewart and Rex Humbard: Miracle Valley and The Cathedral of Tomorrow

The successor to the directorship of the Miracle Valley organization was born in Arizona, the sixth child of Beulah Henness and Roy A. Stewart, on October 25, 1939, and named Donald Lee.[1] His father had drifted about in various occupations and no religions until he met his future wife in Prescott. Although originally a Methodist, she became a member of the Pentecostal Full Gospel Church early in life, and withstood the wandering Canadian's proposals of marriage until he agreed to accept the Lord as his Saviour, too, after which "he never touched another drop of alcohol or a cigarette."

The minister's recollections of his family are not without interest: Ann who was often found "coming home from school with a torn dress or a bloody eye," as a result of her temper and hoydenish character; Mary who would "lace into the dishes with the same enthusiasm with which she would read Deuteronomy"; and brother Bill who "was my idol, and the hardest thing I would ever do would be to . . . turn him over to the FBI . . . when he was a bank robber."

Brother Stewart's introduction to the healing power of the Holy Spirit came when his father laid hands on their ailing goat, saying, "God, this is our only means of supplying milk for our

---

[1] The following account of Don Stewart's life is taken from Don Stewart, with Walter Wagner, *The Man from Miracle Valley.*

children. We ask you to heal this goat." And it was done instantly.

Throughout the various conditions of his childhood, the Stewarts were devoted Assembly of God parishioners, but it was not until he was taken to a tent meeting, when he was ten years old, that he was opened to the glory of the Divine Inspiration.

"Saved and born again! Now I *could* hear the cascading trumpet of Gabriel . . . I had met God . . ."

But once separated from the enrapturing atmosphere, the youth's dedication began to falter. He sought the praise of his peers in worldly ways, began to swear, smoke, and, finally, stole. He had fallen far from his moment of grace. Yet, apparently, his earlier misdeeds affected him far less than the surreptitious attendance of a motion picture which, because of his training, made him feel "dirty and filthy. I was certain the devil had me by the collar . . . I began to accept the fact my final destination would be hell."

A sobering thought for a twelve-year-old. And if he felt his soul was nearly lost, he had no doubt about the deterioration of his character, especially the lack of control he showed over his explosive temper.

Then his leg was injured, and an operation followed. It was successful, but left the hip fragile. In a subsequent fit of fury Don Stewart, during a violent confrontation, struck a teacher with one of his crutches. The victim suffered little damage, but the young assailant reinjured himself and was required to undergo another surgical procedure. This time the mending process was less certain, and, even months later, the physicians would give no assurances that his hip would ever be normal again. There was a reasonable possibility that he might be slightly crippled for the remainder of his life.

Soon afterwards a healing evangelist visited the church the incapacitated boy attended, and, notwithstanding his full awareness that he had not truly repented, he approached the altar to be prayed over. The minister laid on his hands and invoked the pity and the power of the Lord:

" 'But he was wounded . . . ,' " he began, moments later concluding, "It's done. You're healed."

Overwhelmed, Don Stewart felt himself suspended in the
absolute silence, and then strength surged into his leg. "Something supernatural was happening. I slipped the crutches from
under my arms and let them fall. I took a step, and yet another."
He was healed.

Yet, in a sense, he was more confused than ever. He could not
imagine why God had restored the health of one still steeped in
the sickness of the mind and soul, for he in no way deceived
himself that more of him than the physical had been cured—and
certainly the Holy Spirit knew that even more than he. In Reverend Stewart's words, "The answer wouldn't come for several
years."

And during the period before his finally achieving a genuine
relationship with, and for, the Lord the future revivalist piled up
sins "like winter cordwood." He got drunk, lied to his parents,
gambled away his earnings, and frequented the local whore-
houses. It was after a combination of such activities that he
found himself in church one Sunday morning, listening to a
missionary who had spent most of his ministry promulgating the
gospel among the headhunters of the Amazon.

Suddenly, but since such occurrences were becoming habitual
perhaps not unexpectedly, "an unbelievable thing happened.
God spoke directly to Don Stewart:

" 'I want you to go into the world and preach the Gospel to
every creature.' "

And from that instant forward the young man knew that his
life must be dedicated to the preaching of the Divine Word. This
conviction was additionally buttressed a few nights later when he
heard the Reverend Asa Alonso Allen deliver a sermon on the
radio, and raise a crippled woman to health from her stretcher.
The boy took the evangelist as his hero.

Soon he was dispatched to the Canyonville Bible Academy, a
small, essentially Pentecostal school in Oregon, created, constructed, and operated by a hardy servant of God named Dad

Schaffer. The rules verged on the monastic. Chapel for forty-five minutes before breakfast, hair combed straight back, spartan, if nourishing, meals, no smoking, no dancing, no movies, no radio, no drinking, no dating between the male and female students, and everyone in bed by nine o'clock.

Two of the more memorable incidents at the academy were the visit of Reverend Allen in a flashy red Cadillac, a gift from members of the black clergy in appreciation for the evangelist's long-standing policy of integrated meetings, and the raiding of the girls' dormitory to steal a kiss from a sexy blonde pupil from Las Vegas. The first intensified his calling; the second got him expelled from the school.

The fluctuating disciple returned home and managed to graduate there, but persisted in his devilish ways. Yet, as he views those days in retrospect, he feels that God was constantly protecting him. He cites an incident when he and two friends planned to go out on the town, drinking and wenching, but his mother, possessed of some sort of premonition, was praying for his safekeeping, and although he was unaware of this he altered his plans and worked instead. On their return trip, one of the youths, who was sitting in the place in the automobile in which he always sat when the trio went abroad together, was shot through the head with a high-powered rifle. The murder remains unsolved.

After countless digressions, a genial camaraderie with the demons of sin, and a state of remorse and fear following the killing of his friend, the would-be gospeler was guided into an A. A. Allen revival under the world's largest tent devoted to the Word. At last, the glory of God struck him and held. The salvation was completed and the ministry commenced.

Immediately he began making his religious inroads, becoming one of the very first settlers who built Miracle Valley. Despite disagreement with a couple of his administrators, the young man gained the attention and interest of the leader, who nourished his talents into the pulpit. During this period Don Stewart had fallen in love with a beautiful girl who had been an admirer of

Reverend Roberts, and was the subject of divine healing by another Pentecostal evangelist. The couple were the last ever married by A. A. Allen.

A point was reached when Reverend Stewart was ordained by his mentor and went out on his own, with initially small, but growing, success. This period of his eventful life is somewhat shadowed by an unnerving experience which resulted as his temper flashed out during a meeting. While conducting a service in Canada, he was assaulted by the heckling and scoffing of an eighteen-year-old boy. Suddenly, Reverend Stewart's patience broke and he whirled about, thrust a damning finger at him, and cried:

"Young man, unless you repent of your sins *tonight* rottenness will enter into your bones within three days!"

The revivalist recalls that he had terrified himself with the curse, the like of which, he notes, he has never cast again. The boy's response was to laugh it off, but within three days he was on crutches. Six months later Reverend Stewart received word that he was dead of bone cancer.

Yet, strange experiences appear to be as much a part of the evangelist's life as religion. A short time later he discovered that a bank had been robbed by his brother Bill. Soon he received a call from the culprit, who had been caught but had managed to escape the police. He wanted a hundred dollars to get to Mexico. Don Stewart was caught in a state of great conflict, especially when he found out that this was the third bank his brother had relieved of funds. The indecision was resolved in favor of fraternalism, until Mrs. Stewart took a firm, irrevocable stand for turning the fugitive over to the authorities. This compounded her husband's problem enormously. Yet eventually he acceded to her demands and telephoned the Federal Bureau of Investigation, reporting the whereabouts of his brother. Bill spent most of the next ten years in the penitentiary.

Soon after this unfortunate incident Reverend Stewart was contacted by his mentor. Upon finding one of his revivalists unable to conduct a service, Brother Allen called upon his protégé to replace him. Needless to say, the audience was enthusiastic. The incident resulted in the young evangelist's working the gospel tour for the entire ten-day engagement. Then the regular preacher returned and he prepared to go back to his own fluctuating ministry. To his happy amazement, Reverend Allen suggested that he remain with the evangelical corporation and assist its leader in "special work."

Don Stewart was more than glad to be included in the inner circle of the Allen Revivals, Inc., and became the founder's aide in researching sermons, typing notes, preparing texts, and occasionally preaching. According to Reverend Stewart, his idol taught him four major ecclesiastical points of efficacy: 1. First the congregation had to be shocked—an absolute necessity . . . 2. After the gasps subsided . . . prove [your] thesis . . . Scripture was filled with examples proving almost anything; 3. Arouse curiosity . . . Who is God going to kill next? You? And the final injunction of Brother Allen was "the most important of all . . . don't forget your own self-interest." Yet, with all of the advantages of being associated with the much-publicized preacher, Brother Stewart decided that his spiritual evolution required him to pursue an "independent ministry" again, and he set forth on his own once more.

Although there were practical trials to be endured as his new venture into the promulgating of the gospel progressed, the healing powers of the youthful revivalist seemed to come more and more under his direct command. One example is typical and appears to have been the specialty of a number of faith healers, that is the lengthening of one leg which was shorter than its companion. In Prescott, Arizona, Reverend Stewart remedied this discrepancy, and the man, an Alfred Cosette, is said to have departed wholly healthy in his limbs.

Of somewhat less common nature, although not at all unknown—as a matter of fact, one contemporary thaumaturgist specializes in the operation—was the reported medical help afforded Barbara Gregory, a high school student of the area. Having confessed that she was inordinately afraid of dentists, and, as a result, suffered from nine cavities, she submitted herself to Brother Stewart's power. He laid hands upon her and prayed, and she left. On the following evening Miss Gregory returned to testify that all of her cavities were completely filled with, in the words of the evangelist, "material I had never seen before." While an interesting sort of physical improvement, it is difficult not to wonder why the Lord did not simply restore the teeth to their original perfection, or replace them with new ones—especially since occasionally some people, in what is recorded as the normal course of their physical evolution, acquire a third set of teeth, anyway.

Certainly, Reverend Stewart's conviction as to his calling and the manner in which he should approach it strengthened. "In asking Him for healing, I had learned by now that I had to command [who?] in an authoritative way . . . He doesn't expect timidity from His ministers. 'O God, if it be Thy wish, heal this person,' was the Mickey Mouse prayer I'd heard so often from virtually every minister I knew except Brother Allen. Like him, I commanded healing and boldly rebuked sickness and death . . . my power to act as God's agent in healing was a gift, a result of the accumulated faith I had inherited from my folks, from Brother Allen, from Christ coming to me as a brother during my time of fasting, prayer, and meditation. . . ."

On the other hand, after the fashion of most fundamentalist healers, he voices the same explanation for those who are not benefited by his touch, i.e. ". . . but it is not my decision as to who should and should not be healed." During this period in the mid-1960s he numbered among those restored to health at his revivals persons with palsy, and goiters, and was also forced to confront gangs of ruffians, the anti-Pentecostal police and judiciary of Charleston, South Carolina. It was hard times in the American Southwest, and there was a marked decline in the practice and interest in evangelism, especially the itinerant "under canvas" type. In truth, in the large sense, only the A. A. Allen Revivals, Inc. was continuing to prosper. In the minister's words, "the Stewarts bounced along the gospel trail, a preacher and his wife equally afire for God, little Renée [their daughter] and a second child who might or might not [Kathy was pregnant] come into the world to live for Him."

Brother Allen now called upon him again. This time one of the regular staff preachers was unable to accompany the senior revivalist on a tour of Great Britain and Reverend Stewart was asked to replace him, which he did. The expedition was a success, and when it returned to this country Allen suggested that his protégé remain with the organization, although, as Brother Stewart recollects the arrangements, they were unspoken and, therefore, in his mind, somewhat tenuous. Nonetheless, half a year had soon elapsed, but his relationship with the Allen evangelical movement continued.

The Christmas season arrived, and, with it, the annual organization party for the couple of hundred Miracle Valley employees. After the banquet, the apostle of the Pentecostal movement rose and announced that he wished to introduce the "new secretary-treasurer of A. A. Allen Revivals ... Don Stewart!"

From this point onward, the young minister assumed a primary role in the activities of his mentor including arranging for and conducting major meetings, some abroad, aiding in transforming the orientation of it to encompass more youthful spiritual prospects, and assisting in the development of Miracle Valley.

Brother Allen, as has been noted earlier, died in 1970, and was buried on June 15. Paraphrasing Reverend Stewart, the torch passed to him, and he became the practical and spiritual leader of the Allen Revivals and Miracle Valley, over which he retains firm control today. The official journal, *Miracle*, almost invariably features a photograph of him on its glossy, colored cover, and nearly every issue opens with a lead article by him, beginning with a double-page spread. The magazine is the voice of what is now called the Don Stewart Evangelistic Association, and its sixteen pages consist almost entirely of material by or about Allen's successor, including a list of his many television and radio broadcasts, his personal crusades and testimonies purportedly relating thereto, photographs of him with and without other persons, in profusion, and perpetual and usually powerful, hard-sell centerfold petitions for contributions from $10 upward.

Dr. Roy Gray is still the dean of the Miracle Valley Bible College, which, in 1973, graduated "the largest class in the school's history," although the reference did not indicate how many were included in that number. As covered by text and six photographs in *Miracle*, it seemed quite evident that Brother Allen's philosophy of integration has not been dissipated, as perhaps a third or half the class appeared to have been black.

The December 1973 issue contained a lead article by Reverend Stewart titled "I Believe in Christmas," which, rather simply, expresses his preference for the generally accepted Christian religious concept of the holiday to the more commercialized version ubiquitously prevalent today. To any interested in the breadth of fundamentalism in the United States—and most conceive of it in far too narrow terms—a comparison of Brother Stewart's piece and the one by Charles F. Vinson, in the Worldwide Church of God journal, *The Plain Truth*, titled "Why the World Needs Christmas," is worthwhile. The latter is professionally researched and written, and is opposed to the celebration of December 25 by Christians on the basis of the quite accurate argument that virtually nothing relating to it has any connection with the religion it alleges to rejoice or the Saviour it is supposed to honor.[3]

Few evangelical healers assemble the financial resources and create the complex organizations of Oral Roberts and A. A. Allen, but this does not prevent a number from becoming very well known, especially in specific areas, and accumulating capital, or even annual income, in six and seven figures. The majority of these might be classified as "independents." That is, while encouraging missionary activity, as well as other related religious efforts, the primary thrust of their ministry is centered in one place and their parishioners come to them rather than the traditional practice of foraging about the country for lost souls. This is not to say that such figures do not travel from time to time,

[3] The author would like to make explicitly clear that beyond their fundamentalist religious leanings the two publications have little in common. *The Plain Truth*, usually consisting of approximately forty pages, is similar in format to the *National Review*, except that it carries colored photographs. It is among the more interesting publications in the country.

fronting elaborate "crusades," but rather that there is a greater tendency for the modern thaumaturgist to communicate by *television* crusades, rather than big tent tours. In truth, some, such as Kathryn Kuhlman, professedly concentrate their activities in their own church or temple, with only occasional, if regularly scheduled, ventures to other locales. Furthermore, most members of this successful group of revivalists have little, if any, intercommunion with the formal Protestant religions, although they maintain an umbrella policy of accepting, or summoning, persons of any faith, from theosophists through Methodists, to Catholics and Jews, to their Pentecostal parade to the Lord. Still, while there are a few essentially ego-arguments among leading evangelists, the great majority either ignore or praise the work of their colleagues or competitors, with the attitude of any particular minister toward another strongly influenced by the position of each in the fame and financial hierarchy of revivalism.

Rex Humbard is among the more publicized of the second tier fundamentalist preachers who emphasize their healing relationship with man and God, and belong in the category just described. Born of Alpha E. and Martha Bell Humbard in Little Rock, Arkansas, on August 13, 1919, his records indicate that he was only two days old when his parents, both evangelists, committed his life to the service of the Lord. As an infant he was transported from one camp meeting to another, sleeping in a corner of the platform, as services were performed in an endless chain of small communities. Wherever home was, an altar could be found, and, as the years passed, children in increasing number, for the future minister was to be the eldest of a half-dozen siblings. The paternal discipline was strict and corporal, and when the Reverend Humbard decided that Rex, and other offspring, should learn to play musical instruments, to complement the presentation of the gospel, they learned. Soon they appeared on a local radio program, which led to an appearance on a larger station, and by 1939 to a professional, if limited, career in the promulgation of religious music of the fundamentalist order.

It was in that year that the group was to be featured at the state fairgrounds in Dallas. There they met the Reverend Albert Ott, and his daughter, Maude Aimee—for Aimee Semple McPherson, noted female evangelist of an earlier period—who was foreordained to be Rex's wife. In his heart, the young man thought the bond was sealed when, at a YWCA Valentine party a fortnight later, he serenaded her with "*I Want a Girl Just Like the Girl That Married Dear Old Dad,*" and, in terms of "popular" secular songs, you cannot get much more fundamental than that.

Six months later, when he received his high school diploma —she was fifteen and he three years older—they began going steady. They certainly seemed eminently suited to one another as the girl was, if anything, even more religiously precocious than he, having discovered Jesus of Nazareth as her personal salvation at the age of six, shortly following which conversion she began to sing the story of the Lord at services and on the radio. Before the year ended he pleaded for her hand, to which petition she replied with a direct and unallegorical "OK, Rex." Yet, despite their certainty, it was decided their relative youth precluded the immediate assumption of the burdens of marriage.

The work, nonetheless, had to proceed, and the Humbard family were called to disperse the gospel once more in Little Rock. It was during this period, January 1941, that the prominent revivalist Jackie Burris invited the family to display their musical gospel at one of his crusades. The offer was enthusiastically accepted and for six weeks an opening half-hour of the group's music was offered. Still, if positive currents were carrying the clan forward, the youth's life was not without its difficulties. His separation from Maude Aimee diminished his professional happiness in direct parallel to the increasing infrequency of her letters, which, before the new year, had completely stopped. When the family was invited to return to Dallas for a church dedication, Rex discovered that his fiancée was involved with another young man and he assumed all was lost. But fate was not to be deterred and soon after, while visiting the Humbard family, Maude Aimee responded to a new proposal by Rex and they were married shortly thereafter.

Evidence indicates that the future evangelist had done little, if any, preaching up to this point, that task being reserved for his father, while he and the remainder of the family provided the hymnal interludes. One gets the impression that, although a strong Bible-thumping preacher of the Word, the elder Humbard was not a major healer. This is not to suggest that such miraculous events did not occur prior to Rex's ministry, for he has personally recounted one incident which occurred around this time during which a woman who had suffered sixteen years of blindness found her sight totally restored.

Other examples of divine intervention during that segment of his life include the reconciliation of a couple fighting in the divorce courts through numerous more physical improvements, to Rex's prophesying that someone in his audience had but one more chance to be saved. The man whom he had singled out for this ominous forecast hesitated, suggesting perhaps he would soon accept Jesus. As the revivalist recalls the case, later that night, not far from the auditorium, the man was mugged and murdered.

As with most of those who practice the charismatic arts today, Reverend Humbard occasionally throws in a mote of memory regarding glossalalia or foreordination but the emphasis is always upon the gospel and healing.

Reverend Humbard, despite never having attended any seminary nor engaged in formal religious training, was ordained in the independent fundamentalist Gospel Tabernacle, in Greenville, South Carolina, although under the aegis of the family's regular church in Hot Springs. The license of validation was issued by a separatist body of preachers calling itself the International Ministerial Federation. From there the revivalist moved to Gastonia, North Carolina, and across to Louisville to conduct services in the province of Dr. Mordecai Ham, whom Humbard identifies as the individual who converted the person and ministry of Billy Graham.

Following the birth of his first child, his mind was permeated by the divine suggestion that he go to New York, and he followed it. Immediately upon his arrival, he confronted one of the major networks and informed them that he wished to broadcast daily, coast-to-coast, but was rejected with assurances that he was most fortunate that programs of his were aired three times a week. Resolved to have his own way, he tried his demands on a second flagship station and was able to work out a deal which also permitted him to continue his traveling gospel schedule.

The ministry progressed, but with occasional interruptions, such as being burned out of one auditorium, which resulted in loss of many thousands of dollars' worth of musical instruments and other paraphernalia; having its big tent destroyed by a violent Florida storm; and suffering through the contraction of a respiratory disorder by the revivalist's son, which led to a partially collapsed lung, pessimism on the part of the attending physicians, and, eventually, his cure at the hands of the premier healer—Oral Roberts. On the other hand, Reverend Humbard learned to fly, he purchased his private plane, and performed the opening musical segment for a debate between two California politicians, one bearing the name of Richard Milhous Nixon. Not surprisingly, the fundamentalist regards it as one of the most memorable incidents in his career.

The years rushed by, the Word rolled out; the towns and cities visited became uncountable and each new tent was larger than its predecessor, until the Humbard crusade could raise as much canvas "as the Ringling Brothers." Yet, increasingly, the preacher was inclining toward the idea of settling his operation in one location, from which he could go forth soul-seeking when the spirit moved him. After a major service in Akron, Ohio, to which he shrewdly invited Kathryn Kuhlman to be guest speaker, thus assuring a full house, he decided that this was to be his Zion.

Thus it was that in the winter of 1953 Rex Humbard began seeking a location which might serve as a permanent housing for his ministry, ultimately acquiring an old theater in the city of Cuyahoga Falls, north of Akron. Pledges were solicited and forthcoming, and, on April 5, Easter Sunday, the new Calvary Temple opened, crowned by a forty-two-foot-high neon cross. Success followed success. As more than five hundred charter members were enrolled, a nearby elementary school was leased for a Sunday school, twenty-two buses were engaged on a weekly basis to transport persons who had no traveling facilities of their own. Friday-night Bible film programs were arranged, adult Bible classes inaugurated, five television broadcasts were added to the burgeoning network of Humbard radio shows, a Dial-a-Prayer facility was initiated, and the evangelist reports that he didn't miss a service for more than seven years.

It need hardly be recorded that the entire organization rapidly began to outgrow its plant, and soon Reverend Humbard was searching for fresh and larger quarters. Yet, so vast had the following and operation become, it appeared to be impossible to find a building adequate for the exploding parish.

New property was acquired for $140,000. A friend offered additional money to buy up the land and buildings across from the new site to secure the possibility of future development, and, thus, with skillful manipulation, the "Cathedral of Tomorrow" project had accumulated over twenty acres of urban land. Not unexpectedly, control of the various and overall programs deviated little from the center: Rex Humbard, director of the Architectural Committee; Rex Humbard, head of the Finance Committee; Rex Humbard, supervisor of the Construction Committee. Voting for primary administrative office in the church councils obviously provided the members with no insoluble problems. Still, the revivalist learnt that, even in religion, the buck stops somewhere, and he was unable to find an Akron architect who would design his dream of a round building, notwithstanding the existence of hundreds, probably thousands, of them around the world—many of which are spiritual edifices. Undiscouraged, he investigated the possibilities in Chicago and concluded arrangements with the A. L. Salzman Company to create his temple. Singularly philanthropic, the head of the firm accepted the greatly delayed schedule of compensation suggested by Rex Humbard and did not begin to receive payment for his company's contribution until the "Cathedral of Tomorrow" officially swung wide its door five years after the work was begun.

Land, design, labor—all in hand; but no cash. Then a supporter offered $25,000 to initiate the fund-raising, and while this constituted the smallest of pittances, construction was begun, with amateur contractor Rex directing the erection of the building and amateur decorator Maude Aimee the interior plans.

The Cathedral of Tomorrow was opened on May 24, 1958. The four-inch-thick wooden cupola spanned 220 feet (the preacher is fond of noting that the second largest of this type doming, the Cathedral of Florence, is only 138 feet in breadth), constituting a 38,000-square-foot ceiling. From this artificial black sky hang teardrop chandeliers and a cross 100 feet high which is subject to more than 60 color lighting combinations, putting it on a par with Radio City Music Hall, in New York, in terms of theatrical illumination.

Facing the nearly 5,500 upholstered seats is the 168-foot stage into which is incorporated hydraulic operations and automatic contour curtains.

In addition, the operation includes a 200-bed nursery, chapels, prayer retreats, a library, more than 150 classrooms, and various other features, plus all sorts of relatives, friends, and associates—including Jackie Burris, who had been absorbed by the cometing healer he once engaged for his own independent crusades. As Reverend Humbard recalls, the inauguration to completion of The Cathedral of Tomorrow took less than six years, 10,000 people were attracted to it on its opening day, and it cost well over $2,000,000.

A ladies' girdle factory, located in Brooklyn and purchased in 1965, was among his stranger, nonreligious acquisitions.

Yet, while God may help those who help themselves, he may be a bit strict on those He believes to help themselves a bit too much. To pursue his goals, Reverend Humbard had floated bonds with a 1973 maturation date, but rumors of financial uncertainty caused many purchasers to begin asking for redemption, this time fiscal, fifteen years early. Despite having sold almost $250,000 worth of these securities during the thirty days following the temple's opening, most of it was spent or committed, and the minister had never dreamed that this situation would arise within a decade, let alone a matter of months. No bank approached was willing to underwrite the debts and defer the demands, and finally, after having "muddled along" for five years, The Cathedral of Tomorrow arranged a nearly $1,250,000 loan, at 6½ per cent interest, on a fifteen-year term, from Jimmy Hoffa and his Teamsters Union. This may have saved the enterprise for the moment, but it hardly quieted the queries as to why an operation grossing about $60,000 a month, or about $750,000 annually, was unable to remain solvent.

The desire for the convenience of a personal plane had never abated in the evangelist, and three years later a dozen-seat Lockheed *Lodestar* was purchased, but soon gave way to a new *Ventura*. Ultimately a *Viscount* was added to the crusade's facilities. In 1968 plans for the more than 200-unit Cathedral Apartments were prepared, and a few years later were completed. The same year saw Reverend Humbard achieve his ambition of television coverage in every state and across the breadth of Canada, as well as the acquisition of thirty acres more, which was to be converted into a sports and youth complex.

During these years, as with other revival movements, name show-business personalities appeared on his stage, including Mahalia Jackson and Pat Boone.

The beginning of the new decade revealed the ministry had established more than forty missions in about half that many points in the world, and had broadened its television network to over three hundred stations. By 1971 more land and additional facilities were added to the evangelical empire with the purchase, from the declining Moral Rearmament movement, of Mackinac College, situated on more than thirty acres of Mackinac Island, in Michigan, along Lake Huron. It was renamed the Rex Humbard Development Center.

Two months later the corporation assumed a seventy-year lease on the Cascade Plaza, in Akron, for a mere $10,000,000.

The influx and expenditure of monies was enormous, and, among other things, the nature of these transactions was going to bring other burdens to bear on the shoulders of one of the most remarkable contemporary religious entrepreneurs.

As 1973 began, the Ohio State Department of Commerce and the Securities and Exchange Commission brought suits charging that church representatives had been unethically and, in some instances, illegally merchandising unregistered securities in many parts of the country, and the agencies asked that The Cathedral of Tomorrow operation be restrained from further distribution of same. The federal commission contended that expenses had exceeded income during the last half of 1971 and all of 1972 by more than $7,000,000, notwithstanding the fact that, of the total of approximately $12,000,000 worth of bonds sold since 1959, over $8,000,000 had been sold during that eighteen-month period. The state's case was in February 1973 at the Cuyahoga County Common Pleas Court, and the Securities and Exchange Commission's went to court in March.[3]

The United States District Court in Cleveland almost immediately issued a consent order providing for the appointment of a professional business manager to conduct the operation of the financial complex, and on May 25, Judge Paul Riley ordered that The Cathedral of Tomorrow send letters to all of its investors offering repayment for their bonds, by not later than the end of the year. Such a proposal was prepared by the church organization, but it included a suggestive phrase indicating that the recipients could simply donate their holdings to Reverend Humbard's ministry. This understandably proved objectionable to the state, which contended that it was a final attempt to recoup losses and stem the tide of fiscal failure. An amended plan, from which this fillip had been expunged, was accepted by the state in late October, and the decline of the evangelist's extraordinary business establishment continued.

A program for the sale of many of the religious group's mundane properties was instituted, including the liquidation of the Cascade Plaza venture in Akron, the Rex Humbard Development Center, formerly Mackinac College, as well as retrenchment with respect to lesser projects—even the ladies' undergarment concern, the Real Form Girdle Company, had to go.

On January 3, 1974, it was revealed that purchasers of approximately one-third of The Cathedral of Tomorrow bonds

---

[3] *The New York Times*, February 22, 1973.

were demanding the return of in excess of $4,000,000. These claims had mounted only during the brief period from the court's decision in November that the Humbard group must make such reimbursements available to the beginning of the new year's deadline date. The arrangement was understood to have bound the church to liquidate these bonds at a rate of $50,000 a month until everyone who wished the return of their funds was satisfied. As the petitions have exceeded the fund of $4,000,000 set aside for the anticipated requests, the court has indicated that the contribution, by The Cathedral of Tomorrow, of $50,000 a month must continue until all of the claims are fulfilled.

The revivalist with the Midas touch had discovered that the carousel of modern business was more complicated than the healing of the infirm, and that the golden ring had turned out to be plated. Nonetheless, he retained a vast television audience, the use of his temple, possibly whatever quality he had possessed in the first place which allowed him to translate sixty-five dollars into twelve million, and several pewsful of people into an enormous parish. Few who know of him, and fewer who have worked with him, think that Rex Humbard has come to the end of his singular road. The future may not be as flamboyant, but, assuming he is not summoned to his Chairman of the Board unexpectedly early, most suspect his winding sawdust, or golddust, trail will continue for some time.

X

Leroy Jenkins:
"The Arm of God"

The Reverend Asa Alonso Allen was one of the first healers to merge with the times, especially with respect to clothing and music. During the late 1950s he sported sartorial and audio effects in chromatic brilliancies which rivaled his oratorical powers. Rhythm pervaded his services and his hymns were built upon a rock-and-roll base. When the state of excitement reached an anticipated peak, a seeming invalid was helped down the aisle, or, on dramatic occasions, brought in on a stretcher, although in the latter instances it was often difficult to determine why the "patient" was not ambulatory. Nonetheless the alleged cure was loudly solicited, loudly acclaimed, and loudly praised. And while his corporation disclaimed any responsibility for the authenticity of cure reports in the softest possible whisper or the smallest of type, (persuasive) absentee testimonials dominate every meeting, journal, pamphlet, broadcast, and address—as is the case with virtually every other healer from early Roberts, through Jenkins, to Kuhlman, and, even Baughman. For, in truth, among healers—as with Hillel, before the birth of Christ: "What you do not want anybody else to do to you, do not you to them. That is the whole of the law; everything else is only commentary"—healing is the whole of the law; everything else is testimony.

If proof of that contention were required, none would suffice more effectively than that of one who to this day relates his cure at the hands of the late evangelist, although, as the years go by, Allen's name tends to be mentioned considerably less than in earlier renditions of the case. It was a cure of body and an impression of mind so great that it catalyzed the dormant ministry that had lain in the soul of the subject since he was but five years old, at which time the voice of the Lord ordained that the child must someday come into His service.

Instances of second-generation healers are quite infrequent, and usually only one of the people involved has "strong" power; examples of second spiritual-generation healers are almost unknown. Yet, according to his own testimony, Leroy Jenkins is one, and his story derives directly from that of the late Asa Alonso Allen. The prelude, as delivered in a typical tent-meeting introduction, sounds like this:

> In 1960 Leroy Jenkins was a businessman in Atlanta, Georgia. At that time a near-fatal accident occurred in his life. With the knowledge that death was inevitable, Leroy Jenkins came face to face with the realization that only God could help him. Allowing God to take over in his life, this young man experienced the power of God through conversion and miraculous healing. Since that healing and conversion of evangelist Leroy Jenkins, countless thousands of people have been converted and healed. Many times as he stands before the people who gather in great arenas in coliseums and tent cathedrals all across America, the supernatural gift of God enables him to look into the lives of those who stand before him. He sees their sickness, problems, and burdens, many times he tells them things that happened years ago, that only God could know.

Yet, one should be warned that the mesh of such recollections is often loosely webbed and tends to shift about here and there.

According to the A. A. Allen *Miracle Magazine* of July 1960, under the subheading "a supernatural vision given A. A. Allen in Atlanta," the revivalist shouted to the audience of the Divine Presence and the manifestation of the image of a man somewhere in the huge tent.

Now I see Him better! It is Jesus coming! He is walking down between the rows. . . . I see a man standing there with a *stub at his elbow!* His arm is off! . . . As Jesus passes by, he [sic] touches him, and on that stub, instantly, there is an arm with five beautiful fingers on it!

However dramatic Jenkins' accident and recovery may have been, according to him the original seed of spirituality was sown much earlier.

When I was five years old God spoke to me, and He told me that He had this work for me to do. With my young mind, I could not comprehend this, so God waited until I was nine years old and God spoke to me again. And I would go and I would tell different ones that God had spoken to me and they thought I was crazy. They thought that I was having hallucinations, or something. They didn't believe that God would speak to a young boy.

The future preacher might well have raised doubts in the minds of some on the occasions when he related his more remarkable version of the Second Enlightenment. According to one of the more hostile, but nonetheless professional and informative authors on the subject, George Bishop, the recorded report was quite compelling, whereas in this author's interview with the evangelist, and in many of his gospel service renditions, the fact that he was touched by the divine power is merely mentioned and all details abandoned for immediate continuation of the more mundane aspects of his preministry.

This iridescent reminiscence pictures the nine-year-old lad strolling home when suddenly the heavens were cleft and a sweep of sky flared into a kaleidoscope of colors, through which reached a Sistine-Chapel-ceiling-like arm showering golden sparks. In this recollection, the aerial phenomenon was clearly visible to the entire community of Greenwood, South Carolina. Bishop quotes the healer: [1]

[1] George Bishop, *Faith Healing: God or Fraud?*

I became so frightened I turned pale. I thought the Lord was coming. My feet actually left the ground. I was about four feet off the ground and I floated a solid block back to my house.

Rev. Jenkins did not seem to mention the communication with God when he was five years old during the period of Mr. Bishop's investigation, and he did not mention the celestial miracle and the sustained levitation when I spoke with him. Still, it is such an extraordinary series of experiences to have undergone, especially the two of his youth, it is understandable that certain details might be overlooked from one telling to another.

One of the major constants of Jenkins' story is his description and reiteration of how he fled from the Lord, how he sought to escape His foreordained service. He roamed the low and highways of this country, with the "call" following ever after. His aimless anti-odyssey eventually delivered him to Atlanta, Georgia, where he gained employment as an usher, and quarters in the home of his superior's mother. This seemed to work out well for him; working at the theater and being treated almost like another son by his landlady.

Already he had led a somewhat adventuresome existence, and so he decided to get married, although not—as it was to turn out—necessarily settle down. Jenkins met his future wife at work and they were soon married—both at the age of fifteen.

"It is very difficult to explain my life to you," he has accurately observed. "I don't know how I can—to make you understand it. Why God would choose me for this work he chose me for."

As he describes it, he was quite successful in business, acquiring three of them, plus a home, cars, and money, as the result of working constantly to keep his mind off the ubiquitous divine "call." As Jenkins puts it, "It was always misery."

Then as a result of watching Billy Graham on television—who got to him—he decided to go to church one Sunday. At the service the preacher announced that he had a feeling that a young man present, who was running from God, must give his heart to Him that very day, or meet with a great tragedy. According to the evangelist, this so frightened him he fled the church.

He returned to his home and decided to do some work on a dressing room being constructed for his swimming pool, and began removing a large pane of glass he thought the workmen might damage. It slipped and slashed into his right arm. His fingers would not move, he began to go into shock, and blood "was gushing out."

The following words are from a broadcast gospel meeting report by Rev. Leroy Jenkins of his accident, healing, and compact with God:

> I lifted my arm up and it folded all the way back here, [he will recall, gesturing] and I knew it was gone . . .[His wife wrapped his arm in a towel but] before I could go a few steps it was saturated in blood and I had to take it off. I ran across the street to a neighbor's and I beat on the door. And, as I stood there, a puddle of blood formed and turned like jelly. The reason I know is that when I moved my foot it left a print there. It was just like jelly . . . [the neighbors] came and put a tourniquet around my arm to stop the blood and they rushed me to the Georgia Baptist Hospital. On the way to the hospital, the blood was running out of the car and it left a streamer all the way there.
>
> And in that car, I looked and there was an imprint of somebody sitting there, yet no one was there. And I could see this face that I will never forget as long as I live. It was laughing at me—a man. A terrible-looking thing! I never saw anything like it. It was just laughing, and I was scared to death.

Finally, he arrived at the emergency room.

Diagnosis convinced the doctors that the arm was too severely cut to be saved and that amputation was indicated. But Jenkins refused to grant permission for such an operation, and directed his family and brothers to follow the same course should he become unconscious. Therefore, despite the warnings of the physicians, the arm was not removed, but sewed closed. In Rev. Jenkins' words, this decision was to be almost fatal: "I apparently got so weak that I showed no pulse. The doctor said that I was dead. He went out into the hallway and told my family, 'He's dead.' " Nonetheless, the preacher recalls being aware of the conversation going on about him, feeling "two great, big tears rolling down the side of my cheeks . . . and I said, 'God, please let them know that I am not dead. And, if you will save me, don't let me die, I will do anything you tell me to do.' "

At that point he describes how his legs were burning with pain and he was "gradually going into this" (presumably the state of death). He continues: "I can't describe to you what happened, but this started, and this oxygen thing fell off of my nose. It had a feather on it to see if you are breathing or not, and that's the reason they [the doctors] decided I was dead."

Accepting the hyperbolic character of this interpretation of the catastrophe, we find that the revivalist's arm was repaired more or less, and he returned home. Still he was permanently crippled and continued to expect death at any time. Then his sister told him about a recently arrived healing evangelist. She convinced him to attend a meeting despite his embarrassment because "the odor from this arm was so bad . . . it was terrible . . . this stuff was dripping out of it."

They got a seat, and the service was well under way when, in this Jenkins version, "the man [who was Asa Alonso Allen] spotted me and he said: 'Where's that man who cut his arm off? Come up here.' "

Recollecting the indescribable pain, Rev. Jenkins recalls that, as he pulled himself to his feet and started toward the platform, a "lady jumps up and starts speaking in tongues, and when she did the pain left . . . I know she stopped the pain with tongues. She didn't pray for me, she scared them [demons?] away."

As the petitioner continued toward the stage, the woman quieted down, only to be replaced by people shouting that they were "the Lord, Thy God!"

"Lord, they're claiming to be God, now," Jenkins remembers thinking. But soon he realized that they were making no personal assertions of divinity, but were merely touched by the Holy Spirit, and that the fervor was "for him."

Convinced that the healer and his audience were concerned with the restoration of his health, Jenkins reports that he decided that he would not "tell him how bad it is, I'll just let him think it's something simple."

Once on the stage, according to this particular sermon, "he took me by the hand and said, 'Stand over here.' And I didn't say it, but I thought, 'Boy, you ought to talk a little kinder to a fellow who's dying.'" The preacher then went into his supplication, and concluded by asking the tentful of people, "How many of you believe God can heal him?' 'Amen!' Boy, they believed it," recalls Jenkins, adding that, at the time he thought, "If they could convince me now, we'd have it made."

At that moment, he relates that a one-armed man leaped up and began racing about the aisles, shouting, "Glory to God" and other devout exclamations, his face a mask of joy.

"I saw that smile on his face and I thought, 'My Lord, he's got one arm and he's happy. I said, 'Lord, forget the arm. Give me what he's got. That's what I was looking for—happiness, honey.

"I felt something moving over me, and, when it did, it took hold of my mouth and my tongue, and I heard this Voice yell out, loud as it could be, saying, 'No man can heal you, but Me only. Believe Me right now and I will restore your arm.'"

Thus was Leroy Jenkins cured and led into the charismatic ministry—according to one sermon.

A. A. Allen was not mentioned during Rev. Jenkins' recitation of his remarkable experience, but then again the details of one point of view invariably differ from those of another, sometimes to an amazing extent. As was mentioned, years before this sermon, *Miracle Magazine* had devoted a number of pages to the healing of Leroy Jenkins and to how the young convert got into the business himself, including a "Special Note" that he would be at Allen's Miracle Valley camp meeting for the four weeks of August 1 to August 28, 1960.

The publication recounts the accident and how the surgeons sewed the severed portion of the arm together again, and then reports on the meeting between the injured youth and evangelist Allen. According to its story, one afternoon shortly following Jenkins' discharge from the hospital, Allen met him in a parking lot. The arm was in a cast, tears streamed down his face, and the pain was insufferable. Brother Allen asked if the young man believed God could perform a miracle, and received an affirmative reply. The account, phrased in Allen's words, says he told Jenkins to return on the following evening, but, understandably impatient, Jenkins arrived at the service that same evening and the healer called him forth.

"What do you believe God is going to do, son?" Allen asked. "I believe He is going to heal my arm!" the journal has Jenkins responding. There was a further exchange and then Allen is quoted as declaring: "Now he's ready for a miracle." Some further exhortations ensued and, amidst a general praising of the Lord, Leroy Jenkins was healed—as transcribed in the catalogue of A. A. Allen.

Almost immediately the well man began his healing ministry, and according to Rev. Jenkins' own testimony as published in *Miracle Magazine*, a short time afterwards he returned home one evening to discover his son had been in a severe bicycle accident, leaving him with his head "cut open, his mouth cut, and two huge ruptures . . . on his stomach, one on each side! You could see his intestines protruding under the skin!

"My wife asked if we should take him to the hospital. I said, 'No. I will lay my hand upon him, just as God laid His hand upon me, and God will heal him!' When I laid my hand upon him, he was healed immediately!"

From that point forward, the thaumaturgic limb of Leroy Jenkins became "the Arm of the Lord" or "God's Arm," and in the words of the healer and his associates it has cured thousands of people of hundreds of diseases and disorders. His hand has sown miracles and reaped the harvest—mundane and spiritual.

In speaking with Rev. Jenkins in October 1973, I was interested in updating his previous comments and gathering from him his sentiments on, and evaluation of, various subjects of as contemporaneous a nature as possible, but my usual clarification of a particular point—which I had not obtained earlier—came first.

"Is your particular gift unique with you, in your family, or—as you know, the healing power is occasionally hereditary—"

"No. We didn't know anything about all of these gifts, you know, of the spirit, until, in 1961, I believe, when I had an accident . . . where plate glass fell on my right arm, almost severing it."

As we spoke, Rev. Jenkins told me the story of his injury, going to the hospital, being sent home with his arm sewn up, expecting to die, and how the cure came about.

"This lady [in this version apparently *not* his sister] had seen in the newspaper where I was going to die, and she knew me because she had worked for me. She came to my home and told me about the Allen crusade being in the city of Atlanta, at the ballpark.

"So I went. Not too impressed in the beginning. Then he [Allen] called me up on the platform, and I went, and he handed the microphone over and said, 'Tell the people God's going to heal you tonight.' And I said it, but I didn't believe it. He never prayed for me, or anything. I just was standing there and I started believing and started feeling this tremendous sensation all over. And I had said, 'If this is real . . .' I had said, 'God, if this is real. If God is real. If all this is real, then give it to me.' And, sort of suddenly, it started happening.

"I received the Holy Spirit at that same time," he explained. "And I lifted my hands and started praising God and started speaking in tongues [which he sometimes describes as an effect of this healing when recounting the event at services]."

"Other than the cure of the arm, was there a physical characteristic?"

"There was a tingling sensation, like needles. Like an arm, or something, had been asleep, and was waking up."

"As you know so much better than I, sometimes cures are almost instantaneous, and sometimes they are progressive and they take a few days, a few weeks, a few months—"

"My arm was black and blue, and swollen, almost like to burst. Immediately it started changing colors, and the swelling started going down until the cast on it started getting loose."

"Right there onstage?"

"Yes. And by the time I got to my mother's house, my hand looked the same as the other one," he remembered.

"And you never had any problem with it again?"

"No. None at all," he assured me.

"Was that the beginning of your ministry then, or did you start later on?"

"That was the beginning of it. I started the next night."

"And you were with Reverend Allen for a while?"

"I went in and gave my testimony a couple or three times, in his crusade. Then I went out on my own."

"How long has it been, now?"

"Thirteen years," he replied.

"Was your initial ministry a healing ministry, or did you begin simply as a gospel preacher?"

"It was healing, right in the beginning."

Rev. Jenkins is widely known for his musical services, like his healer, A. A. Allen. But in his case he is the musical star himself, writing country hymns and singing them in a folk-rock style. I inquired about the combination of his two forms of expression.

"Would you speak a moment on how you combine your musical talent and your healing ministry? How did it begin, and how do you integrate them?"

"I just started singing there in the crusade, you know, because I had nobody to help me."

"Had you been a performer previously?"

"I had done some, yes," he acknowledged.

"Where?"

"I had sung in a show in San Jose, California, on a TV show. That's the only thing," the evangelist explained.

"Precisely how did you incorporate the music into your services?"

"Well, I just, you know, liked good singing and music, so I just started singing with the organ. And then we started adding pieces to it and it just built from that."

"I see. Now, you write some of your own songs, don't you?"

"Yes. Yes, I do."

"Do you write most of them?" I pursued.

"The ones that I record, I do."

"Is all of the music you do gospel, or do you do any nonreligious material?"

"Just for my own enjoyment. I don't record anything except gospel," he emphasized.

"I know you have a regular group. What is the instrumentation you use to get the holy-rock and sometimes rock-ballad effect?"

"We have two trombones, a [tenor] saxophone, and two horns, and an organ piano. Also a guitar. Then there's a choir." (The ensemble also includes banjos, and perhaps other instruments on occasion.)

"You are known to attract the young. Is that the intentional aim of your ministry, or is it incidental?"

"No. They like the way I dress and everything, and they sort of dig it because I'm not one of these, you know, real way-out-type ministers with the dull sense of humor, you know."

"You mean you can talk to them in their own language?"

"Yeah. See, I got married when I was just fifteen years old, and I have some kids that's big as I am. So, I understand kids pretty well, you know. My own, plus a lot of kids I affiliate with."

"You travel pretty much today, don't you?"

"Yeah, I go all over."

"And you have your own radio shows as well, I believe. Is that a tape you do which is distributed around the country?"

"Yeah, and TV too. Texas, California, Florida, Chicago—a lot of places." (A recent brochure listed about twenty-five radio stations, almost all broadcasting the show on Sunday.)

"Do you think the whole sense of religion is changing now, reverting to the more fundamental?"

"Oh, yes. It's all changing. There's lots of Catholic people, Catholic nuns and priests that come to my meetings, you know. Everybody's changing."

"Do you think there is a really great religious movement in

the United States?" I asked. "Perhaps a religious revolution?"

"There is. People are going to church more and more, now."

"In England it is not uncommon for healers to use trance states in their work. Have you ever employed that technique? That is, are you ever merely a channel or are you always fully aware of what's going on?"

"No, I'm always fully aware of all things happening."

"Your healed arm has frequently been referred to as 'God's Arm.' How do you think the healing actually takes place? When you were healed were you personally given the power to heal, or do you only function as—"

"No, I knew that when I was five," he interrupted, and spoke of the incident related earlier on in this chapter, and he concluded his reiteration of his inherent destiny after I asked if, like Allen and other revivalists, he had experienced a vision.

"It wasn't a vision. This was just something that I knew, just like something that was instilled within me, something that was borned in me. And I knew that I would do this someday."

"I gather that you have cured a great many different kinds of things. Would you name some of the diseases or disorders you have healed?"

"A lot of people are healed in my meetings with cancer, and a lot of deaf and dumb mutes. A lot of blind people. A combination of all—everything."

"What about those who are sick in mind rather than body?" I asked.

"Psychosomatic cases?"

"I was thinking more of actual mental illnesses such as schizophrenia—"

"Oh, yes. I've had a lot of success with people like that, too."

"Are they more difficult?" I inquired.

"Yes, they are."

"Are your healings always quick?"

"The ones that I've experienced are."

"It happens all at one time?"

"Yes, most of the time it happens all at once," he echoed.

It would be difficult, if not impossible, to find an evangelical minister who lives a spartan existence, but the entrepreneurial activities of Leroy Jenkins outdo most. In 1974 his association offered to the public five professionally produced record albums—one with two disks—of his gospel singing, preaching, and healing for donations of from $3 to $10; books, posters, and photographs of Jenkins are available and cost from $1 to $5; the reverend's "personal testimony" is offered for $7 per tape; and the ten "best radio shows of the 1971–72 season" for a contribution of $21.

Among the most interesting items for sale is one of the recordings devoted to a broadcast service conducted by Reverend Jenkins at the Church of What's Happening Now in Columbus, Ohio, the revivalist's home base.

The meeting opens with the minister singing a hymn and continues with various declarations of an awareness of the presence of God, interspersed with many and random "Hallelujahs!" "Praise the Lords!" "Amens!" and like jubilations. A colloquialized Biblical parable is then delivered, wherein Jenkins tells of the woman who thought she had been cured of an affliction by having touched the hem of Christ's robe. Then the evangelist tells his audience, "Jesus didn't say, 'I healed you' or 'God healed you,' or anyone healed you. He said 'Woman, you healed yourself!' " He develops this story into the thesis that with *faith* all things are possible. Yet, almost immediately, he states: "I want everyone of you to know something right now—God is the healer!" But also, frequently he makes it quite clear that Leroy Jenkins or his Arm of the Lord performs the miracles, with expressions such as "you didn't think I could do it, did you" or "now you're convinced that I can do what I say I can."

In the sermon in question, he points out, "You are the instrument in the hands of God," but moments later he reveals, "He is the instrument that does the real work," which is a comment not on the inconsistency of his accreditation but on his diction.

The oration continues for different lengths of time, varying with the service, before getting into the healing. He may preach on nearly any religious or secular subject. He often admonishes those he apparently regards as "book Christians," suggesting—with obvious justification—that much hypocrisy exists among those who merely attend church, but fail to see and practice the broader, deeper intentions of the religion.

"Many, many people think that when you become a Christian, that you're supposed to go to church on Sunday and stay in the house all week, and never, ever have anything to do with anybody else . . . Jesus Christ had friends that were nonbelievers, they were not Christians [any such expectations, perhaps excepting the apostles, might have been premature]. And He went in and had fellowship with these people, and because He did they called Him a winebibber, that's just a mild way of saying 'drunk' . . . and they called Him all kinds of things because He lived in the way that He felt that He should."

The culmination of this particular rhetorical preparation being—"and the thing that makes me different than anyone that you know of, I do what I feel like doing."

This then leads into how he is attacked and vilified, how he suffers quietly, but then the real objective of his oration emerges in clear light.

"There's a lot of old, jealous, belligerent people in the world. They're mad because they can't get it; they're mad because they don't have it," he scorns in a Paul Lynde voice, and it becomes increasingly apparent that Reverend Jenkins is speaking of nothing spiritual, at this juncture, but is defending his material acquisitions. "And if I lived in a little old shack on the side of the road," he continues, "and went around with rags, people wouldn't talk about me, except [to say] 'that's a sure humble man, bless him, he doesn't bother anyone . . .'

"But does a man of God have a right to have something? Or is it just the members [of the congregation] that can have all the goodies? . . .

"A man [cried out] once in a crusade: 'Jesus didn't have a Cadillac!' I said: 'I know, but He had a jackass when the rest of them were walking. Amen.'" Moments later he provides a further insight into his concept of the ministry of Jesus, when he observes: "And, if there had been Cadillacs back in those days, I'm sure—that sharp as He was—He'd a had one.

"I believe that God and Jesus Christ—I believe that They're People, and I believe that They're not the type that are holier-than-thou."

Following this remarkable theological analysis, he shoots off into a rather confusing, and wholly unrelated, discourse on the misapplication of religion with respect to children, and a general dissertation on how they are led down the sawdust path by false prophets. He then explains that his personal gifts, which came at such an early age derive from a natural anointment and appointment by God and from the fact that he "had gone through all these experiences" and "had done everything twice" very early in his life. Yet, Reverend Jenkins' diction, syntax, and nonlogical verbal approach are such as to make anything other than an emotional response virtually impossible. (In this respect his oratory is often reminiscent of the writing of Mary Baker Eddy.) Yet, into his moderately lengthy sermons, the revivalist drops indisputable truths. "I never, ever had one inkling that Christians are the way that they are—'I'll forgive ya', but I'll never forget it,' " he growls his satire of the clerics he regards as too puritanical.

Suddenly, he turns to a man in the front row and inquires how he is, receiving a husky-voiced "Aw right." The minister then identifies the parishioner as one whose vocal cords had been paralyzed for years—and the healing aspect of the meeting is under way.

The evangelist then asks for a "total nonbeliever" (although one would not imagine that the crusade would attract many true skeptics). The nonbeliever is told that he has had the religious call all his life, but has resisted it; that he has had an experience where he might have been killed and is suffering from an injured leg.

The man assures the audience of the truth of this quasi-clairvoyance and diagnosis by chanting "Amen," "that's the truth," and "so help me," a few times, and the miracle process is inaugurated.

"Father, save this man," begins Rev. Jenkins. "Anoint him, and bless him, and keep him, and heal him, in Jesus' name. Let it be. Praise God."

Obviously, the congregation has no way of knowing the accuracy of the history given by the psychic man of the cloth, or whether the physical condition, obscured by the patient's trousers, has been improved, let alone cured. But that there is little doubt throughout the crowd is strikingly evident.

Then Jenkins proceeds to tell a series of individuals, in extremely vague terms—in effect, you-and-I-know-what-is-wrong - so - we - needn't - be - specific - in - public - regarding - so-personal-a-matter sort of diagnosis—that they suffer *some* physical disability or, occasionally, an emotional or psychological disorder, and delivers them his miracle-evoking incantation.

Much is made of the fact that Jenkins could not possibly know anything about the persons, especially that he would be ignorant of their sicknesses. While there are ways preparatory information might be obtained, it is never even raised for consideration, for this *awareness* is a key element of his ministry and is called "the gift of knowledge," which is merely an alleged divine clairvoyance, or, as he puts it, "only God could tell me, isn't that right?" (It is not a question, naturally, except rhetorically.) He occasionally breaks into song, supported by the organ that is constantly and deftly accenting his words and phrases.

Rarely is the disorder described in any but an indeterminate manner, although, from time to time, one of his congregation claims to have been crippled or blind. In one instance, a thirty-six-year-old woman, who asserted that she had never had sight from the day she was born, vowed to all that vision had been given her. Yet it was difficult—notwithstanding a moderate degree of excitement in her voice—to accept the relative calm with which she accepted this astounding phenomenon.

So Rev. Leroy Jenkins selects one after another of his transient parishioners to be healed and completely convinces the subjects and the audience that he accomplishes just that.

The evangelist and his supporters contend that he is clairvoyant, is spoken to by God, and that he heals all diseases and physical, mental, and spiritual corruptions with an "Arm of the Lord." Thousands believe he has cured them. Whether true or not, tens of thousands have had at least a fleeting happiness, which they would have otherwise missed, because of his assurances and their faith.

Leroy Jenkins lives very well—and not only admits it, but flaunts it, and is criticized for it. Many dismiss his performances and the results they seem to elicit as mass hysteria or a catalogue of completely unproven claims. Certainly the commercial aspects of his operation are among the most developed, promoted—and often blatant—in the business.

Whatever one's opinion, Leroy Jenkins moves toward larger and larger audiences, with his Arm of God outstretched and his hands wide open.

XI

Kathryn Kuhlman: The High Priestess of Healing

Kathryn Kuhlman has never cured anyone in the world. She has no power to remedy the physical, let alone the spiritual, ills of a single individual. And the impression that she is a "miracle worker" is wholly without foundation. All this according to Kathryn Kuhlman—sometimes. On other occasions her disclaimers are either less specific or are merely more ambitious. Of course, attributing the gift to superior forces in nature —from gods to God, from cosmic vibrations to senses of value—is ubiquitous among healers and healing groups, but Miss Kuhlman is unique in how widely divergent her opinions of her own powers can be.

"If you are seeking a faith healer read no further," opens the third paragraph of her Foreword to her book *God Can Do It Again*.[1] "I am not a modern-day . . . worker of miracles," she explains. "No one knows better than I that in myself I am nothing. . . . *I am not your point of contact*." (Emphasis added.)

According to Miss Kuhlman, she was born in Concordia, Missouri, an indeterminate number of years ago, where her Methodist mother was a housewife and her indifferently Baptist father a one-time mayor of the community. She actually found true religion at the age of fourteen while attending a church service accompanied by her mother. Nothing exceptional happened to commemorate the enlightenment, and as Miss Kuhlman's recollections make clear, the presiding minister was pos-

[1] Kathryn Kuhlman, *God Can Do It Again* (Englewood Cliffs, New Jersey: Prentice-Hall, 1969).

sessed of no great spiritual or oratorical persuasion. Nonetheless, as she stood among the pews singing a hymn, she was suddenly struck with the power and presence of the Holy Spirit and, trembling with emotional intensity, gloriously cleansed of sin by the blood of Jesus Christ, she wept wildly in her awareness of having been forgiven.

During the remainder of the service, and as she walked from church, she felt that the whole world had been changed. Entering the family house, she went into the kitchen, where her father was, and announced that "Jesus has come into my heart." Although not especially responsive, he was glad, the future preacher recalls.

Early in life she began promulgating the gospel. One gathers that these formative years were frequently trying and that the material deprivations made a considerable impression on her, the marks of which she carries quite consciously to this day. She speaks intensely of this period in her ministry, particularly of Idaho and the parishioners who heard her long ago but still occasionally write telling her that "she has never changed." If that is accurate, Miss Kuhlman must have been an extraordinary evangelist to watch when little more than a girl. In point of fact, she regards that era as the time when she "really began her religious education."

Yet, in conversation she seems preoccupied with the physical situations she remembers, such as being "hungry all the time" and often having nothing more for dinner than a bowl of soup, rather than any spiritual evolution.

One of her reminiscences is especially interesting. She speaks of the old portraits of grandparents which so often gazed sternly at her from the walls of bare, unheated bedrooms provided her by local ministers where she was preaching. Sometimes, she recalls, "somebody's grandmother would be staring down at me with their high, lace collar, almost frightening me. And those mustaches on somebody's grandpa almost scared me to death. I almost felt like I was sleeping with them, you know. Kind of like that," she adds, chuckling, more to herself, it seems, than at any humor in the situation. "Ah, my friends," she adds, "those were the days!"

Still, confronted by the suggestion that, because of her present wealth and position, she has had a most fortunate life, she responds emphatically and somewhat enigmatically,

"It wasn't luck, my friend. I know the price I paid. I know the price," she repeats, without further explanation.

Even she has wondered why good fortune did not come to her earlier on. She speaks of how recently she was sitting alone, reading her Bible, when that thought occurred to her. And, in effect, she asked Jesus why He had not given her the gift in those initial and difficult days of her ministry. Explaining emphatically that her Saviour neither appeared before her, nor actually spoke to her in an audible voice, she assures one that the response within her mind was as clear and distinct as if it had been enunciated by a present Christ. The reason why she had not been anointed with the power in those previous days, Miss Kuhlman heard the spirit of Jesus say, was:

"Kathryn, if I had given it to you then, you would have blown the whole thing."

Miss Kuhlman's pilgrimage for a greater understanding of the power of God proceeded from her initial enlightenment, through her years as a novice gospel preacher, and even into the observation of supposedly more charismatically gifted persons of the cloth. "I saw healing," she remarks, "but I could not see *scriptural* healing." Nonetheless, she reiterates, "I knew it was in the Word. I knew that whether or not I would ever see a miracle in the healing of the physical, it didn't alter God's word one iota." The reflection of the minister's opinion of some of her colleagues and contemporaries in the field of evangelical thaumaturgy are more than evident in such comments. Yet, should any doubt regarding her evaluation of certain of them remain, it dissolves as she continues.

"I shall not betray confidence in giving the name of one who was conducting a service under a great big tent. I went there to see, but I didn't find what I was seeking. I began weeping. I left weeping. And all that I can say were these words: 'They've taken away my Lord, and I know not where they have laid Him.' " She relates how she continued to cry all that night, and all the next day; then, pulling herself together, she pressed forward in her search. Ultimately, she affirms, it came to pass. Or, as she puts it:

"And then it happened! It happened in Franklin, Pennsylvania, in the old Billy Sunday tabernacle. Think of what a place God chose!

"I was standing on the same platform where Billy Sunday,[2] years and years previous to that night, had stood preaching the gospel. I had gone to Franklin not knowing what I would find ... The first service there were thirty-eight people there; the next service there were nearly two hundred; after that the tabernacle never held the crowds.

"It was in that third service, as I was preaching the gospel on the Holy Spirit ... a woman stood up and said ... 'Last night, while you were preaching, I was healed.'

"I was shocked and said: 'How do you know?' " remembers Miss Kuhlman. She then reports that the woman revealed, at that time, that she had been previously diagnosed by a regular physician as having a malignant tumor that, during the aforementioned service, had been cured. According to the minister, the parishioner stated that she had been engulfed in a strong bodily sensation and was convinced that her condition had been rectified, and that, on the following day, her optimism had been verified by her doctor who could no longer find any evidence of the tumor.

"That was the first healing that took place in this ministry," says Miss Kuhlman. "Without the laying-on-of-hands, without any [specific] prayer, just a woman sitting in the audience, in Franklin, Pennsylvania, while I was preaching on the power of the Holy Spirit."

That was but the beginning, as her records indicate.

"Since that time there have been thousands and thousands of healings. The secret? The Holy Spirit!"

2 William Ashley Sunday (1863–1935), one-time professional baseball player who became one of America's most prominent and notorious tent-style revivalists.

Her most famous book, *I Believe in Miracles,* which many believe to be an autobiography (or, at least, a biography), is actually more than 90 per cent "case histories." The foreword opens with the line: "Kathryn Kuhlman is an institution." Obviously this can be regarded as accurate only in the most colloquial sense. However, she certainly is a *foundation*—the Kathryn Kuhlman Foundation.

Her present ministerial and organizational achievements began when she rented the auditorium of the Carnegie Library, in Pittsburgh, Pennsylvania, a number of years ago. She has appeared in that same location countless times since then, attracting hundreds of thousands of listeners. About her she has gathered a group of followers, which is evidence of her ability to convince people of her good intentions and her communication with great powers. They number a handful of physicians, some members of the legal profession, as well as numerous others possessing degrees of one kind or another. As with virtually all mystic healers, the overwhelming majority of her supporters are drawn from the less-educated segment of the population.

Still, regardless of how one evaluates her disciples or her "parishioners" (including those who tune in on her professionally slick radio and television productions which appear regularly on hundreds of broadcast outlets throughout the United States), there are former medical patients *and* orthodox physicians who claim that they or their patients have recovered from disabilities, from the incidental to the terminal, in a manner that defies standard scientific explanation. Cancer of every description, tuberculosis, goiter, liver conditions, and so on—almost any disease, or malfunction of an organ, or cellular degeneration—appear responsive—of course, only on occasion—to the healing of Miss Kuhlman, or the power of the Holy Spirit passing through her, or, if you or she prefers, through the Holy Spirit's presence, with herself only obliquely involved.[3] Further, malformations of bones, malfunctions of joints, muscular injury, and other such

[3] According to Miss Kuhlman, persons who have attended her services have been cured of all manner of afflictions before entering, during, and after her services. Yet the implication is that the proximity to her and the cures were by no means coincidental.

problems seem to have about equal chance of correction. On the other hand, simple injuries—a broken leg, or shoulder bone, or rib, or a severe laceration, which medically would require a couple of dozen stitches—do not seem to appear in Miss Kuhlman's published records.

The second instance of healing in her ministry was perhaps more persuasive than the first. As she relates the surrounding circumstances and the "miracle" itself—

"It was Sunday morning . . . twenty-one years and five months prior [to the actual initiation of healing] . . . George had suffered an accident in the foundry where he worked in Grove City, Pennsylvania," when molten iron splashed into his right eye, blinding it. He consulted several doctors, including a specialist, and, based upon their opinions, was, in 1927, "awarded workmen's compensation by the state of Pennsylvania for the industrial loss of his eye." Eventually, according to a specialist in Franklin, Pennsylvania (where Miss Kuhlman's early experience with healing had occurred), the double demand on the remaining eye was jeopardizing its efficiency. Briefly, that is the history of the case according to the minister's records.

In 1947 one of George Orr's daughters who lived in Butler, Pennsylvania (in which another of her published cures took place a couple of years afterwards), heard the evangelist on radio and suggested her father attend a meeting. His first visit convinced him that "Kathryn Kuhlman has something." This persuasion motivated him to participate in seven services within the following few weeks. "All my doubts were removed when I saw the scope and depth of this ministry," he is quoted as having remarked. "I knew it was the real thing."

Shortly thereafter, while at a meeting, Orr pled, "God, please heal my eye." Immediately, Miss Kuhlman explains, the orb was permeated with a burning sensation and tears poured forth from it. Still, it was not until the automobile ride home that his vision began to be restored; by the end of the trip the cure was complete.

"You will note that I never prayed for George Orr. I had never touched him. His healing came to him as, unknown to me, he sat in the auditorium that May afternoon in 1947," specifies Miss Kuhlman.

Upon visiting the successor to the late optometrist who had examined his eye a quarter of a century earlier, he was told that "the scar on his right eye [had] completely disappeared and that the other eye was normal."

Miss Kuhlman asserts she had nothing to do with the cure. As she is the expert in miracles, who is to dispute her?

Eugene Usechek apparently contracted Perth's disease when he was nine years old, early in 1950. About eight months later, after two periods in the hospital in traction and a chest-to-foot cast designed to correct a one-and-one-half-inch discrepancy in the length of his legs, he was brought to a Carnegie Hall (Pittsburgh) service. He had been wearing a brace for several months, but midway through the gospel meeting his leg began to twitch. Immediately his mother removed the cumbersome hardware. His health was restored, and eleven years later he was accepted into the United States Air Force.

In the same year, at the Penn Theatre, in Butler, Pennsylvania (where George Orr's daughter had lived when she directed her attention to the possibility of spiritual healing), one Carey Reams, "a man on crutches, who said he had not walked unaided since 1945, was told [by Miss Kuhlman] to throw away his supports," did so, and walked freely up and down the aisle.

The ministerial records indicate that during World War II Reams had been subjected to a severe concussion from an explosion, which cost him use of his right eye, displaced all of his teeth, fractured his jawbone, broke his back and neck in several places, resulted in pelvic injuries, and necessitated brain surgery. And that was but the first operation; he was to undergo forty more. Additionally, after frequent and prolonged hospitalization, his lower body became paralyzed.

The day following his deliverance he helped to load a truck containing some of his wife's furniture and drove it back to Florida, from Pittsburgh. He was successful in life and business for eleven years following the restoration of his psyche or body, at which time the report of his case was published.

"The miracle woman of Pittsburgh" has a legion of supporters. They include members of virtually all professions. Her most famous book about her ministry has a foreword by a former congressman who was a Pennsylvania judge at the time of the writing. Another of her books has an introductory chapter by a self-described reporter who stipulates that one of Miss Kuhlman's successes was an individual who had been physically examined by Dr. Martin L. Biery, "a specialist in general surgery for thirty years, with degrees from the University of Michigan and Michigan State University," who, as quoted in the book, testified to the extreme pedal debilitation of the subject and to the inexplicable improvement in her condition. Both examinations were apparently conducted onstage rather than in any sort of medical surroundings.

One psychic researcher notes the support offered her ministry by an Episcopal priest and psychologist, and by the cleric's father-in-law, a Dr. E. B. Henry, a Pittsburgh physician of fifty years' practice. The same writer cites a number of other medical men who believe in Kathryn Kuhlman's charismatic gift for healing, including Dr. Cecil P. Titus, head of the department of oral surgery, St. Luke's Hospital, Cleveland, and ophthalmologist Claire King of Columbus, Ohio.

In *God Can Do It Again* Miss Kuhlman alluded to an unnamed Catholic priest who extolled her powers and, while regretting that he could not invite her to speak at his own church, was anxious to arrange for and financially underwrite her appearance in a local auditorium so that his parishioners might hear her preach and, one must assume, see and participate in her presentation of a "miracle" service.

Other men of the cloth, of many denominations, named and unnamed, are cited—in books and articles by and about her—as believers in her ability to catalyze the spiritual healing process.

Yet, in at least some instances, their enthusiasm must be in spite, rather than because, of her rather unorthodox theology, a subject which is rarely delved into during public services on radio and television testimonial programs.

As has been noted earlier, Miss Kuhlman did not begin with the gift of cure, it came to her some time following her youthful entry into the pulpit. Therefore, when it did descend to her, she was both deeply gratified that this additional instrument with which to do God's work had been placed in her hands and very curious about it—precisely how it functioned, and explicitly from whence it originated, other than the obvious ultimate source, God.

Soon, however, she realized that it was not God, Himself, nor even specifically Jesus, who was responsible for the anointment of the healing power, but rather the third aspect of the divine Trinity, the Holy Ghost. Miss Kuhlman claims to be quite unschooled in the history of spiritual healing, and even less acquainted with mystical philosophy. Yet much of what she propounds as her theological conviction reflects the early church writings, particularly those concerning themselves with the concept of God as *Logos* and *Logos* as manifested in Christ.

Her visualization of how the Son of God was Man is worthy of note. Recalling her awakening to the true process of the terrestrial origination and development of the church, she says:

"I saw, for the first time, that there was more than God, the Father, giving Christ [as a sacrifice for the sins of the world] . . . but something else had happened before God so gave His Son, and I like to think of the three Persons of the Trinity sitting down at a great conference table [presumably in heaven] planning Man's salvation. It would have to take sinless blood, perfect blood. Only the Son of God could measure up to it, and Jesus said: 'I'll go. I'll take the form of flesh. I'll take the form of man.'

"Absolute Deity, Absolute Divinity, the very Son of the living God. But to pay the price for Man's salvation, it would mean He would have to come in the form of flesh! But before God gave His Son, before Jesus consented to come, He offered Himself first, the Word of God says, through the Holy Spirit.

"We fail to see this, sometimes. I often think of those who try to minimize the power of the Holy Spirit, who refuse to accept the power and the person of the Holy Ghost.

"Remember, if Jesus could trust Him, if Jesus could stake

everything He had on the Holy Spirit, surely you and I can afford to trust the Holy Ghost. [It is somewhat unclear, within this context, how the ultimate protection of God, Himself, might have been withdrawn or otherwise not be available to Christ at any moment of true spiritual need.]

"He knew the Holy Spirit, He knew the mighty Third Person of the Holy Trinity in a greater degree than any human being has ever known. Even the apostle Paul, with all of the spiritual insight, with all of the glory, with all of the secrets that God trusted him with—yet, the apostle Paul, methinks, never knew the power and the person of the Spirit as Jesus, the Son, knew Him!

"He was the resurrection power; Jesus knew it. He was the power of the Trinity! [Apparently rather than God, the Father, as is usually conceded; i.e., within this theological framework, it appears to be flatly stated that the Holy Ghost is the *first*, not the *third*, aspect of the Trinity.] Jesus knew it. Jesus had faith, Jesus *had confidence in Him,* and so He turned, first of all, methinks, and said to the Holy Spirit: 'If you be with Me. *If you come, too, I'll go.* I'll go. [It is not resolved whether Jesus would not have given Himself for the redemption of Man had the Holy Ghost declined to accompany Him. In either event, it can hardly be avoided that, for a moment there, Man was in his greatest jeopardy since being cast from the Garden, or, *at least,* since the Deluge.] And, methinks, the Holy Spirit nodded His head. [Again, the possibility of considerable confusion is raised in her: is the Spirit possessed of physical qualities, is He shaped in the image of Man or some other creature? Or may we assume this is merely a matter of metaphor?] And then it was that God gave His only begotten Son, that you and I might have life eternal."

Following this extraordinary bit of anthropomorphic theology, Miss Kuhlman notes the Nativity, the growing to adulthood of Jesus, and then adds to her singular thesis:

"Yet, methinks the three [elements of the Trinity] *were not united* until that hour when Jesus came up out of the waters of Baptism—Oh, glorious moment! ... and in that moment ... a Voice spoke—It was the Voice of God—when He said: 'This is my Beloved Son in whom I am well pleased.' "

Miss Kuhlman's suggestion that the *Trinity* (i.e., the three divine aspects of one God, or, if one prefers, the three entities who were one and that One was God) did not exist as the Trinity of One before that and only unified into the one God in three "persons" at the moment of Jesus' baptism must give pause to many theologians despite the subsequent quote from the Father specifically depicting Jesus as "My Son," since that could be used semantically as support for the multiplicity of the "Trinity." But, then again, this is not within her thesis since Jesus was already baptized and in her concept the moment of fusion had already occurred.

The evangelist's interpretation of Christ's emergence from the river is as intriguing as other of her metaphysical conjectures, for, according to her, it was then that ". . . the Holy Spirit came upon Him in the form of a dove. Methinks He [the Holy Dove] was saying: 'I'm here, now. I'm here, now. Things will happen. We're really on schedule.' " At this point Miss Kuhlman chuckled, understandably, as the dove continued: " 'I kept my part of the agreement, you keep yours [was divinity suggesting to divinity that the Spirit was waiting, but the flesh might be weak?]— and Man will have salvation for the whole body.' " The mercantilistic aura of the entire contract between the Holy Ghost and Jesus, with the former seeming to be playing the dominant role, is a most original reading of the Bible, and, as that work is still rife with mystery, any new light shed upon possible inferences to be drawn from it cannot but fascinate the interested reader. Miss Kuhlman continues:

"Oh, it must have been such a reassuring time for Jesus [are we to deduce from this speculation that Christ had recurrent moments of doubt throughout his ministry, when we usually restrict consideration of the possibility that the Son's confidence in His Father wavered, if, actually, at all, when he cried: 'Father, why hast Thou forsaken me?'] . . . and then it was that miracles began happening." Presumably this is with respect to the Christian ministry, unless Miss Kuhlman has dismissed the entire Old Testament.

"I know the secret to the power in this [her] ministry. I know the secret in those who are healed by the power of God. The secret is found in the person of the Holy Spirit. *I have chosen to accept the gift that Jesus left for me,*" she declared, although at other points she absolutely rejects the idea that she, personally, has any "gift." Or to refer to her personal testament, as found in her own writings: "No one knows better than I that in myself I am nothing."

Kathryn Kuhlman shares with Mary Baker Eddy a quality of personality able to exert great influence over other people. I am not referring only to the countless patient/parishioners each attracted, but to the individuals immediately surrounding them. Yet, while the founder of formal Christian Science was, despite her greater organizational genius, unable to translate that charismatic quality into a functioning "gift" of her own and thus had to work through others, Miss Kuhlman, from a ministerial point of view, like virtually all evangelical healers, operates alone, notwithstanding the large number of persons who contribute to the overall preparation and management of her activities.

Other than her countless personal appearances, Miss Kuhlman's most effective and comprehensive access to the public is her weekly television programs. They are intriguing—if not unnerving—to watch. For instance, the broadcast of July 28, 1973, opened with Miss Kuhlman standing in the semidarkness of a highly elaborate and expensive set reminiscent of those used in big evening variety shows for a major female personality about to sing a ballad, or a more polished version of the atmosphere films used to create for somewhat mysterious housekeepers and governesses in the tradition of Dame Judith Anderson at Manderly.

Lush music rolls out from behind the scene, smoothly amplified by a substantial chorus (drawn from either the Kathryn Kuhlman Concert Choir of a hundred voices or the Kathryn Kuhlman Foundation Men's Choir, which is four times as large), with Miss Kuhlman turning to the viewers, rapturously speaking her spiritual slogan: "I believe in miracles."

Then a male voice-over is heard:

"Miracles. The supernatural power of the Creator, God, intervening in human affairs. Restoring lives in a material world.

Each week at this time Kathryn Kuhlman presents guests whose unrehearsed testimonies are a rich source of hope and inspiration. And now the voice of I-Believe-in-Miracles, Kathryn Kuhlman."

"You know exactly what I'm going to say," she begins, moving forward in her floor-length, simply cut, high-fashion gown, smiling most of the while.

The evangelist then reaffirms her acceptance of miracles, attributes the belief (although not specifically the miracles) to God. "Christianity is not a religion," she then pronounces, emphasizing with "always remember that," continuing by admonishing those "thousands of people who put Christianity in the category of a religion. It isn't. Christianity is a marvelous spiritual revelation [chuckle]!"

The sermon then continues mostly in a quiet hallelujah (praise God) tradition, with Miss Kuhlman using her hypnotically effective voice as the quasi-musical instrument it is. This is not to suggest that it is melodious; the pitch and quality are quite far from that, as her speech, notwithstanding its being carefully, even meticulously, rhythmed, is devoid of the poetic feeling. It is pure prose. Yet, in a way it achieves certain effects expected from poetic phrasing, and elicits many responses anticipated from music. Some of these vocal results can be recognized and monitored. For example, she employs three devices essential to music: her voice runs, sometimes sweeps, and occasionally leaps from an almost unintelligible whisper (as this is often overexecuted it is the lesser of two real flaws in her extraordinary oratorical style) to a shout of jubilation; her range of pacing is as versatile as the careful direction of her decibels, with some syllables requiring as long as five seconds for completion while immediately before or after Miss Kuhlman may machine-gun out three or four words in a single second. (This is the most deficient aspect of her elocution. Often these spurts of sounds are nearly impossible to translate into intelligible meaning, although for regular followers the practice probably constitutes only a minor problem, because the phrases are ones which constantly recur in her sermons and conversation.)

Following the paean, there is a musical interlude featuring a most competent singer, Jimmy MacDonald, accompanied by a highly professional pianist, in the rendition of a concert-styled hymn. Mr. MacDonald then defers to his accompanist, who does a solid medley of "Onward, Christian Soldiers" and "The Battle Hymn of the Republic." These performers are presented in a setting consonant with the overall elegance and artful execution of the program, including a completely revolving segment of the stage which rotates as they display their talents.

As she prepares her audience for the "testifier," Miss Kuhlman emphasizes that all of such individuals to appear on her broadcast are "thoroughly investigated," presumably by the Kathryn Kuhlman Foundation. Then she recites her guest's medical history, which is one cancer problem after another, including mastectomy, cobalt radiation, and, finally, her physician's pronouncement that "he could not promise her six months." Scheduled for twenty-five radiation treatments, although she was in a condition of carcinomatosis, the patient abandoned therapy and prepared for death.

There follows a detailed interview by Miss Kuhlman which elicits a catalogue of pathological details, a confounding reiteration of the most depressing and sickening minutiae, punctuated by the evangelist's grins and chuckles. Doubtless the continuous amusement, seemingly at what were patently the most gruesome medical details, was no less than joy at hearing once again the case history she knew would have "a happy ending."

Having thoroughly crisscrossed the terrain of her guest's traumatic experience with cancer, the interview turns to how the patient was attracted to attend one of the miracle services, how she was in unendurable pain during the trip to the auditorium, wasn't able to gain entrance because of the crowds, and returned home without seeing the healer. She came again and failed in her pilgrimage (although she did see the service on a closed-circuit television monitor in a nearby hotel), but finally, on the third attempt, supported by her daughters, the poor guest got past the doors and found a seat in a remote area of the balcony. Carefully guided, but not obviously prompted, the guest then recalls how

Miss Kuhlman suddenly turned on the stage, hundreds of feet away, and "stopped, and you shook your finger, and you said, 'There's someone right up there, in the center, about ten or twelve rows from the top, that has just been healed of bone cancer. Stand up and accept your blessing.' "

Needless to say, the woman concludes by saying that she had been completely healed and was in excellent health at the time the broadcast was being taped.

The program concludes with another brief exercise in exultation, with a rising musical coda of piano and choir, and imprimatured by the voice of the announcer informing the audience where they might write letters for further knowledge of the healing ministry and identifying the Kathryn Kuhlman Foundation as the sponsor of the show.

Despite these programs, if anything is difficult to believe —and most things relating to the life and ministry of the "miracle woman of Pittsburgh" must be accepted with more than a mere grain of faith—nothing so strains credulity as the assertion of psychic investigator Allen Spraggett in 1967 [4] regarding the evangelist's age. Extrapolating from his direct quote of her statement concerning it, Kathryn Kuhlman would now be about ninety years old. To the readers who find nothing especially singular in this, I can only offer the recourse of watching the television service or attending one of her live meetings and taking along a powerful pair of binoculars.

For after all of the positive reports of her work have been read and evaluated, her unique theology examined, the attacks on her alleged cures perused, at least one can still say, "If that woman is ninety years old, *I* believe in miracles!"

[4] Allen, Spraggett, "Kathryn Kuhlman Loves People to Health," *Fate*, November 1967, pp. 64-65.

XII

Dr. John Lee Baughman: The Church of the Truth

The Church of the Truth is representative of countless "independent" pentecostal churches in the United States. It was under the direction of Dr. Ervin Seale for a great many years, during which time it achieved an international reputation. Almost as soon as the structure was completed the famous Sunday services of the church were moved to Philharmonic Hall, at Lincoln Center, generally filling the vast hall with its thousands of seats. Recently, after over three decades of dedication to the calling of the cloth, Rev. Seale accepted the grateful accolade of minister emeritus, and gave the spiritual and operative direction of the church to his successor, although he dismisses the idea that he is "retired." Rather, he has embarked upon new adventures and, at the moment of this writing, is touring and lecturing in South Africa.

Dr. John Lee Baughman, a prominent voice of the Unity movement in the country and a member of the executive board of the Association of Unity Churches, has taken the torch, and is moving the New York church forward in many ways. He is eminently qualified to continue his predecessor's efforts as he has helped to build and served Unity churches in Boston, Worcester, Miami, Beverly Hills, and Fort Lauderdale.

While the programs of the organization are many and include Sunday Musical Meditation, Sunday Devotional Service, Sunday school, a Dial-a-Prayer facility, Sunday evening radio broadcast, and the publication of a regular bulletin, it was because of the healing aspects of the ministry that Dr. Baughman was selected for an interview, portions of which appear below.

As an important aspect of the formal schedule, the church offers a special Healing Service on the first Sunday of each month. This ceremony consists of four primary portions: Dr. Baughman's recapitulation of "the outstanding points of spiritual knowledge of the past month" [presumably gained personally, or in reports from other scholars of the church association, or from benefited parishioners] and a trio of "healing pools, one for the body, one for human relations, and one for business." The practice is for all of those present to give themselves up to the force of spirituality until a "tremendous healing pool of response Godward is created," upon the achievement of which any member of the congregation "is invited to drop his problem into that [analogic] pool, and leave it there with no strings attached . . . and let God take over." The essential point being that in the philosophy of the Church of Truth, and in the Unity movement collectively, a concentration of believers is worth at least the power of its assembled parts, and, quite possibly, considerably more.

In addition, the church offers private classes for those who wish to become "practitioners," but, of more consequence here, Dr. Baughman, personally, conducts a facet of it devoted to the development of students "whose 'unfoldment' and devotion to Truth make them great channels for God's Power to heal and to bless." While schools to teach the art of healing exist in England, for example, this is one of the very few such operations in this country. This fact tends to produce individual healers who usually feel that they have been singled out, from on high, for the quasi-divine role.

The offices of The Church of the Truth are located on two floors of Carnegie Recital Hall, and Dr. Baughman's personal sanctuary is high up, overlooking the day-long congestion of humanity, pedestrian and mechanized, which throngs through the Fifty-seventh Street and Seventh Avenue intersection. The minister greeted me warmly and we chatted for a few minutes before the actual interview began. He is of middle age and stature, with a faintly Pickwickian roundness and, at fleeting moments, manner. He was dressed in a well-cut gray suit, rust tie and pocket piece, and brown alligator shoes. Large, finely worked cameo cufflinks adorned the French cuffs of his immaculately white shirt.

"I know you are acutely aware of the rapid rise in the art of charismatic healing in recent years," I began. "Would you like to make an initial and general comment on this revitalization, Reverend?"

"Yes, there has been such an upsurge, in our time, that I've been interested in [the approach of] taking it from the top, namely Jesus Christ who has the greatest record of anyone of whom we are aware [with respect to the performing of 'spiritual' healing]. I have asked myself why there occurs through his consciousness, this power, that all of the healers lean to in such fabulous fashion. The essence [of this phenomenon] . . . is the great crisis in his life, and it is in crisis that you get a real understanding of the person."

"In the beginning of his healing ministry Jesus was using a laying-on-of-hands technique. As time went by, direct contact seems to have been less and less necessary, until in its final stages there was no physical contact with the afflicted," I observed. "Do you regard this as spiritually or therapeutically indicative?"

"Yes. I will share with you these thoughts I've had on the general subject of healing, including all of the people who are currently involved in it. My desire would be to give to your readers a *rational* view . . . I call it the *three levels of healing*.

"Healing takes place on three levels: the physical level, the mental level, and the spiritual level. The physical is the easiest way to procure healing, but it is the least lasting."

"By that do you mean that such cures tend to dissipate themselves and the illness returns, or do you mean they are more transient in the broad, spiritual sense?" I asked.

"I mean that, on the physical level, the practitioners in this field are seeking the allaying of the effects, not necessarily the causes [of illness].

"This would include our wonderful doctors, surgeons, and other orthodox medical people, for whom I have the greatest admiration and respect . . . [although] again, I would say this is the easiest way to procure a healing, but the least permanent, in the sense that it has not produced anything of the Person who produced the malformation in the first place."

"Which I suspect advances us to the next plane. Would that include those identified as 'faith' or 'spiritual' healers?"

"I will clarify this as we progress. The mental field, the psychic field of healing, is better for the individual, in the sense that it is a level higher. At least those who are practitioners in it deal with causes, rather than just allaying the effects, to be very strict about it. Since mental healing is a work done solely by the individual and his particular unfoldment, there is obviously a time gap involved, for all the work is done by the practitioner."

"Would you clarify that—the 'time gap' phrase?"

"Well, the condition returns again and again and again, on the mental and the psychic plane . . . but I do want to say that the psychic and the mental levels of healing can, and do, work, but it is so involved with the individual and his patients, the very level they are functioning on makes the process quite lengthy."

"Might we conclude that in many instances the results are derived from an alleviation of essentially psychosomatic conditions rather than any divinely inspired cure?"

"You could say that to a degree, but I'm quite sure that some of the practitioners of the mental-psychic level really believe that they are manifestations of God, too."

"But you would not hold too strongly with the supposedly instantaneous cures— 'I - have - a - complete - restoration - of - hearing - in - a - previously - totally - deaf - man - in - the - balcony' sort of thing?"

"Of course, that kind of thing is not new, it has been widely written about. Many reporters have followed up on such cases and found that the person has returned to the same condition in a relatively short time. However, in fairness to all practitioners, I believe there are all sorts of possibilities along this line," conceded the minister.

"And, to complete your initial detailing of the three levels of therapy?"

"Yes. The highest level is the spiritual one and it has the fewest practitioners, because it requires the most, in the sense of processing the consciousness of God. The value in the spiritual level of healing lies in the fact that it shortens the time gap. In it, instantaneous healings can happen, because they are not procured by any human being, but by God Himself. And it depends entirely upon the processing of the individual consciousness to the point where it can get powerful realization of Divine Grace, which merely means a higher action delivered to the patient.

"When I suggested that there are three planes, and that each I have mentioned in sequence is higher than the one that preceded it, I do not mean to belittle the physical approach to health, for I pray for the unfoldment of all of our fine doctors, surgeons, and research people in the medical field who have made such astounding progress. Speaking only for myself, there can never be a quarrel between the doctors and the surgeons and me. With all of their science and their knowledge, they work from the outside in; my work, on the other hand, has to do with operating from the inside out.

"The second plane, the mental or psychic one, has had various kinds of practitioners, functioning at different levels. Let us take the case of the fine write-ups we read of the work in the Philippines [Eleuterio Terte and Anthony Agpaoa are two of the known 'psychic surgeons' of that country] where a person called a doctor performs operations on the human body using no instrument, only his hands, as he exerts mental influence over the patient, who feels no pain, somewhat comparable to Mesmer [this refers only to the hypnotic aspect of the 'anesthetic,' for the German physician did no surgery]. Whether this takes place or not, this is the reporting that we have. Trying to ascertain what level of healing this is, we may conclude that it involves two things: the psychic dominance by the doctor of the patient, plus the use of his hands, giving us a combination of the mental and the physical. Obviously, this is a psychic level of healing.

"Then we have reports of healing 'guides,' most of whom seem to be Indians."

"We're now speaking of spiritualism or spiritisim?"

"Correct."

"Here the practitioner makes contact with the Indian guide who has some hold on healing processes. So, when a patient comes to this person, he, in turn, opens himself to the spirit guide, and these healing vibrations pour out and the subject is helped.

"Let us think that through. Whether you go along with the thought that such a thing happens or not, this is the reporting.

"If you were to accept such as fact, again you would have to be dealing with the mental or psychic level of healing, because death is no diploma. Should you and I pass through death, all that happens is that eventually we wake up on the other side with our head on the same pillow. If there is any great good in what we call death, it is that it has the ability to help you to forget that which you stubbornly refuse to forget, the things you should drop from your consciousness, the scars, the things you've been through, the beliefs—all that has been holding you back and are what we might call, in today's language, hang-ups. Death enables you to drop those away and make room for further growth without negating your progressive unfoldment.

"I make this point in reference to the healing guide to explain that the fact that he is on another plane does not make him superior to being here, save that through death he would have dropped off some of his inhibitions and carried with him only his unfoldment, and if his unfoldment had to do with healing processes he would have it there as well as here. He is still the same individual. The patient is asked to believe in the Indian guide, so, frankly, you are short of God, and thus you're dealing with psychic healing."

"In other words, the consequential consideration is the evolution of the spirit, not the education of the entity?"

"Exactly.

"Many people who have risen to some fame through the

healing of hands have a rather primitive educational background. Yet, it doesn't really matter how they started to believe that they have healing hands, whether from a parent or grandparent. The point is that they begin to believe at an early age that something in their hands helped people. If you will look over the long list of such reports, from the most primitive to people from our highest churches who lean this way, you find that they nearly always connect themselves with God, and think of themselves as a channel for God.

"The hands, like any other part of the body, do not perform of themselves," he noted, observing that, having lost its brain power, a corpse cannot raise its arm. "The hand is raised by one's mentality. From this we can readily understand that the hand is not the healer; that is the consciousness of the person. The hand is a sensitive instrument for his consciousness, that is all. Now the question is whether the healer, by use of hands, leans to God, as most of them do, or simply believes in his hands, or in the idea that somewhere along the line there came a force which goes out through him.

"That would include several varieties of so-called 'psychic' healers. What are some of the others?"

"We have so many levels here, in order to be objective we almost have to isolate and analyze individual cases. Now, I have just spoken of the 'primitive' type; also current among recent reports have been a number on a 'mystery man,' whose name is never given [generally referred to as 'Mr. A'], who seemingly has been helpful for many people, including Governor [George] Wallace, and I have no question in my mind about his sincerity and the work that he does produce. He is interesting, perhaps, because he represents a higher type. He appears to have fixed his attention on energy that flows from the pelvic region of the body, and, regardless of the nature of the condition, he is able to transmit the force from his person, or to call it forth through the subject's also, whether it's for the eyes, the throat, the heart, or whatever."

"Just why do you define this technique as a higher type?"

"Since he doesn't speak of God, in particular, I have to think that he believes himself to be a mental or psychic healer, and that is how he is usually described. Nonetheless, just a little bit of knowledge of spiritual things would indicate the term 'spirit'—which is the means by which God acts through Man—is compiled [sic] of life and energy, distinct from matter. Therefore, this fine gentleman is really an instrument for energy; life, which is energy and intelligence, distinct from matter. Whether he calls it God, or not, he really is utilizing the idea of energy apart from matter, which is purely spiritual."

Dr. Baughman reflected on several theories, which, in general terms, coincided with his own, relating to the incapacitating nature of such subjective attitudes as fury, jealousy, and other negative states of minds. During this exposition he concentrated mainly on some ideas expressed by others and on a book which had dealt with the hypothesis. However, the clarification for which he strove was to be found in his contention that the idea of many illnesses and diseases being caused by negative attitudes within the patient was "only one-third right."

"In this field, whether you speak of it from the mental or spiritual plane, we are the ones who are growing—especially on the latter level. What is there already *is*, and it is a matter of our cultivating the consciousness to receive it. It's an expanding thing, a progressive thing, for all of us in this field. Many young ministers come to me and remark, 'There is only so much to say in this field, is there not?' and my answer to them is 'I'm sorry, you have come to the wrong man. I don't think we've touched the hem of the garment yet.'

"The idea we have been talking about, this aspect of the mental healing, is, as I noted, only one-third right. Not wrong, merely one-third correct. There are three ways to procure the same ailment in a body: one is by bad disposition—that, seemingly, has a relation to physical organisms. The other two ways you can have malfunction in the body are suggestion and fear.

"Let me illustrate suggestion. A little boy overheard a doctor diagnosing his younger sister as having a goiter. This could very well have played on this youth's consciousness, although men are not usually prone to goiters. Much later he had to have a goiter operation—interestingly, it was of the type that grew inward and was not visible. It could very well have been that the suggestion of the overheard remark worked like a depth-bomb in his sub-consciousness, since we are apt to take in that which is given to us indirectly more than that which is given to us directly."

"Since the unconscious aspects are rarely analyzed, would you like to elaborate on that theme?"

"When something negative is given to us directly we put up a conscious defense. Unless we're schooled to keep the lid of our kettle on, we're very apt to pick up the incidental influence. That being a good illustration of how suggestion can play a role in the malfunction of a person's body. Also, it explains how 'family heirlooms' blossom in people's lives. That is, we're all aware of people who say that 'Uncle Joe had this, and Aunt Bessie also, so it's in our family,' and you rather get the impression that he's waiting for the affliction to descend to him.

"The third variety has to be classified as a general *fear* complex. We've all met such people, ones who have many known apprehensions, but, obviously, much of their fear is unknown to them. We might take the case of a lady who had this type of consciousness and the havoc it played on the physical. In her case she had nine cats, all of which developed St. Vitus's dance. She was the dominant, in fact the only, factor in the household and the cats performed in keeping with her consciousness, showing the power of the general fear outlook.

"Now, I mention *disposition, suggestion,* and *fear* as three different ways by which you could produce the same ailment. Yet, while we are still speaking of the mental or psychic field, I want to give credit where credit is due. In this kind of work, the individual is asked to change his own consciousness, to change the cause. I have a way of describing this sort of program; it's substituting the virtuous cycle for the vicious cycle."

"I wonder if we might concentrate on your own area of interest and practice?"

"Spiritual healing? Yes, to get back to Jesus Christ. I'm not a narrow person, and neither was He. His disciples, who were not so well unfolded, at the time that they worked with Him, found people down the road who were healing by another method, and He said, 'Well, if they're not against us, they're for us.' He obviously represented a consciousness that released the healing action of God to a greater degree than anyone of whom we have record. When I think of the Bible, I think in terms of those who actually demonstrated the 'truth that sets free,' that which they all talk about. In this context I think of Moses, Elijah, Elisha, who followed him, and Jesus as being the four who best demonstrated this power that all healers talk about. One may take Paul, a great intellect, but he never performed any important miracles. Take Isaiah, perhaps the greatest intellect of the Old Testament, but you don't identify any great healings with him. On the other hand, these four seem to represent man growing up in the spiritual sense. Each did a little more than the one who preceded him. Yet, they were beholden to those who preceded them—certainly Jesus Christ. People forget that."

"In speaking of the miracles of Jesus, is it your conviction that the miracles were performed by his own divine power, or simply, again, as the ultimate, the highest level of contact with God?"

"My answer to that would not come from me, but from Jesus. He said, 'I, in myself, can do nothing, but the Father within me, He doeth the work.' At no time did he claim, and it wasn't any attempt to disguise his own glamour—always he gave all credit to God, designating Himself only as an instrument.

"Those who aspire to the higher level of healing, the spiritual action of God, Himself, through a person—those who may be called *spiritual* healers—in no sense ever believe that they perform the results. They are merely instruments for God, as was Jesus Christ."

"What is the subconscious consideration in spiritual healing, in contradistinction to mental or psychic healing?"

"Spiritual healing does not cut out the subconscious in procuring its healing, any more than mental or psychic healing technique. We started off with my saying that practitioners in the physical field largely work to allay the effect in the body. For example, taking an actual case, a patient once had a tumor removed from his body, which proved benign, but he had the temerity to ask the doctor if it would return. The doctor said 'No, that one won't, but I can't guarantee that your system might not produce another.' That is to say, the physical deals with alleviating the effect, not necessarily the cause in a person, whereas, in the mental field there is a very serious attempt, however limited it is, to unlock why it is the person is having these conditions and clarify the causes. Now, this is equally true in the spiritual field, but it does not by-pass the subconscious in producing healing.

"Spiritual healing begins in the subconscious of the person, not in the body. Of course, the public isn't interested, they only want their hand healed, or their eyes healed, or their ears healed, or their lungs healed, but whether they know it or not, the first healing that takes place is in their subconsciousness, which relays the effect to the afflicted spot in the body. You see, no process can breach divine law, the natural law—that's what divine law really is.

"There is no process used through a person that can breach that. They all have to heal the subconscious if it is going to be permanent. Jesus, or an Elisha, or an Elijah, or a Moses, they were interested, as a consciousness, in the higher use of that part of the body of their patients. That's all they saw; that's all they believed in. They saw what the Father wanted done there; they became it totally. God does not force Himself; He has to be invited."

"How do you relate this thesis to the more sensational cures?"

"Instantaneous healings can take place, from this point of view. They don't always, but they can. Further, when they do it is understandable, because spiritual healing has the capability of shortening the 'time gap' that the psychic plane, where everything is being done by the mental process of the practitioner, obviously could not have."

"In this spiritual healing, which does not bypass the subconscious, is the subconscious divinely stimulated to assume control of the disharmony of the body and correct it, or is the body directly—via the subconscious—divinely repaired?"

"It happens in the subconscious. There are many passages in the Bible that express this, saying such things as 'I will make darkness light before you,' 'I will straighten the crooked path,' or 'I will write my higher law in your inward heart'; those are almost exact statements of what is done. But I have been as a channel only—I have had great privilege—with five people, including an eminent physician, who was desperate because he operated on his own wife for cancer—and that's unusual, because they don't, they hire another doctor. Still, he is one of the greatest on the East Coast, and he operated on his own wife, who, incidentally, had been his assistant in his own office. Afterwards, he was convinced that he did not get out all of the cancer, and this was evidenced by the fact that she then dissolved into nothing but skin and bones, and was approaching the end."

"What occurred then?"

"He joined with me and three others who were completely devoted to spiritual healing. If I mentioned who they were, everyone would recognize their names, but that's enough on that. However, we 'rhythmists,' through a system we all agreed on—a very simple system of responding to God, which he could follow—we even used medical terms to gradually acquaint him as to what we were after, then letting God come into her. Basically it was seeing what God was doing to the cells that had gone awry. We didn't even have to know where they were. God knows His own. When He is invited, there are those who really respond; they only make entrance for Him to this plane and to a particular case, that's all."

Dr. Baughman explained some of the more technical supertherapeutic and complex medical considerations, remarking on how "all cells are alike," and emphasizing the nature of their disorder with relationship to the debilitation in the patient, especially as it resulted from these physical components "going awry." He then continued describing the inception and progress of the curing of the subject.

"We saw these cells under the influence of God, and the action stemming from the subconscious to the cells, wherever they were, and they were being fed their proper direction again, and their form, and their movement. We used this medical approach because of the doctor."

"This was conducted in collective prayer?"

"Yes, five eminent people, including the doctor, whose wife was the patient. Cancer is not like disorders caused by faulty disposition, suggestion, or fear—elements I have spoken of earlier. When you have cancer, or something comparable, such as leprosy, of years ago, and other vast epidemics which have long since passed because 'crash' programs were directed at them—as long as such crash programs have not been applied or have not worked, it is a great bubble in the race, and everyone is afraid of it. The dearest, sweetest, kindest people can come down with it, because it is *in the race*. When *materia medica* catches up with that, the bubble is popped, and you'll find less and less cancer once the crash program proves effective on it. Until then, people will continue dying like flies. Just as leprosy was cured by Jesus, cancer is being cured. I'm not talking about quackery now, I'm talking about the highest level of healing. Of course, it depends a great deal on the patient, too, that he is receptive."

"Did the fact that there were five of you participating in the healing quintuple the power of your effort?" I wondered.

"It substantially increased it, yes. But I wouldn't want to give the impression that great groups of people are necessary. While we prayed, her sister did a reporting job to us by phone. The other four of us began to hear from her, and the first information was that she was taking on weight a little at a time, then that she was gaining weight rapidly—"

"Am I to understand that the patient wasn't even present, that this was, in actuality, an absent healing?"

"Oh, yes. She was in Virginia and I was in Miami with the others, at the time. That is, she and the doctor were there and the three of us were in Miami. Time and space had nothing to do with it. It was just that the five of us really wanted this. We had that simple procedure that these cells were now under the spell of God again, and that we were seeing them being fed direction, form, and movement.

"A few months before I came to New York, when it had been five years and eight months since she returned to work as assistant to her surgeon husband, she drove down from Virginia to Florida to see me."

"Has this group ever worked together since?"

"Yes, I have used them on other occasions. But I saw the greatest run of spiritual healings in my entire life during my three years in Beverly Hills. There I conducted a special set of four weekday classes, apart from my Sunday duties, of forty people each. We gave ourselves completely to the deepest side of spiritual knowledge, over a period of three years. As we went along, all of those people in the four classes developed great empathy for one another, toward one another.

"One day it was decided that we had gotten so deep and had such feeling that we really ought to try it out [the collective spiritual power of the group]. We had never planned it, but I suppose it was natural that someone would bring it up. Anyway, we began to use it. I then saw more miracles in three years than I saw in the thirty-eight years of my ministry. Still, when I speak of it, people think of one hundred sixty people. Therefore, I brought it down to five, and they still procured it [the cure]."

"To shift to a different facet of your involvement in the healing ministry, I would like to ask what is usually one of my opening questions. How were you introduced to your power to be a corridor of healing from God to man?"

"Actually my initial contact with healing was personal. I was healed of blindness when I was very young. I was operated on both eyes, but that couldn't offer but so much. Then I went to a natural eyesight institute and studied in it. Still, I didn't get my healing until I came into this field and was in it about a year."

"Before we move on, I would like to ask a little more about your personal cure, which I think makes your opinions so much more pertinent than one who has had no direct experience with the phenomenon. Did it consummate when you found your own enlightenment as far as God was concerned?"

"It was a beginning, but I will tell you of another case, if you are interested," he offered.

"Definitely. Is it related to your first activity in healing others?"

"It is. You know, you can be a minister for years and never get engaged in healing. You just go through the forms," he noted in a manner which suggested to me that he felt that such a "non-charismatic" service might be less than a true fulfillment of the ministerial possibilities. "Mine was an intense desire to find something that made sense for this life."

"What was this initial healing experience that led to your healing ministry?"

"I was in Boston, at the time," he began. "I was just a young minister, although I did spend twelve years there, all told. One day this lady, a classic Beacon Hill dowager, entered in a wheel-chair. Immediately the maid who had rolled her in withdrew and she spoke in brisk, authoritarian tones, saying: 'Young man, I don't want to hear a lot of words from you. I'm eighty-four years old, and I once had a healing in the spiritual field, way back in the days of Phineas Quimby, by an associate of his.'"

"That is interesting," I interjected, as it suddenly gave our conversation a century-long sweep across the subject at hand. Reverend Baughman, who did not question that the true founder of the thesis of Christian Science and, in some very tangible ways, the progenitor of mind healing in America was Phineas Quimby, was also fascinated by this historic figure.

"Now, this lady, who said that she had been cured of a problem by an associate of Quimby's forty years ago, said, 'I don't want to hear any talk from you. I'm not here for that. I have a fuzziness in my mind and I have a congestion in my stomach, and an obvious congestion in my knees and they won't support me anymore. I cannot get up. In the time I'm with you, I'd rather not hear any words. I've heard the best. I'll be very candid with you, I realize that people of eighty-four have such problems, but I can't seem to die, and so I am trying to get a start again for the remaining years I have. Just do whatever you can during the silence which we will both enter, and I'll be beholden for whatever help you can bring through from that.'

"As I said, I was a very young minister and I had never been confronted with such a situation, but we both sat there, with closed eyes, for a while. I looked in the silence, eyes closed, past her forehead to the image and likeness in which her brain was made. And then to the digestive part, and then to the knees. It was immediately apparent to me that this was a remarkable individual, open to the greatest. And when we finally came out of our silence I just sat there and looked at her. Then, slowly, this eighty-four-year-old lady rose from that wheelchair, thanked me as only a Bostonian dowager could, walked out of that room in the grandest manner, told the maid to wheel the chair away, and departed."

"Did you ever encounter her again?"

"Some years later, I think about eight, which would have made her around ninety-two, when I was serving in Miami, her daughter called me from New York. She introduced herself and asked if I remembered the incident. Needless to say, I told her I would never forget it. She then told me that her mother had contracted the flu and had said to her, 'If you will call that young man. . . . I will be very open [spiritually] tonight at eight o'clock, and I expect him to give it the try he did then.' The daughter asked if I would do that, and, naturally, I said I would.

"Of course everything of the first experience came back to me, the remarkable woman, the incident—and I made a full effort."

"What was the result?"

"The next day I got a wire from the daughter saying that her mother had responded magnificently and that she was up and fine. Ninety-two. Interesting."

"Had you been practicing any healing in the interim?"

"That was my first, and afterwards I was back into my regular ministry."

"So there was the initial healing, and then the lapse of several years, before you returned to the charismatic work? However, today, isn't a good deal of your ministry specifically in healing?"

"Well, I'm the only one in my particular field—the metaphysical field, that's instituted a special healing service once a month."

Dr. Baughman then graphed out his schedule of three Sunday services a month, culminating in the fourth healing and unfoldment one, as well as his numerous other activities, which include weekly radio broadcasts, a number of courses, and educational efforts for young and old alike. He further detailed some of the techniques he employs to lead the responsive up the ladder of spiritual enlightenment. As the idea of a *metaphysical* minister may confuse some, a bit of Dr. Baughman's theology is in order. By instruction and spiritual direction he leads his followers "very carefully up the ladder to this knowledge, to this action, and then this utter stillness. We call it the great healing pool." He then compared this monthly service to a period at the end of a sentence. "We need that in religion," he emphasized, "instead of just going on and on. One must take time to digest what we learn."

"Do healings occur during these services?"

"Oh, yes. I have had all kinds of reports. But mine is not of the old school of religion, you understand. It's coupled with the very latest things—psychology, psychotherapy, all the latest knowledge."

"Would you give me a thumbnail sketch of how the church differs from the orthodox religions?" I requested.

"With the greatest respect [to other denominations], for me, on the question of the Will of God, there is much to unlearn." Then, mentioning that he was raised in the great traditions of the American church, he observed that the entire history seemed, even in prayer, to be concerned—perhaps even *intimidated*—by "the Will of God"; that mankind collectively and individually had been taught to fear it. Further, when His Will was not feared directly, it was called upon for individual or group preference. "It probably stems from the old days of unfoldment," he offered, "when we knew that [in war] God was on our side and He punished the armies on the other side. The Will of God is for all people," he said. "The Will of God is good. Diseases, the troubles, the disappointments, all of the negative things we have are simply consequences of being apart from His Will."

"Products of man's *free will?*" I put to him.

"Yes. And we use it badly or wrong suggestions are put upon our persons. We have to get back to His will."

"Does The Church of the Truth, which you head, accept Jesus Christ as the Son of God?"

"Not in the classical sense. But in the sense that you and I are His sons and that He was the way-shower to that Sonship."

"First among equals, that is, in terms of unfoldment?"

"Yes, but don't get the wrong impression, for He was far more mature, in that sense. We're still growing up today."

"But not ultimately divine?" I attempted to sum up.

"Let's put it this way. Refer to your older Scriptures, Psalm 86, verse 2: 'Ye are gods'—with a little *g*,—'and all of you sons of the Most High.' It is the way-shower, and is very serious. What He was getting at is this. When you understand secretly and privately that this should be the premise for your life, then the things of God flow more easily to you."

"How does the church feel about other enlightened religious figures? Perhaps, taking as an example Buddha, *sans* the pervasive corruption of his original teachings?"

"If they're not against us, they're for us," he replied immediately and succinctly, elaborating on the fact that most major moral teachers have taught much the same things.

"Might I conclude, at least in part, that the church is returning to what may be the oldest concept of Deity, and that is there is a God, and there have been voluntary and involuntary messengers, persons who have been anointed by God, but not messianic figures who actually partook of His *divinity?* One God and humans who represent Him for given tasks?"

"I like to call them 'way-showers,' " concluded Dr. Baughman. "Whether it is Buddha, whether it's Mohammed, whether it's any of the other great leaders throughout the world—they are the way-showers to divinity. One God."

XIII

Harry Edwards: The World's Greatest Healer

"The greatest spiritualist healer in the world" was honored by nearly 6,000 colleagues, disciples, and beneficiaries gathered at vast and elegant Royal Albert Hall, in London, in the spring of 1973. The event celebrated the eightieth birthday of internationally renowned thaumaturgic therapist Harry Edwards. And while consensus is not always the most prominent emblem of the psychic world, virtually every figure in its English hierarchy lauded the character and career of this remarkable man, including Thomas Johanson, who directs the Spiritualist Association of Great Britain, Gordon Higginson, president of the Spiritualist National Union, and Maurice Barbanell, perhaps the most noted of journalists and authors on such subjects now working in the United Kingdom.

The highpoints of the commemoration included the treatment of eight subjects, the presentation to Mr. Edwards of a bronze cast of his famous hands, and the gift by him to a trio of close associates of a painting showing the four of them healing a patient.

The sparkling affair was a distinct departure from what has been Harry Edwards' life and work for some years.

Friday, July 6, 1973, was a pleasant day, for London, gently fluctuating from mildly sunny to vaguely cloudy. The journey from Waterloo Station to Guildford, Surrey, where the healer lives and conducts much of his practice, was only a half-hour trip, but several aspects of England glide past the window. Suburbs

live. The wife contacted me and explained the circumstances. Then she sent for all her family to come . . . all a sort of last-visit business. However, she knew me as a healer and requested my help. Of course I agreed, and I went to work. The sum of the story is that the next morning the man got up himself and made his wife a cup of tea. He never looked back from that moment, living for many years afterward, making violins. Perhaps the most interesting aspect of this case is that he never knew of the help that he had received. He was an adamant atheist and his wife dared not tell him that she'd sought spiritual help for him. Even if she had, he wouldn't have acknowledged it.

"The third case was a consultation regarding a girl who had an undiagnosed condition. The doctors only knew she was dying. Her sister summoned me and I said, 'I'll see her in the morning.' The next day I went around. Remember, this was my very first contact healing, that is, where I was present. I was very self-conscious, you know, putting my hands through the bed veils onto her head. Nevertheless, I told her mother, 'She'll be up by Sunday.' A very foolish assurance to make. Still, she *was* up by Sunday! Interestingly, she was also tubercular. She'd never had a full lung of air 'til that day. Later, she got married; she has children, grown-up sons, now, and she's still living. Today she has a healing sanctuary of her own in Wales."

"To return to the second case a moment. Did the cancerous patient know what had happened to him?"

"No . . . he never knew. And that brings up the question of whether . . . or the difference, rather, between 'faith-healing' and 'spiritual healing.' Faith-healing has an advantage—that is, if the person has some faith or confidence they're going to get well. Just like a doctor's bottle of medicine. But this does not apply to, and is not an essential for, spirit-healing. Otherwise, we should not see the benefit to the agnostic. We couldn't help the atheist, or the third-party patients—individuals who are brought back to health, even though they don't know the healer's been getting to them.

"Spiritual healing is a *science*. It does not depend upon a person's faith. To overcome a given condition does require a specialized treatment to induce change that is needed and to overcome the affliction. Therefore it is a *planned* effort. To carry out a plan needs an intelligence. To a healer the curable is only the so-called 'incurable.' It indicates that an intelligence superior to man's is operating. Therefore, it also implies that the spirit intelligence who carries out the healing has a knowledge far superior to human science. It also means that it has a much more extensive knowledge of the laws that govern physical science, energies, and things like that."

"Would you stipulate that this is the force of God, or merely the intervention of an entity, or forces, from a higher plane?"

"I think all healing has a divine source. It comes from God. But I question whether any specific healing is the direct act of God on behalf of a certain individual. I think healing is part of the conflict between good and evil, which exists on this earth, and 'upstairs' as well, I imagine. Therefore it is evidence of divine favor. But when God has things to do, He gets His agents, His angels, to do them. The people who carry out these acts, the 'healing intelligences,' I believe are doctors who are ministers of spirit—God's ministers in spirit who are carrying out part of the divine plan."

"How long a period do you work each day in healing, and is it personally invigorating, exhausting, or just plain hard work?"

"I am usually at healing almost the whole day. It commences after breakfast and goes on until one or two in the morning. I like the nighttime for absent healing, because everything is very quiet and nice. I do have a break, a rest, now and then during my schedule, but otherwise it is fairly continuous. At the end of the day there is no depletion at all. No depletion whatsoever . . . for the simple reason that *I* do not heal. *No* healer heals. He hasn't the knowledge or the ability to diagnose and then prescribe the right treatment, to bring about a particular change. Still, I do get refreshment. I feel more rejuvenated *after* a session than I do before I start!"

"That is most believable looking at you. It is difficult to envision a man of your age presenting a healthier image.

"In any therapy, some percentage of patients—under medical

science or anything else—will be helped, some will not. Can you give a rough percentage of your success rate?"

"Yes ... yes. Yet, you want to remember that the types of patient that we receive are those, generally speaking, for whom the doctors have abandoned all hope.

"There are advanced conditions referred to me. Of those patients, repeated researches have found that 80 per cent show signs of betterment in varying degrees. They lose their pain. They're more at ease. Their minds often clear of whatever might be bothering them. Their circulation's better. And of the 80 per cent, a third—roughly 30 per cent—report they're well, completely recovered.

"And 20 per cent do not appear to yield. There's as much reason for why they do *not* respond, as there is for those who do. You have to study each case individually to find a good sign. Generally speaking, I say it is owing to physical conditions that the cause still persists. The cause persists and the effects are all the more certain to continue. For some reason—old age, it might be, or through the disease becoming very, very advanced, causing wastage or paralysis, or the absence of the existence of an organ or nerves ...

"Although, on the other hand, it may be that it is not within the scheme of things for a healing to take place.

"It is of vital importance, I think, to remember that a healing can only take place within the framework of the laws which govern us," he emphasized, leaning forward.

"In other words, you regard healing as a *natural* phenomenon?"

"Natural? Yes, of course. Perhaps a little bit *super*natural. No, not super*natural.* Super*normal.* Yes, supernormal."

"Coming back to the types of illnesses. Tuberculosis and cancer have already been mentioned. What are some of the other serious illnesses that come to you, and the victims of which you help? What would you say were the major ones that stand out in your mind?"

"The major ones? Well, I think the simplest ones are those dealing with physical deformities—for example, curvatures,

slipped disks, arthritic adhesions, locked joints, breathing difficulties, and general functional troubles. The more difficult ones
that may take longer are those where there is a psychosomatic—
definite psychosomatic—cause, although they are also very vulnerable to the spirit."

"You find the psychosomatically linked illnesses *more* difficult than the physical?"

"The reason is simple. It takes a little longer to overcome a
psychosomatic problem than it does a physical one, which is
purely a matter of chemistry."

"Have you actually worked with psychotic patients, patients
that faced these problems?"

"Oh, yes. Many times. Many times."

"Do your methods have any relation to psychoanalytic techniques, or are they completely separate approaches?"

"I don't think you can necessarily compare a spirit-healing
with physical or mental techniques, for instance, psychiatry. A
spirit-healing comes from a spirit dimension, not a physical dimension. And all our knowledge is, as it were, pertaining to the
physical dimension."

"Mr. Edwards, in the United States some of the most publicized healing is done rather theatrically. Oral Roberts, and
others, practice with large, often enormous, crowds collected
together in one place. The impression is that no one here works
that way, but rather deals singly with people."

"True. Over here, healers essentially work by themselves.
They may work in groups under a leader. Small groups as a rule.
There is a distinct difference between the healing of an Oral
Roberts and ours, although I do not deny for one moment that
under those circumstances healings take place. They may take
place under any kind of technique which has a sincere healing
intention as its source. If the intention is to seek healing, then it
will take place in spite of whatever the healer or person does.
While I regard Oral Roberts as more of a—oh, what's the word I
want—an *evangelical* healer . . . I still think healing can only take
place through the *science* of spirit-healing, as I have advocated,"
he clarified, with an expansive gesture.

"Then, again, he will disagree with that. He will say that it is the hand of God that is stretched out to that particular individual."

"In very brief terms, how *does* a spirit-healing event take place?"

"Ah," he chuckled, softly, "that is a question! Well, first of all, there must be the application of the patients, or their relatives, to a healer. There must be the beginning, to start the wheels rolling. The healer then receives the request and what knowledge can be given to him of the person's trouble. The healer will have developed an art of attunement—this is the important word, I cannot ever stress too much. He has developed *the art of attunement to the source of healing.* The spirit-doctors, or the spirit intelligences, are able to read the patient's mind as easily as if they were listening to his words. They receive the knowledge. Then, in the way that they do—which is difficult to explain in an interview like this, we have to take it as writ that they can and do—the spirit-people are able to contact the patient, wherever he or she may be. Remember that absent healing with us takes place all over the world, in America, particularly in Canada, all over. Distance is relative, but irrelevant. All the limitations of physical conditions vanish . . . sight . . . sound . . ."

"Once you change dimensions?"

"Yes, yes. One can say so. You have to accept that they find the patient, and having found the patient, then they make their own diagnosis. They must do that in order to know the character of the treatment to give, or the strength of the energies to give. Healing is a matter of energies, or directed forces."

"In recent years in America there's been an upsurge in healing—a revival even in the orthodox churches of their healing ceremonies, but especially among the evangelical sects. What do you think at this point is going to happen—within terms of religion—with respect to the future of healing?"

"From what I hear, I think spiritual healing is clouded by too many techniques, too much technology. Too much 'do this or that.' I think the healers in America have to learn the lesson our healers have learned in this country. Primarily, *they* do not heal.

If there is any lesson that I've learned, it is that healing, as far as the healer is concerned, is a matter of *utter* simplicity. You don't turn it into an act, and I'm given to understand that takes place frequently in the United States."

"You mentioned before that the spirit physician will contact you. Do you think these spirit presences could be some of the great healing personages of the past?"

"Well could be. We understand, for example, from evidence I've received, that both Pasteur and Lister are working through our group, at this moment."

"Then healing actually functions on two levels. The mediumistic contact with the other world and, also, the particular spirit physician working through the healer as a separate branch?"

"That's correct."

"There seems to be a greater number of male healers than female healers. Do you have any reasons for it?"

"I gather in England there are more female than *male*. You want 'Women's Healer Lib' in America!" he laughed. "With the advance of human science—especially regarding the ecology and energies—knowledge of body chemistry, atoms, and so forth have made more readily understandable the way of spirit and how spirit-healing is able to work. To induce a chemical change near an afflicted joint, for example, it must require the same character for remedial energies, regardless of whether it comes from one source or another.

"Take a joint which is locked with arthritis—calcium carbonate. In order to remove that structure which is cementing the joint, it means that another molecular energy has to be directed to that adhesion in order to change its status, that is to remove it so the joint will move. Whether the healing comes from us or any other source, from America, or from the Philippines, or anywhere else, it must be more or less the same remedial energy, because all things *are governed by laws*. Therefore, as science advances, so we're able to understand more easily and more readily the way of the healer. I could go into more detail about this, but I want to stick to a single point. As we receive from spirit . . . no, just as spirit receives from us, so we are able to intuitively receive information from spirit. It is based on this that we've been able to put forward a thesis for *the prevention and cure of cancer.*"

"A cancer cure?"

"Yes. In putting this forward, we have to agree one does present new concepts. The most conservative organization of all are the doctors. They are very, very reluctant to admit any new idea. Usually they say it's medically unsound. Now, from the evidence we have we believe the actual cause of cancer is *definitely* not physical. It is *non*virus. It is *not* a question of infection at all. It is purely a matter of psychological frustrations.

"This is where we want *a new look*. There's a cell. Let me get down to one thought, to a different thought. Take the mammary cells in a woman's breast. Regard each cell as a living unit. It is *in tune* with the mind, and with the senses, because if the woman's eye sees an erotic subject the cells will become operative. The same with the voice, but *especially* with the touch. So they are in harmony and they are communicating with the senses, and especially with the mind. As the mind works, so we get the cell coming to life. Therefore, a cell is a human unit. Its life is governed by pituitary glands, or some other way. It cannot reproduce itself until it's told to. It wants oxygen to breathe. It has to have the RNA protein for its food. It projects waste. In all these ways it is a living unit.

"Now then, the majority of women who develop breast cancer either wanted children they can't have, or had them and didn't want them, or want to be married and settle down and can't, or have had too strong a maternal control limiting their lives and preventing their associations with the male sex, for example, setting up in their minds a deep frustration. Now *remember the cell*. The mammary cell is linked to the person's mind. When that female realizes she cannot have a baby, ... when she realizes that her fundamental purpose in life cannot be achieved, she becomes depressed and frustrated. That feeling of frustrations is conveyed to, or is received by, the cell, perhaps one particular cell, probably all cells, but especially one particular cell."

"How would you differentiate this hypothesis from the psychosomatic theories of—for example—Karl Menninger, which are not on a spirit plane at all, but based on psychological arguments?"

"Well, it's more or less the same, isn't it?" he replied.

"Apparently."

"So, when this cell becomes frustrated, it throws off the discipline of a cell—it becomes rebellious. It becomes a 'bolshevik,'" he chuckled "and therefore starts reproducing itself as quickly as it can, thus producing a tumor. It becomes a lunatic cell and a malignant cell. This I offer as an explanation of the means by which an apparently normal cell changes its character and its function to become an *abnormal* cell. This is what the doctors will never believe because they can't put it under a microscope."

"*Is* it possible for the spirit physicians, for example, to be part of the investigation of precisely this thesis?"

"People say to us, if the spirits know so much, why can't they tell you how to cure it. Well, *here they're doing it.* We're answering their question." He opened his hands, palms up, as if it were so clear, and again gave way to his infectiously amused manner. "The value of this is that once we can find out the *character of frustration* which is associated with the particular organs of the body, such as I've just described with the breast —incidentally, you notice, especially with women, how the majority of the sites of cancer are all linked in with the organs of reproduction—it ties in *absolutely* with what I've been saying. The interference with their purpose, with the main biological directive of life—if we can discover that, as we are hoping to do through our research—isolate the kind of frustration associated with particular organs, then we can provide for the patient an alternative life directive. We can offer a substitute to replace the other drive, introduce another dominant feature of interest in their lives. Then we shall be able to *prevent* cancer."

"Many medical scientists tend toward the argument that cancer is not a single disease, but a series of diseases. Do you have any opinions on that, sir?"

"What I've been saying really applies to the malignant

cancers and not necessarily to leukemia or Hodgkin's disease, which medical science is making great progress in overcoming. These are a particular form of cancer, insofar as you are creating a malignant cell, a lunatic cell, whereas the other forms of cancer mainly have a genetic origin."

"In Britain, do you find that the British medical establishment welcomes your work or that of other healers?"

"*In spite* of the efforts of the British Medical Association—" he chuckled again—"we healers of the federation have permission to visit patients in over 1,500 of our national hospitals. And that has the agreement of the Minister of Health. The medical profession as such does not even know us. It will not even see us. No, it entirely ignores us. It will not even answer questions or acknowledge our existence. The reason is obvious. The weight of evidence today is so massively in favor of spiritual healing. Remember, its growth has been phenomenal during the past decade. And it has arisen alone from successes in healing sickness where medical science could do no more. So they don't dare know us.

"Unfortunately, in a way they view us as a threat. Because once they admit the principle, that a person who is not a registered physician can heal the sick, once they admit that, then their prestige or high position declines. They're *answerable*, no longer 'untouchables.' "

"Have you in your personal experience worked with any specific physicians who became convinced of spirit-healing as a viable method?"

"There is an ever-increasing number of individual physicians who bring their patients to us, who come to us themselves for healing, although it has to be kept entirely confidential. Otherwise they're liable to disciplinary action by the British Medical Council. Now we have *hospitals* sending their patients here in official ambulances, accompanied by nurses, because generally our patients are very advanced cases, often thought to be terminal cases. But that is *taking place*, now. It can't be held down forever. They'll have to acknowledge it before long."

"There's been a great deal of interest in the United States

recently in death, the idea of the dying patient and the process of dying. Have you had any experience with the business of the preparation of people for death?"

"Yes. Ah, every question you ask opens up endless avenues." He smiled, but took a deep breath and pressed on. "You see, when we get terminal cases of cancer—painful, unendurable agony—when the healing is unavailable, invariably the patients receive inner fortitude, a kind of peace. They do not experience pain. Pain is taken away. They sleep, and the passage is peaceful. Oh, it might be said that the healing had not succeeded, but that which is more important is the contentment. Also, it prepares people for surgery.

"The activities of a healer will prevent operational shock in surgery. Invariably the patients come through it speedily. Frequently hospital personnel call them 'miracle' patients. Therefore, healing helps that way, as well. It also helps in the mind, because, as healing deals mainly with the basic cause of disease, that is, the psychosomatic causes, we are able to influence minds in order to overcome frustrations, in order to give new attitudes, in order to soothe the mind's trouble, especially those of the discontented. As that takes place in the individuals, they will contact the *actual*, and with the passing, mental peace is due. What we often find now is that when a person is approaching the passing they're quiet and without pain. No drugs are needed. Invariably they begin to see their relatives who have passed on before them. Their father, their mother, their sister, their child—whoever it might be. They become conscious of their presence while still lying here . . . during life. In other words, the two forms of life are already together. Does that answer your question?"

"It does. Thank you."

XIV

Thomas Johanson:
The Healing Medium

Thirty-three Belgrave Square is a most elegant address in London, and there, sharing, with embassies, consulates, trade mission offices, and other important enterprises, the perimeter of a broad, oval avenue is the Spiritualist Association of Great Britain. As is the case with its many illustrious neighbors, it is housed in a grand, several-story building of grey stone, across from which is a lovely park, situated in the center of an oval drive.

Mr. Thomas Johanson, who presides as executive secretary over the largest organization of its kind in the world, is himself among the most prominent mediums and healers in England.

Our conversation was conducted in a rectangular demonstration hall of the SAGB known as the Sir Arthur Conan Doyle room, as it featured, upon its speaker's platform, a carved oak chair from the study of the creator of "the world's first consulting detective." [1] Sir Arthur was among the best known early supporters of spiritualism.

"Mr. Johanson, since my arrival I have had the opportunity of speaking with a number of persons in the psychic and spiritist fields, and it appears there is an ever-increasing growth of interest and participation in them."

"Absolutely correct. The number of younger individuals being attracted is greater every year. Some are even becoming mediums."

[1] Arthur Conan Doyle, *A Study in Scarlet.*

"Do the majority of sensitives, whether young or more mature, function on the conscious plane or in trance?"

"They work mostly on the conscious level. Trance is a phenomenon that is dying out. Thirty years ago, in this country, physical mediumship was extremely prevalent. However, it has dwindled away. Clairvoyance, clairaudience, and psychometry—that is, mental phenomena—have taken over."

"Now, regarding your own talents, is there a history of spiritualistic power in your family?"

"Yes. My father, who would not have called himself a spiritual healer—"

"You do not care for the phrase 'faith-healer,' do you?"

"No, because it is not accurate. I am a *spiritual* healer. There is a world of difference between these two characterizations, and it is this. It is stated by certain religious sects that, as God is perfect, and He created everything, [He] therefore created everything perfectly. However, as we do have a lot of disease and disharmony in our lives, this was obviously created by man, himself. Therefore, these religious bodies say that if you have *complete* faith in God, have utter faith and no fears, and live simply and peaceably, then all of the undesirable conditions will automatically disappear. But we know from experience that man cannot live like this. Man does worry, he has problems, he fears. So, the difference between the *faith*-healer and the *spiritual* healer is this: the spiritual healer is a sensitive who believes that around him and above him there is a spiritual force, call it what you will, and he is convinced that through the power of prayer and meditation he can tune in on that superforce, thereby becoming the instrument which relays the power to the ill person. It is only by the power of prayer that he may open the channel to heal the sick."

"Then, the spiritual healer is a transmitter through which flows whatever therapeutic spiritual energy is available?"

"Yes. Every person who has love for his fellow man, and has the natural instinct to want to help him, is a spiritual healer. Incidentally," he continued, "I want to mention this vitally important point. A spiritual healer is never ambitious to take over from an orthodox medical man."

"Yet earlier on you told me something of spiritual healing, in Great Britain, in terms of hospitals?"

"Over the past seven or eight years, we have been allowed to work in nearly 2,000 hospitals. If any patient requests the services of a spiritual healer, it is forwarded to the matron or sister [nurse] in charge and she will contact the National Federation of Spiritual Healers. A healer living in that area will be directed to the hospital and the particular patient."

"To return to your personal career, you said that your father seemed 'gifted,' although he never thought of himself in those terms."

"He was. He had a remarkable talent for healing animals. The neighbors used to bring their children and their animals to him. He would not have recognized the term 'spiritual healer,' but that is what he was."

"As a child, were you aware of your father's skill?" I asked.

"Oh, yes."

"When did you first realize the presence of your own gift?"

"I actually never did, to be honest. I simply became interested in psychic matters, not healing particularly. I was concerned with what the clairvoyant was seeing and what the clairaudient was hearing. Having learned that these perceptions really existed, I discovered a growing urge to develop myself."

"How old were you when you began?"

"I was about twenty-seven or twenty-eight when I joined a class of instruction and I studied there for six years. Needless to say, I never saw or heard a thing. Still I was intrigued by what others were doing and saying. Then, one day, the leader of my group was invited to form a healing clinic and, out of some thirty people, he had to select six to cooperate in the new work.

"Now, he was controlled by his guide," digressed Mr. Johanson for a moment. "Incidentally, I should mention that this particular leader had been a Roman Catholic monk, but he was such a natural clairvoyant he felt he had to leave the monastery and try to help people with his gift.

"Now, while this leader was in a trance state, being guided by his control, he selected six individuals to assist him in this fresh venture—and, to my utter amazement, I was one of the six. I was totally convinced at that time that he had made a dreadful mistake. A, I had no ambitions; B, I had never thought about being a spiritual healer. My speculations had never once strayed in that direction.

"On the day they put me into one of those private consulting rooms and sent in a patient, I felt a complete fool," he recalled, leaning back in his chair and smiling. "I really did not know what to do, and so I placed my hands on the patient's head, or wherever he felt the pain, and prayed. Still, I was convinced that nothing would happen and that the mistake in judgment would soon be discovered, and that they would send me packing. Don't you see the situation?" he chuckled.

"Lo and behold! the patients returned and said they felt a peculiar heat coming out of my hands. Then they appeared to get well. So we carried on and got a bit more confident over the following months. Now, I have developed into a healer and I travel around the country giving public demonstrations of spiritual healing."

"How many persons would you imagine you help a year?"

"That is difficult—ah—well, I would say between 800 and 1,000. I have my regular clinic at the association [SAGB] where I deal with—although it has been as high as twenty persons—an average of eight or ten a day. However, in addition, I have patients who come to my home."

"Do you do all of your work through direct contact?" I inquired. "I know that there are healers here in Britain who operate by spiritual proxy, as it were, often conducting their therapy via post."

"As all healers do, I devote a little part of my evening, perhaps a half-hour, to sitting quietly, sending out thoughts to patients. This absent healing is quite a potent force. I remember a lady telephoning me about her little doggie which was very ill.

He wouldn't eat, neither would he move. The vet feared that if he were not improved by the following day he would have to be put to sleep.

"This lady was desperate, and so I sat down and sent out my thoughts for this doggie. She rang me early the next morning and said a miracle had happened. The little creature had just jumped from his basket and displayed a ravenous hunger, and after that need was satisfied she had taken him for a long walk."

"From which one may deduce that distance isn't a pertinent factor?"

"Distance is a phenomenon confined to earth," he emphasized. "It is not concerned with thought or spirit."

"This remote approach brings to mind the practices of Edgar Cayce, the so-called 'sleeping doctor' of the United States [see Chap. VI]. Is there much interest in him in England?"

"We are certainly well aware of him—there are books about him in the association's [SAGB] bookshop. However, personal contact with someone such as Harry Edwards [see Chap. XII] makes a difference. He is very real to us since we see him working."

"Most healers in the States seem to work consciously," I remarked. "What is the custom in Great Britain?"

"A large majority of healers operate on a conscious level," replied my host. "Yet we do have trance healers. George Chapman,[2] for example, works eight hours a day in trance."

"I know that many mediums find one sitting quite exhausting, and even some clairvoyants and psychometrists restrict the length of their interviews. How is your physical and spiritual strength affected by your work?"

"Healing has no debilitating effect at all. On the contrary, the more patients one treats, the more alert and refreshed one feels afterwards. Before I came to the SAGB I was working in the advertising field, but would frequently leave my office feeling very tired and come here to do an evening's worth of healing. By

---

[2] George Chapman is another prominent British healer.

the time I had finished with the clinic, I was a new man. I was walking on air."

"Do you think there are any limitations to the healing power of a sensitive with a strong gift? For example, would there be a great difference in the problem presented in the curing of a common cold in contradistinction to treating some severe disease? It occurs to me that a minor, a major, and a chronic disorder might fall into three different categories."

"First of all, there are two points we must make abundantly clear. First, *no healer, himself, no matter how powerful, can decree that a specific person shall be cured* [emphasis added]. Every healer, including Harry Edwards, the greatest healer in the world, has had to admit to failure at times.

"Second, there is no set pattern of behavior in spiritual healing. A, *the healer is only a channel through which the power may pass to create whatever effect is destined to happen*. B, *the pattern cannot be anticipated* [emphasis added].

"On occasion," he began to elaborate, "I have had two nearly identical cases—one has cleared up almost instantly, while the other dragged on, and on, seemingly never to get better. Some patients respond, some don't.

"Human beings are subject to many natural physical and spiritual laws. You know, it is true that many diseases, many disharmonies of the body—a great percentage are created psychosomatically. The way people think, the manner in which they live, does establish conditions. Therefore, unless we can get them to alter these self-made climates of existence, we cannot really achieve a cure."

"Then the psychosomatic disorder would tend to be a more difficult problem, less responsive to spiritual treatment, than something that was actually physical?"

"Well, you know, it's not easy to classify a disease by simply saying 'psychosomatic.' The question is, 'What degree of psychosomatic emphasis is involved?' "

"Understood, but what about the hysteric type, an apparent invalid without any apparent organic problem? Does such a person present additional complications?"

"He does. My specialty has been psychological distress, and I can testify that it is more complex than treating arthritis."

"When you say 'psychological healing' are you speaking of physical disorders caused by mental or emotional problems and attitudes, or are you alluding to purely nonphysically symptomized illnesses of the mind?" I asked.

"The second. We are talking about psychological problems, which, incidentally, have increased tremendously in recent years. Particularly acute depressions, fears, suicidal impulses—usually deriving from no material—i.e., financial, employment, etc.—cause. And these conditions take a long time to resolve."

"What about serious or more advanced conditions in purely physical healing? Do you assert, as do many healers, that the spiritual approach can really be of help in really grave diseases such as tuberculosis, cancer, and paralysis? Generally one gets the impression from sensitives in therapy that, given a true rapport between the patient and themselves, virtually any disorder can be eradicated."

"I have been associated with the practice for a score of years, and there is no shadow of a doubt that every condition has, at one time or another, responded to spiritual healing. Yet, I cannot say that I have cured every case of cancer that has come to me," Mr. Johanson granted. "But cancer has been cured by spiritual healing," he reiterated. "It has been almost miraculous, you know."

"I would think the 'almost' an unnecessary modification," I replied. "Such a case would certainly deserve to be termed 'miraculous.' Now, your own specialty is the psyche, in the medical sense—that is, the psychological. What of instances of exceptional psychological disorientation? Perhaps schizophrenia? Have you had an opportunity to work in this area? If not, do you see a possible future for your kind of therapy among such tragedies? Take the catatonic schizophrenic, about whom little or nothing can be done because the avenues of communication are barricaded by unknown etiological blocks. Presumably, spiritual healing would not be forestalled by this wall of vacuum, as it were."

"I am very glad you raised the subject of schizophrenia, because I have had a tremendous amount of experience with it. The doctors talk about this complaint as a 'split personality [sic].' But this is totally wrong, it is not a 'split personality,' meaning that it is one mind split in two.

"I have noticed over the years that there is a direct pattern concerning these people. First, they are very intelligent. Second, they are extremely sensitive. In other words, *there is a definite mediumistic material present* [emphasis added]. When I have observed these persons, there is not a shadow of a doubt in my mind that I am communicating with two different individuals."

"Not merely different aspects of a single individual, but separate entities?"

"Not two aspects, two persons," he reaffirmed.

"Are we speaking of invasion or possession?"

"I wouldn't say 'possession,' because this is a definite term, but I would say that we are talking about a direct infringement by one mind upon another mind."

"Do you mean two mundane minds?" I asked. "I mean, obviously one is earthbound, but are we entertaining the idea of an additional psyche from another living human being, or are we describing a personality moving from another plane and attempting to house itself in a new body? Or are we speaking of something entirely different," I posed, "namely, the *Doppelgänger* phenomenon, the counter-personality, the mirror image which everyone is alleged to have—either as a wraith, astral separation, or corporeal twin?"

"Well, we know, because of the enormous amount of research we do in the psychic field, that all dying means that the etheric body vacates the material one. Now, in the normal course of events, this etheric body would move into the proper spirit world."

"That is frequently characterized as 'the other side'?"

"Yes. However, there is a state that is neither the material world, nor the complete spirit world."

"Would it be the equivalent of, or at least analogous to, what was once called 'limbo' by theologians?" I inquired.

"Limbo, or what we call it," he clarified, "the lower astral world."

"Do I understand that it is populated by personalities who have failed to make the complete transition from one full state to the other?"

"Exactly. The transition has not been completed for a number of reasons, and the etheric body is suspended in between the two worlds. The subjects are in a most difficult situation, because they cannot express themselves. It is as if they were in a sort of pea-soup fog. They can remain thus for many years."

"How may they extricate themselves?"

"When they see a sensitive—sensitives emit a kind of light —an aura.[3] When suspended personalities see the emanation they instinctively know they can express themselves through it. They are drawn to the individual, recognizing a line of communication. Still, they don't exactly enter the body, although they come close. There is some defect in the aura, which we know is a protective field, whereby the entity is allowed to transmit to the mind of the person on earth. Therefore, when you observe a schizophrenic —and any medical doctor will confirm this—you are always aware that he is a suspicious person, and he will always blame this or that relative, friend, or neighbor for his apprehensions, although he never really knows who or what is actually causing his fears. The result is an intricate pattern of the two personalities, each trying to gain the upper hand.

"I also find in the schizophrenic some sort of weakness in character," he elaborated. "On one occasion my success lay in my being able to establish a rapport with the character of the earthly person, who happened to be interested in art and music. Being a trained artist, I was able to give him drawing lessons and I arranged for a friend of mine to instruct him on the piano. Attention to things of this earth strengthened him and his character until we were able to eject the intruding spirit entirely.

"I don't pretend to know exactly what the defect is," he

[3] Alleged to be an invisible (to all but sensitives), ethereal glow surrounding all—or particular—individuals, which is interpreted in various mystical ways.

conceded. "All I do know is that I have had conversations with *both* of the personalities, not merely the patient.

"In one instance, I had a sweet, young girl," recalled the medium. "She was of excellent background and upbringing but would converse in most coarse language, quite foreign to her. At another time, I treated a different girl, only twenty-one years old, but extremely stout. She visited me with her mother and, at one point, cried out: 'Don't identify me with that fat thing!' and, also, 'That's not my mother over there!' Again, we had an entirely new personality coming in."

"These were both instances where you had diagnosed the subjects as schizophrenics?"

"Schizophrenia is the impingement of a wholly new personality upon the weakened character of a person on this earth."

"Have you been able to ascertain what does happen to these semidiscarnate, 'limboized' inhabitants of 'the lower astral plane'?" I queried. "Do they finally traverse the bridge to gain full citizenship in the spirit world?"

"Let me clarify something. We are not interested in 'getting rid' of these entities. We are concerned with helping them. It's the same, in many instances, with a poltergeist. A poltergeist is not necessarily some spirit gone berserk, but it is a spirit needing aid. The churchman—the priest or minister—will attempt to get rid of it [exorcism]. Now, we don't want this. We wish to direct the entity so that it will discover its proper place, aiding it to move into its destined total astral sphere.

"In one of these cases," recalled Mr. Johanson, "a woman had been playing with a ouija board,[4] a very dangerous device. She was not a spiritualist, merely curious.

"Her husband, who was a scientific man, president of an astrological society, brought her to me in a kind of a trance state. I was able to communicate with the intruding entity who, incidentally, was male. He told me that outside of the host patient it was dark, unfriendly, and that he had attached himself because

[4] A divining instrument introduced in the late nineteenth century, based on earlier home-made techniques, consisting of a board covered with letters and numbers across which moves an indicator spelling out messages, allegedly motivated by spirit forces.

through her he could have communication, even conversation, and the proximity of another personality, through which things he got comfort. This exchange between us lasted for nearly two hours, during which time I explained that he was causing a great deal of distress. He admitted that he realized that, but asked, 'What can I do?' I told him that I would tell him what to do and that, as I only wished to aid him, he must trust me."

"What was your advice to this disembodied presence?"

"I told him, 'Now, in a sense close your eyes, and then imagine that you are looking upwards at a tiny spot of light towards which you must will yourself. When you move outside this lady you will feel the darkness, the loneliness, but you must rise toward this light.'

"He said he would do as I instructed," remarked Mr. Johanson. "There was a violent shudder from the patient and I thought him gone. However, she gave a deep breath and the entity's voice exclaimed, 'Oh, it's dark out there!'

"We went through the entire thing again," my host continued. "Finally, as the girl heaved a profound sigh, he departed. She was perfectly all right after that."

"We may assume that playing with ouija boards, or other aspects of the spiritualistic, in which one is unskilled, is dangerous."

"Absolutely," he agreed. "Like leaving the house open at night."

"Have most of these cases been hospital confinements, or were you dealing with them outside of an institution?" I asked.

"This particular woman had been to a hospital, but such people are often regarded as merely neurotic."

"Was she viewed as schizophrenic by medical doctors?"

"No, no, she wasn't."

"What about conclusively schizoid cases?"

"There have been hospital cases. Dr. Carl Whitman [a doctor with an orthodox practice in London] handled such cases very, very successfully. His wife, fortunately, was an excellent trance medium. She used to sit beside the patient and the doctor, who was a medical man, used to pass a wave of electricity through the subject. For some reason this caused a very uncomfortable feeling for these entities. Apparently it was a kind of vibration which was close to theirs."

"Electricity introduced mechanically?" I inquired.

"Yes. This impulse used to reject the intruding personality, and it moved into the unelectrified trance medium next to the patient. Soon the entity got into the habit of seeking sanctuary thusly and this enabled the doctor to speak with and help it. The technique had a very high percentage of success, but, also, many failures."

"When one encounters an advanced stage disorder, such as a catatonic, where the patient, too, is in a trance state, as it were, and he is nonconscious sensorially, neither perceiving visually, nor audically, and all efforts to break through with a line of communication have failed—shock treatment, chemotherapy, and all psychiatric approaches—do you think that, because of the extramundane nature of your discipline, through spiritual healing an avenue might be found via which one may enter the arena of perception of these seemingly totally inaccessible persons?"

"Yes," he replied, "but I do think, apart from the actual healing, you do need a good medium to make the contact."

"You mean that it would best be a cooperative effort between a medium and a spiritual healer? A medium to breach the physical barrier and establish a rapport with the alien consciousness, and, then, a healer to deal with the actual problem?"

"Definitely. You see, what you've got to realize is that, in every case, these entities are in rather a bemused state. They're lost. You've got to help them find themselves."

"Mr. Johanson, many mediums, trance mediums particularly, have controls, or rather exotic spirit guides, and in the past frequently of American Indian origin, less often Eastern Indian, or Chinese, or Egyptian, or something comparably fanciful. Recently, more European, and also American, controls are being introduced, and they are less esoteric, often being professional men, from medicine, the clergy, and so forth. Is this a definite and permanent trend away from the more extravagant concept of guide?"

"Well, I, personally, dislike the term 'guide.' It's somewhat archaic, not in keeping with the modern spiritualism. In the early days we did have these guides with rather exotic names—the red Indians, the Zulus, and so on—and it was right for the time, you know. However, this is a new era. Today I prefer the term 'helper.' The idea of guides with colorful names is passing away and I would like to see it dropped entirely. I would like a trance lecture simply to be presented as an address by Mrs. So-and-so, or Mr. So-and-so, rather than 'There'll be a lecture by White Feather, guide of person So-and-so.' And what you say is true, the 'helpers' are coming more and more from the West."

"It certainly seems to be the evolving pattern," I agreed.

"We had so many red Indians and Eastern people because they lived very close to nature. The red Indian, in particular, was a natural psychic. He accepted life after death as a natural part of existence. He did not have to be taught this as the European has to be taught it."

"Do you have a regular helper yourself, or do you draw from a number of contacts on other levels?"

"Over the years, I have established a reputation of being one of the 'big five' healers in the country. I have this reputation. I know, of course, that there must be helpers with me. I have never inquired who they are, what their names are—I don't care. I am only interested in the quality of the work that comes through."

"Mr. Johanson, in conclusion, what is the future of the spiritualist movement?"

"I have been involved in spiritualism for nearly twenty years. I have never ceased to be a researcher, and so I would remark that one shouldn't accept everything without question. Examine everything. This movement is growing at a fantastic rate. In years to come, the philosophy of spiritualism will eventually take over orthodox religion.

"We have no dogma, we have no creed. We do not say that if a man is a sinner he will be destroyed, we do not believe that. We believe, most ardently, that the sinner is simply ignorant—that is, he is a man ignorant of the ways and purpose of life. This man will ultimately suffer his own ignorance, and this suffering will be the means whereby his ignorance will be transmuted into wisdom and understanding. In this way his soul will progress. He most certainly will not be destroyed, but will continue to evolve. Thus, we differ with the orthodox [Christian] church. We do not hold that God is vengeful. We believe that every man is a god in the making. Obviously he is looked over by a greater intelligence than himself, but regardless of how wicked or evil a man is, he will suffer his own failings, and through this finally evolve."

"Thank you, Mr. Johanson."

"Thank you."

XV
Charisma and the Established Church

Orémus. Réspice, Dómine, fámulum tuum, _____, in infirmitáte córporis laborántem et ánimam réfove quam creásti: ut castigatiónibus emendátus, contínuo se séntiat tua miseratióne salvátam. Per Christum Dóminum nostrum.

No, it is not the mystical incantation of an exotic sect, for those to whom the passage is not familiar or do not read Latin. It is an incantation of the Catholic Church, the most orthodox of religious orders; it is an excerpt from the blessing of a sick adult *(Benedictio Adulti Aegrotantis)*.[1] In English it merely says: "Let us pray. O Lord, look upon your servant [the patient is indicated and named], laboring under bodily weakness, and cherish and revive the soul which you created, so that, purified by her suffering, she may soon find herself healed by your mercy. Through Christ our Lord."

The same manual contains the ritual for the administration of the sacrament of the anointing of the sick *(Sacramentum Unctionis Infirmorum)*, which details gospel passages (Matthew 8:5-10, 13) to be read during the petition for healing, plus the remainder of the thaumaturgy, which includes the individual anointing of eyes, ears, nose, mouth, hands, and feet, and various prayers and exultations.

As remarked in the initial chapters of this examination, charismatic healing has been an essential aspect of orthodox religion, especially Christianity, and, perhaps, the Roman Cath-

---

[1] *Collectio Rituum.* (Collegeville, Minnesota: The Liturgical Press, 1964), pp. 447-448

olic Church, for millennia, although, in the United States, it has long been the special province of minor fundamentalist sects, and, in England, very popular among spiritualists.

The pagan health shrine of the goddess Sequana, later converted into a chapel of Christian cures, was razed more than a thousand years ago, but Catholicism has always had a substantial catalogue of such miracle markets. Fatima, in Portugal, is one of the most recent and best known. According to the accounts, between the dates of May 13 and October 13, 1917, three small children claimed to have been afforded visions of the Virgin. Shortly thereafter, Monsignor José da Silva, bishop of Leiria, decreed:

(1) parish of Fatima in this diocese on the thirteenth day of each month between May and October, 1917 are deserving of credit; (2) that the cult of Our Lady of Fatima is officially permitted.[2]

Since that inaugural recognition many other apparitions are reputed to have appeared, and the sick have journeyed there from far points of the earth. A hospital has been built to accommodate them, and a miracle investigation board has been instituted—much after the fashion of Lourdes, to which it may well rank second in fame and popularity. The committee of inquiry was originally under the supervision of Dr. Pereira Gens, assisted by numerous other physicians and staff during the years. Since his retirement a considerable list of medical men have maintained his efforts. Between 1926 and 1937 an estimated 15,000 petitioners passed through inspection, and the official journal, *Voz de Fatima*, claimed about 1,000 cures, including cancer, tuberculosis, and blindness, among countless other diseases and disabilities.

One well-known case exemplifying the asserted power of the shrine to restore health is that of Margarida Rebelo, which occurred in 1944. The young woman was recognized to have been

2 François Leuret and Henri Bon, *Modern Miraculous Cures*.

the recipient of a miraculous cure from "paraplegia due to compression of the spinal cord; purulent cystitis; fistula formation" (presumably a paralytic stroke resulting from vertebral pressure on a major nerve, accompanied by an inflamed bladder or urinary tract with discharge and swelling).

While it is true that a majority of healing shrines are found in the warmer countries, there are exceptions, such as the one at Knock, at Tuam, Ireland. It was there that, in 1879, fifteen people swore they saw a visitation by the Holy Mother. After a proper period of time it was declared a valid miracle by a canonical court. A large number of persons were attracted to it over the next half century, although, needless to say, the traffic never remotely compared to that directed toward Lourdes and Fatima.

The Knock Shrine Medical Bureau was impaneled in 1935 to survey the claims of cures, and a hospital was erected to house the more seriously ill patients. A *Knock Shrine Annual* was begun to record the results of the investigations and a notable number of miraculous restorations of health have been detailed; e.g., in 1925, John O'Grady was cured of "rachitic deformity of the legs," i.e. rickets.[3]

Naturally Italy has many thaumaturgic shrines. Our Lady of the Rosary, located in the village of Valle de Pompeii, was founded by Bartolo Longo in 1873. It has had a long history and one of its better-known wonders was the elimination of a cerebral tumor from Mother M. A. Falletta in 1940. Yet, while each shrine must be regarded by the believer as fabulous in its own way, it is difficult for any to surpass the fascinating background attributed to Our Lady of Loreto. Religious history has that it was the original house in Nazareth of the Blessed Virgin, and that it was levitated and transported, or teleported, from the Middle East hamlet to Tersat, in Illyria, next to Macedonia, on the Ionian Sea (on the west coast of Greece), in 1291. But that was only the initial flight, for three years later it was miraculously removed to a site near Ancona, on the Italian side of the Adriatic. Today it constitutes the heart of a basilica which was constructed

[3] Ibid., p. 43.

about it by the popes of the fifteenth and sixteenth centuries.

The European healing shrines, and, to a lesser extent, those of Latin America, received an unceasing stream of publicity, and so it is not surprising that many Americans are unaware of many such holy places in their own country and in Canada.

While not quite so exotic as the history of Our Lady of Loreto, Our Lady of Perpetual Help in Roxbury, Massachusetts, founded by the Redemptionist Fathers, has an intersting history. It boasts a copy of, and its name derives from, a thirteenth- or fourteenth-century portrait, the original of which hangs in the Church of St. Alphonsus Liguori. The miraculous cures began on May 29, 1871, when a child—one Louise Kohler—was healed of asthma and lameness. Many healings ensued and are recorded—from their initiation until 1920—in *The Glories of Mary*.[4]

The Shrine of the Little Flower, in Nasonville, Rhode Island, was created as a remembrance of Thérèse Martin, "the little flower of Jesus," who was canonized at Lisieux, France, in 1888, and about whom accounts of supernatural wonders abound. The shrine, it is claimed, has been the motivating factor in a series of "extraordinary cures . . . [two of which] were so extraordinary that a report of them was forwarded to the Sacred Congregation of Rites in Rome." [5]

Perhaps the most frequently cited North American shrine is that of Sainte Anne de Beaupré, which was established in Quebec in 1658, although the original chapel was never completed. The permanent church was constructed, and, again, dedicated to Saint Anne, in 1662. Miracles have been attributed to the site for centuries, giving it a longer history of healing than the overwhelming majority of shrines, including those situated beyond the shores of this continent. The Ursuline nun, Marie de l'Incarnation, wrote in 1665—only three years after the edifice's completion—that "seven leagues from here, there is a village called 'Petit Cap' where there is a church dedicated to Saint

---

[4] *The Glories of Mary*. Boston: Boston Mission Press. 1921.

[5] Francis Beauchesne Thornton, *Catholic Shrines in the United States and Canada.* New York: Wilfred Funk, Inc., 1954.

Anne, in which our Lord vouchsafes to work great prodigies by the intercession of the Blessed Virgin. There the paralytic are made to walk, the blind to receive their sight, and the sick, no matter what their ailment may be, regain their health." [6]

A post WWII example of the miracles of Ste. Anne de Beaupré was a cancer cure, diagnosed by one Dr. Simard. The patient, Evariste Langevin, visited the shrine after declining an operation. About two years later the physician wrote, "There is no doubt that this cure is above medical interpretation." [7]

Among other shrines, on this side of the Atlantic, which have achieved a healing reputation may be counted St. Joseph's Oratory, in Quebec, the Sorrowful Mother Shrine, in Maywood, Ohio, and the National Shrine of the Little Flower in Chicago.

Doubtless, it should be remarked that several of the episodes by which certain of the described shrines were established occurred in the late nineteenth century, and that after that period few cases have been reported. Still, there are exceptions. One dates back slightly more than a decade, but has become one of the most discussed and publicized.

The date of the inauguration of Garabandal, Spain, as a place of Virginal visitations differs from one report to another, but all delineate unbelievable spiritual phenomena with a presentation that borders on high-pressure publicity; e.g., a half-page advertisement that appeared in 1968 in a full-size (not tabloid) New Orleans newspaper (New Orleans *States-Item*) advising that "there will be a supernatural warning made to every human being, believer or nonbeliever. There will be a public message at Garabandal, Spain, on the anniversary day of the child who died defending the Lord Jesus Christ ... this miracle will be announced eight days in advance. There will be a divine chastisement of the entire world, if the above warning and miracle are not heeded."

The advertisement also announced the appearance of Joey Lomangino—accompanied by Rev. Archangel Sica, chaplain of the New York Garabandal Center—who, it was printed, is "the

[6] Ibid., p. 248.
[7] Ibid., p. 252.

apostle of Garabandal, the blind man whom the late Padre Pio, Stigmatist, sent to Garabandal, Spain, and who was informed by visionaries there that he will receive *'new eyes'* at the time of the above-mentioned Garabandal Miracle."

The entire half-page radiates a strong Billy Sundayish, ranting revivalism far more than the usually (at least in recent years) conservative and cautious approach of the Catholic Church to miracle visionaries, regardless of whether they merely bring divine messages or attempt to translate their alleged experiences into doorways to holy health. As a matter of fact, there are at least two lines of seeming retreat, if not outright disclaimers, should the Church bring its restrictive authority to bear, in the notice. One concedes that while "Paul VI has spoken favorably of Garabandal" on several occasions, and "has *not* banned" it, this is obviously less than unqualified approval and validation. The second caveat notes that Roman Catholic law was revised, as of November 17, 1967, so "that regarding apparitions, etc., the imprimatur [sanction] is no longer requested."

The story of this particular promotion of Mariolatry began in a small village of a few hundred persons, named San Sebastian of Garabandal, where, before 1966, there was no permanent cleric or even a physician.

On the evening of June 18, 1961, four young girls from poor, but deeply religious, families—Conchita Gonzales, Jacinta Gonzalez, Maria Cruz Gonzalez (unrelated to one another), and Maria Dolores Mazon, none older than twelve years—were playing in a small pasture when they heard a thunderous sound and saw the Archangel Michael appear. He directed them to be at the same place two weeks later to receive a visit from the Virgin. At six on the specified day they appeared and so did she, as Our Lady of Carmel, accompanied by her herald.

An account of the miracles would be lengthy and complicated, but they include various forms of supernatural manifestations, imperviousness to pain, prophecy, levitation, and the blessing by the Holy Mother of religious objects which were subsequently credited with being responsible for the cure of various afflictions. Yet collectively weighed, it appears clear that the overwhelming emphasis of Garabandal is the dire warning to mankind, as received through Mary, that her Son would bring about great destruction if humanity did not correct its evils.

If viewed only historically, certain of these phenomena are of interest in their obvious relationship to one another, for it is impossible to be unaware of the similarity of the origin of Lourdes, Fatima, Garabandal, the Miraculous Lady of the Roses of San Damiano, Italy, and the experiences of the nuns of Mexico City who have been the recipients of visitations by Jesus and whose messages from the Lord are conveyed via the newsletter *Vers Demain*.[8]

Lourdes is indisputably the most famous of all healing shrines, and among the best-known small towns of any kind in the world. Yet, even today and within the structure of the Roman Catholic Church, it is a catalyst for dogmatic, theological, and medical dispute.

The story of the shrine of Lourdes began on February 11, 1858—another to fall within that quarter-century which produced a series of such phenomena—when an unschooled, sickly girl named Bernadette Soubirous purportedly was blessed with the first of nearly a score of visions of the Virgin. Again, a pattern is apparent: the age, education, social station, and general physical and psychical characteristics of the children of Fatima and Garabandal are repeated.

Shortly after the initial vision in a local grotto, enormous crowds—some have claimed as many as 100,000 persons—began parading after the girl to view her ecstatic trances. It is said that the Church began to be persuaded of the authenticity of the divine nature of the incidents when it was reported that Bernadette had said her apparition identified herself as "the Immaculate Conception." It seemed unlikely that so young and untutored an individual would be familiar with a phrase she had probably never heard and certainly would be unable to comprehend. This argument is persuasive, in a general sense, since the dogmatic proposition of "the Immaculate Conception"

[8] *Vers Demain*, Rougemont, Quebec, Canada. Maison Saint-Michael.

was not included in the mythos of the Church until the issuance of the papal bull *Ineffabilis Deus*, by Pius IX, on December 8, 1854—four years earlier. Of course, the more esoteric theologians had remarked on the idea in their Latin speculations for some time before the announcement from Rome, but we may even more safely say that these were not familiar to her.

Bernadette, it is said, was instructed by the vision to direct that a chapel be built at the springs by the cave, in which she was also to go and immerse herself. Others followed her act of bathing in the sacred pool and were cured of diseases of every imaginable description. Miracle after miracle was recounted and eventually the high authorities recognized that the Mother of Jesus had truly visited the site and ordered that a basilica be erected there, as well as equipment which would separate the watering places for men and women. That is, while thousands, perhaps, over the years, millions, of individual men and women have plunged into the waters which have poured across every conceivable wound, and carried all the contagious corruption and plagues of the race, the sexes have been kept apart. Later in its history records were kept of the "cures" of Lourdes. None, as far as is known, has ever recorded those new disorders and afflictions contracted at the grotto by those who came there to be "purified."

Naturally, the shrine is credited with many famous "cures," like that of Pierre Bouriette's "traumatic blindness" and Louis Bouhohort's "teomalacia and febrile wasting," in the same year the spring was sanctified by the claims of Bernadette.

Journalists have used phrases like "yet medically inexplicable cures do occur at Lourdes...," when, obviously, what they mean—or certainly should mean—is medically *unexplained*. In part, it is such inaccurate reporting that attracts several million people each year to a town of about twenty thousand, with inadequate hospitals, but over three hundred hotels.

The first three decades of the shrine supposedly produced countless healings, but no one kept any accurate track of how many, or to what sicknesses they were directed, or to whom they were granted. Methods of recording were hardly improved through the period preceding the First World War, yet local authorities averred that 2,500 supernatural restorations of health took place. Even the Vatican thought that this quantity suggested divine lack of discrimination, or, at least, an improbable degree of supernal intervention in the affairs of man, and so an investigation was initiated. The conclusions of the confirmation committee reduced the number to thirty-two demonstrable cases, and caused there to be established, in 1917, a permanent review board to validate all such claims. There followed three decades without one confirmed occasion of a miraculous cure.

Immediately after the Second World War, a more elaborate bureau, including two dozen medical specialists, was given the task of such verifications, and it has placed its imprimatur on approximately a single cure annually since then.

Of interest is that particular types of problems seem impervious to the holy treatment and they include almost all instances of birth defects which cannot possibly be attributed to traumata or nerve disorders, examples being mongoloids, macrocephalics, microcephalics, and teratism. Despite scores of thousands of such cases being brought to the miracle bath of Bernadette, not one has ever been made whole.

Ironically on the mundane side of the ledger quite different and surgically exciting progress has been made, and only a few hundred miles away.

Dr. Paul Tessier of Paris has devoted much of his professional life to reconstructive plastic surgery, in some instances employing power tools one might more readily think of as belonging in a hardware store than on a surgical tray. Recently he dismantled and reassembled the nose, forehead, upper jaw, eye sockets, and several other aspects of a twelve-year-old patient's head, re-creating near-normality.

A great deal of his work has been on such congenital unfortunates who have pilgrimaged to Lourdes, and other healing shrines, in endless caravans of misery—but have not benefited by the divine touch. Arriving as "monsters," so did they depart. But the incredible hands of Dr. Tessier have restored, in part, or virtually completely, more than 300 cases of pathetic deformity by the miraculously skillful "laying-on-of-hands."

Yet, from these examples, it must not be assumed that all of the official or even simply condoned healing of the Church is derived from holy shrines. In some instances it is as of the Biblical times, i.e., charismatic, laying-on-of-hands as practiced by the evangelical figures described earlier or by nonphysical contact common to the technique of such thaumaturgists as Harry Edwards. Among the most notable of these within the Roman Church recently was the late Father Pio.

This unusual cleric was born on May 25, 1887, in Pietrelcina, Italy, and baptized Francis. A sober child, he entered the Capuchin order when he was an adolescent, and subjected himself to great deprivation despite his poor health. It is said that in one instance when he was quite ill his temperature broke two thermometers by rising to 119 degrees Fahrenheit! Allegedly that continued to occur throughout his lifetime.

Ordained a priest at twenty-three, he also had to serve in the army, which, considering his uncertain physical condition, proved to be a trial. His suffering was, of course, compounded when, on September 20, 1918, he was marked by the visible "stigmata" (see Glossary) which, it is said, never stopped bleeding for the rest of his almost half-century of life. *That such wounds existed is not subject to question,* as they were examined by numerous physicians; only the explanation is moot. Despite their fame, the stigmata of Father Pio were never officially recognized by the Vatican to be of divine origin.

Examples of purported healing by Father Pio are plentiful. One, dated September 6, 1956, had as its subject a girl whose bones were atrophied. Following mass, the stigmatist paused and blessed her as he passed. Suddenly, it is reported, the girl leaped from her chair, in which she had been carried into the church, and ran to him, kneeling to kiss his hands.

On another occasion a dying child was presented for his aid.

Making the sign of the cross over the patient, the priest moved on, and the child was cured.

A curious instance is told of a woman who suffered from extreme pains in her head. She attended a mass celebrated by Father Pio, and slept with his picture beneath her pillow, anticipating that this would be sufficient therapy, considering his miraculous power. Yet the headaches persisted. In human impatience, she angrily thrust the picture into her mattress, complaining that he was not helping her.

Eighteen months later she went to the cleric to confess, only to have him open the window slightly and then slam it closed. Startled, she asked Father Pio the meaning of his behavior. The window was opened again, and the smiling face replied that just as she had been offended by having the window slammed in her face, so had he been by her shoving his photograph into her mattress.

In September 1956, a notable case of healing occurred at Father Pio's hands. Some time earlier a lady from Grenoble, France, had a dream featuring Father Pio, of whom, so the records state, she had never heard. In this dream he foretold of her giving birth to a child with malformed legs, adding that she should not be overly distressed, but to come to see him and he would tell her what to do. Subsequently such a child was born, all varieties of medical help failed to offer any hope, and—after a rather confused series of events—she went to visit the priest. At the time, about a decade and a half ago, the woman had to wait for over a month for an audience with the stigmatist, although men usually were granted a visit quite expeditiously. This being the case, a gentleman whom she had encountered in her travels to the church offered to take her child into Father Pio's presence during his own interview with him. Yet, when confronted with the child, the priest remarked that it had not been christened, therefore had no name, and so must be removed. After some effort, time, and exchange of communications with her husband in France, the woman received his consent for the baptism, which Father Pio agreed to do personally. In the words of a

European writer on the subject: "When he spoke the last words of baptism, suddenly a sound was heard as if something had broken asunder, and as the woman laid the child's legs free, they saw that the splints which it had carried on its legs were broken and that the legs were straight." [8]

Another recorded case concerns a man who had abandoned his wife and children to establish a home with another woman, only to fall ill of cancer. At the approach of death, he took the final sacraments. Here there was no intervention by Father Pio. The man died. Yet the priest was to have an opportunity to exhibit further his remarkable supernatural skills when he was visited by the man's legal wife who, despite her spouse's infidelity, showed great concern regarding the disposition of his immortal soul. She had to seek no more, for the cleric's clairvoyance was not confined to this sphere. "Your husband's soul is condemned forever. When receiving the last sacraments he concealed many sins, had neither repentance nor good resolve," he announced.[9]

Yet, should this revelation by the divine healer have an echo of gratuitous harshness, one must recall that he was most compassionate on occasions. In the words of one of his biographers: "Father Pio has not only sympathy for Italians, he prays for all." [10]

At the age of eighty-one, on September 23, 1968, the stigmatist died. Three days afterwards, according to newspaper accounts, 3,000 priests and 100,000 laymen mourned his passing as he was buried.

Two sudden cures were announced on the day of his funeral.

The United States is not wholly without its saints, even a healing one. (The miracles which must be accepted as authentic by the Church in the process of canonization are not necessarily ones of cures.) Mother Frances Xavier Cabrini, an Italian immigrant, was the first citizen of this country to be canonized. Not generally included among the factors determining this action on the part of the Vatican, in 1946, almost three decades after her

[8] Karl Wagner, *Report on Father Pio*, pp. 27-28.
[9] Ibid., p. 42.
[10] Ibid., p. 55.

death, is a report by the late Mother Delfina Graziola. According to her account, she was confronted by death following an operation on her stomach for cancer. She had been administered the last rites.

Then she had a conversation with Mother Cabrini, who was directing the hospital where she served, during which her superior instructed her to do some work. The young nun explained her physical condition, but was told that she must begin eating immediately foods which her medical condition had precluded. Despite her apprehension she was assured that she would not suffer pain as a result of resuming a normal diet. Sister Delfina obeyed and her health began to improve at once. She survived more than forty more years, dying at the age of seventy-seven of generalized cancer of the bone.

The key factor to this particular supernatural cure lies in the allegation by Mother Delfina that her encounter with the nun who became a saint was during the experiencing of a vision.

The parameters of charismatic healing relating to the Roman Catholic Church are difficult to determine, as they may be vague, variable, or both. A simple example is the contention by many Argentinians that the late Eva Duarte Perón, or "Evita" as she was affectionately known, possessed the power to cure. Masses are celebrated in her honor, and altars adorned with her pictures to commemorate her alleged ability to heal the sick.

> "I was with her when she visited a leper in a clinic," recalled an elderly man ... "The doctor said the leper was dying. But Evita kissed him, and we heard later that he was saved." Others ... affirmed the incident and recount-[ed] a few of their own.[11]

One of the most unusual centers of healing is Geel, Belgium, which has two distinguishing characteristics. First, it is for the mentally infirm; second, it is no longer actually a religious or specifically mystical shrine. Ancient tales record that an Irish

[11] Reported by Jonathan Kandell, *The New York Times*, May 9, 1973.

Christian princess, Dympna, was pursued and slain there by her mad, pagan father, whose sanity was instantly restored with her murder. Thus did the locality have bestowed upon it the reputation of being where the mentally unbalanced might come to their senses again. Dympna was made a saint over seven centuries ago, a chapel was erected in her memory, and the site became the shrine for the mad. Until 1860 the supervision of the patients was the responsibility of the Roman Church, but from that time forward the community has been operated by the government. While miracles have not been claimed for Dympna's town for a very long time, they were once, and the fact that more than three-quarters of the families of the town of over 30,000 have participated in this program throughout the years is a healing miracle—if merely of a social kind—in itself.

XVI
American Churches, Cults, and Sects

The Pentecostal movement, with its reputation for healing and glossalalia, which in the past has only been associated with fundamentalist Protestant sects, today is permeating all branches of contemporary religion. Recently more than a hundred Roman clergy met at the Catholic University in Dayton, Ohio in a symposium to weigh the implications and impact of the revival of the charismatic preoccupation. It is estimated that 250,000 Catholics are involved. Somewhat unexpected, at least at this juncture, was the seminar's serious consideration of the possibility of incorporating some of these fundamentalistic phenomena into the Roman Catholic experience.

Although, as has been clearly shown, the Church of Rome has maintained a continuity of charisma, particularly healing, via shrines, individuals, and rituals, throughout the centuries, in this country most people are much more conscious of it in the evangelical form, and, if not there, then in the simpler forms of Protestantism. In the General Assembly of the United Presbyterian Church, of 1968, both glossalalia and cures were studied, and the national organization, the Fellowship of St. Luke, devoted to the investigation and encouragement of the charismatic skills, may have 25,000 members today.

Episcopal clerics—over 300 priests—gathered at St. Matthew's Cathedral, in Dallas, during February 1973, for the initial convocation of the National Episcopal Charismatic Conference. Among the conclusions reached was that at least one-tenth of the entire clerical body was oriented to, or being affected by, the rising movement. "In the event that the Holy Spirit directs us to meet again, I am issuing an invitation to convene at the Washington Cathedral, Washington, D.C.," announced Rev. Charles Taylor, of Maryland.[1]

August saw the assembling of elements of the movement again, and in another area of the country, Minneapolis. Large portions of the Second International Lutheran Conference of the Holy Spirit were dedicated to its study and discussion of Pentecostal practices.

"The conference, which ended today, was part of the fast-growing Neo-Pentecostal movement in major Christian churches, which stress the activity of the Holy Spirit and such 'gifts' as speaking in tongues (glossalalia), healing . . ." [2]

One of the contributions to the meeting was the verification that the movement was truly becoming one with which to conjure; this evidence took the form of a warning against ominous opposition. Assemblies of God minister Rev. David Wilkerson warned that he had experienced "a vision from the Holy Spirit" which foretold of great persecution of the charismatics, plus additional worldwide catastrophes that could generally be represented by the allegorical Four Horsemen of the Apocalypse. He anticipated the Vatican's adamant opposition to the revivification of the ancient Biblical practices. On the other hand, an internationally known Pentecostal figure and visionary, Rev. David du Plessis of Oakland, California, discounted such negativism, assuring the convention that if a pope was to set himself up against the rising theological tide it would not be the one occupying the throne then, and he traced the origins of the major thrust of the movement to the reign of John XXIII and his ecumenism.

Dr. du Plessis was among the principal speakers at the February 1973 first National Episcopal Charismatic Conference,

---

1 *The New York Times*, February 18, 1973.
2 *The New York Times*, August 12, 1973.

which convened in Dallas, and at the Second International Lutheran Conference, held in Minneapolis six months later. Recently du Plessis headed a ten-member group of Pentecostal and Neo-Pentecostal leaders in a discussion with Roman Catholic scholars on the developing movement.

In addition to the religious bodies mentioned, other major spiritual groups in the United States being directly affected by the Pentecostal or charismatic renaissance are the Methodists, the various Baptist churches, and the Congregationalists.

The Theosophists, on the other hand, have *always* shown a great interest in healing. In *The Science of the Sacraments* ("The Completed Eucharistic Form") a number of pages are devoted to the Holy Spirit, as a healer, appearing in priests and other persons. It notes that certain cures require more than a single effort and makes the surprising observation that "even the Christ Himself had to apply His treatment twice in the case of the man born blind." [3]

The text observes that, because of human frailty, some attempts at cures are unsuccessful, at which time invocation of the Archangel Raphael is particularly helpful, alluding to the Book of Tobit: "God hath sent me to heal thee and thy daughter, for I am Raphael."

According to C. W. Leadbeater, a prominent Theosophist, his summoning caused this glorious heavenly figure to appear, and Leadbeater proceeds to relate an extraordinary religious experience, a portion of which is certainly pertinent to "spiritual" healing.

He was a very tall and dignified personage . . . His aura glows chiefly with green and purple . . . I noticed he took especial advantage of the singing of the *Veni Creator*, the traditional call to God the Holy Ghost . . . it is most interesting to watch the working of the consciousness of

[3] C. W. Leadbeater, *The Science of the Sacraments*. (India, The Theosophical Publishing House, 1957), pp. 428-433.

this great Healing Angel, but it is very difficult to explain
. . . the mind of an Angel works in many compartments
and he can keep them all going simultaneously . . . while
he was working in our church . . . he was also equally
present in a number of other places—at least thirty or
forty—all connected in some way with the curing of disease. All these scenes . . . [were visible like] colored moving
pictures.

One episode revealed a surgeon making an incorrect incision
which was remedied as "instantly the Angel sent him a flash of
blinding lightning . . . so that the patient's life was saved."

Another frame of this supernatural cinema revealed a mother
superior being restored as "prayers wove a lovely colored
network about" her. Another described a shipwreck.

Among the more esoteric and controversial religious bodies
prospering in the United States in the last few years are the
Assemblies of God, which, while generally autonomous, have a
broad sort of collectivity, not unlike the amorphous interrelationship between the New Thought groups, as exemplified by
The Church of the Truth, founded by the noted Dr. Ervin Seale
and now under the direction of Dr. John Lee Baughman (see
Chap. XI). Revivalist A. A. Allen was a minister of an Assembly
of God until a confluence of the bottle and the law caused him to
be dismissed from it, an incident in no way particular to the sect,
as alcoholism is quite common among a number of Catholic and
Protestant denominations.

The Rock Church may well be the best-known church of the
Assemblies of God, having an affiliation with the national body,
in the City of New York. It is administered by Rev. J. J. Vick,
with the aid of Co-pastor Sister A. A. Scirmont, and conducts
regular healing services. In an exclusive interview with the latter,
the position of the Assemblies of God groups, in general, and the
Rock Church, in particular, was explained.

Despite being sandwiched between two buildings on East Sixty-second Street, the Rock Church presents a pleasing appearance to the arriving parishioner, with its centered double doors, flanked by single entrances on either side. The greeting from Sister Scirmont, whose spacious and well-appointed office was several flights up, was warm, but businesslike. She is a very attractive woman of fewer than middle years, and was dressed in a simple, knee-length, white-collared dress as black as her skillfully coiffured hair.

"Sister, my understanding is that the church accepts the idea, and the practice, and the efficacy of individual healing through a representative of God, although it is fully understood that it is His power that heals, not the individual's."

"Yes, that is correct," she replied.

"Would you give me a general, or specific, example typifying experiences you have had, or seen, here at the church?"

"There was one case where a little boy came to service and I sensed that there was something bothering him. It proved to be that his hands were covered with warts. We prayed for him, and, overnight, God delivered [see glossary] and set him free from them. And his hands were made clear."

"Are a great many people drawn to the Rock Church because of its reputation for achieving cures?"

"Yes. Yes, many in the past have also been healed. For example, cripples. Pastor Vick, one morning, prayed for a lady who came with two crutches. She couldn't use shoes, never used shoes in all of her life. She had brought a new pair with her and placed them under the pew. After the morning worship Pastor Vick laid hands and prayed for her. She sat down in her seat and removed the shoes, which she had bought that night, from their box, put them on. She left her crutches and walked from the service."

"Are there more adults than children healed?"

"No, there isn't any pattern, although many young have come and have been healed," replied Sister Scirmont. "Many from physical sicknesses, distorted minds. We've seen lumps disappear. Hands that couldn't be used because of arthritis limbered up. One little old lady who was going blind because of sugar diabetes got her full sight restored immediately. A young woman with glaucoma got her deliverance. This glaucoma took several days, and several times of praying, but eventually her doctor said there was no longer anything wrong with her."

"Have you found that there is anything that cannot be helped?"

"No. I believe that any sickness of any form, any person with any kind of disease can be delivered. Because Jesus says, 'You can do all things in My name. If you act in My name you can receive deliverances of sicknesses, or disordered minds.' Any form of sickness or disease can be cured."

"Have you had any instances of what medical men have regarded as irreversible illnesses, or terminal conditions—tuberculosis, cancer, and such—where recovery was achieved by praying and laying-on-of-hands?" I asked.

"Yes. We had one young lady here—she's also an ordained minister—who was taken to the hospital by one of our leading physicians who had diagnosed that she had cancer and that it was malignant. He gave her five years to live. She has now lived about eight years. And after he examined her, and re-examined her, he said, 'Unbelievable!' I talked to the doctor. He told me to call the family and tell them that she had only five years. But I said that he should go and tell them. Pastor Vick and I came to her hospital room, laid hands on her, and believed that she would be delivered—and to this day she goes periodically to the doctor and he says, 'You are a dead corpse *living*.' He says that it is beyond his understanding."

"Are all of her symptoms gone?"

"Yes. There is no trace of cancer whatsoever, but she goes . . . once every two years for a checkup, and every time she comes in she's regarded as a living miracle."

"You mentioned some of the mental healings . . . this sort of cure often seems to be set aside by those who believe in the charismatic revival. Does an instance of an encounter with a seriously psychologically unbalanced person come to mind?"

"We had a young lady that came here who was under a doctor's care, and, as a matter of fact, was also a patient in

Bellevue. We visited her a number of times and, when she was finally released, she came to Rock. We prayed with her, and asked her to sit and to listen to the word of God, for we believed that the word of God would give her deliverance. She did. She came, and she sat, and listened to God's word. We laid hands on her, and prayed with her, and today she is normal."

"My impression is that you have really had a great many healings, considering the size of the church, which, I believe you said, was regularly about five hundred persons. Would that be a fair statement?"

"Yes. Yes. We have had a tremendous amount of deliverances, really. We like to call them deliverances, instead of cures."

"Meaning deliverance back to health?"

"Right. Deliverances from maladies, diseases, sicknesses, disorders, oppressions—we never keep records of them, but we've had tremendous healings. At the moment, of course, no specific case comes to my mind, but there is not a service that we conduct that someone is not healed, or delivered from some sort of a malady or sickness," Sister Scirmont emphasized.

"Would you say that one of the essential aspects of a deliverance is the complete conviction of the subject that he, or she, is going to be cured?" I suggested.

"Correct. By all means. If they have belief, invariably they will walk out whole."

"Is it possible for a skeptic to be restored to health?"

"That, of course, is quite a question. I believe that if he comes into a service, and listens to the word of God, and the Holy Spirit descends upon him, that he can receive something from God, as well as a healing."

"Could you amplify that thesis?" I asked.

"I don't want to use myself as an example, but I could give you a good aspect to the question you asked. My mother gave her heart to the Lord, and was prayed for—she had a goiter. At that time my background was Greek Orthodox, and so when she told me she had deliverance, and had accepted the Lord, I couldn't believe that—this goes many years back—but I noticed that she wasn't taking her pills anymore, she wasn't sleeping anymore on three or four pillows because she couldn't rest properly at night. After she was prayed for and had received deliverance she went to a doctor for an examination. The doctor, who happened to be Baptist, looked at her throat and remarked that she had had an operation, but said that he could find no scar. My mother told him that God healed her, and he acknowledged that the lines of an operation were barely visible, and conceded that God had done something for her.

"Of course, I couldn't see that. I was not a believer. I was not of her faith. To me it was dubious. Then came the day when I began to cherish and accepted Christ as my Saviour. My doubt turned into faith."

"Tell me, sister, although healings have gone on uninterruptedly for the past millennia, prior to a few years ago they were rarely heard about, and when one did hear about them it was usually from the Southern Midwest and from a terribly carnival-like atmosphere. Now, it seems to be sweeping the country in nearly a religious revolution. Do you have any idea why there has been such a renaissance of the charismatic gifts—healing, glossalalia, and, even, prophecy?"

"I think first that back there years ago they didn't have the news media, and religion was always sort of hidden. You'd go to church, and that was it. According to the prophecy in the Book, God said that there would be a time when the gospel would be preached and everyone shall hear it. I believe that we're coming to the end of time. I believe that more people are accepting Jesus Christ and that they are heralding the message, not only of Jesus, Saviour of the World, but also as our physician and our healer.

"It goes way back to the beginning when God revealed Himself to Israel, saying, 'I am the Lord that healeth.' People today ... [have the facilities to] broadcast—television and the radio media; they can publish a book to tell of the wonders God has done ... they are more educated along these lines ... they can commercialize what God is doing in the church today."

"Do you conclude that it is, then, merely broader awareness of the impact of charismatic gifts, or are there actually more healings occurring?" I inquired.

"I think more cures are happening today than they did in times back," she responded. "We have a greater population, therefore more ill, and more healings."

"Do you have any reservations about the exploitation and commercialization by so many of the individuals, perhaps they might be designated as the 'unaffiliated' professional healers, often self-ordained, who distribute interminable pamphlets and brochures, sell several books, merchandise often as many as a half-dozen records, and generally engage in high-powered retail product operations related to their so-called ministries?"

"Personally, I don't agree with it, because way back in the time of the disciples and Jesus Christ, when He walked on this earth, the disciples came to the Lord and they said, 'Lord, they're not one of us and yet they're casting out devils in your name.' And He said, 'Leave them alone,' which I thought was a very wise statement. Of course, I don't think it's right for some of them to capitalize on the Lord, but their day is coming, and we feel if we can do good for people, why not do good. There is so much evil and harm in the world, and our job is to bless people. And if they are blessing, and they are frauds, it will show up, eventually."

"Do you think that the country has gotten close to a Sodom-and-Gomorrah sort of state and that has catalyzed the revival of the charismatic movement, and, perhaps, a new religious epoch?"

"The Bible does say that at the end it will be like Sodom and Gomorrah, and we see a lot of that . . ."

"Do you think we are at all near to the time of Armageddon?" I asked. "Or the Second Coming?"

"I think we're very near to the Second Coming," she replied slowly and thoughtfully.

"Near in terms of years, decades, hundreds of years?"

"Oh, I wouldn't say hundreds of years. I would say just years."

"Conceivably in our lifetime?"

"Conceivably in our lifetime," she echoed.

The time allotted for the interview had expired, and Sister Scirmont had a service awaiting her in a matter of minutes.

"May we have a moment of prayer?" she asked.

"Most certainly," I replied, and she reached out her hands and grasped my forearms, and I responded in like manner as we closed our eyes and she petitioned Jesus Christ for our, and then especially my, spiritual, physical, and financial well-being, asking the Divine that the work I was doing be guided by the Holy Spirit and that such aegis would lead it to Truth and great success.

We exchanged farewells. I descended the several flights of stairs, moved through the double doors, onto the street, and out among the racing bodies, the grim faces, the automotive fumes, the architectural monstrosities, and the collective ugliness that has become the City of New York—even on the Upper East Side.

XVII
The Psychic Surgeons

If all healers do not achieve such remarkable success in their mundane careers as Oral Roberts, A. A. Allen, and Rex Humbard, a rare few do not even strive for it. Between the superstars of charismatic evangelism and those who actually claim to be the Ultimate Mentor is a wide and extremely varied assortment of thaumaturgists. One may be a pseudo-gypsy dealing greasy tarot cards in New York's Spanish Harlem and performing "miracles" by what is essentially voodoo magic; another, Reverend R. W. Schambach, for example, may conduct a revival just off the Major Deegan Expressway, in the South Bronx. A third might pose as a Greenwich Village yogi, with a Tennessee accent. But each and every one of them claims the power to restore health.

They are to be found almost anywhere heterodox healing is sought: for example, the Holloways—Dr. Gilbert and his wife June—are in New Mexico, and Rev. Bonnie Gehman resides in Orlando, Florida. And there are specialists as well. Brother Willard Fuller, for example, boasts scores of testimonies which support his contention that, with God's help, he does spiritual dentistry.

Now risen to the realm of final rewards, "the Rasputin of the Dutch court," Miss Greet Hoffmans, began her therapeutic career later than most, when, at the age of fifty-one, while working in a factory, she was given the power of healing during a face-to-face conversation with God. Although never belonging to a recognized religious organization, she soon became celebrated, and set up operations on the estate of Baron van Heeckeren van Molecaten. After a number of healings, she was brought to the attention of Prince Bernhard, consort of Queen Juliana, who gave the faith healer an audience with his royal wife. It was his hope that Miss Hoffmans might be able to do for the Princess Maria Christina, born partially blind, what the orthodox physicians had failed to accomplish.

The strange guest was invited to live at the palace, and was appointed secretary to the queen. Her influence on Juliana (who had once invited the premier flying saucer contactee, George Adamski, to come and tell her of his experiences with the extraplanetary aliens) rapidly increased, and she had soon formed her own courtly coterie. However, her failure to improve the condition of the princess, compounded by her excuses for failing to do so, finally caused a distracted Prince Bernhard to expel her from the royal home. Nonetheless Miss Hoffmans was allowed to remain on the estate of Queen Mother Wilhelmina. She continued her own practice and met with disciples who styled themselves "Peace Through Christ." There the queen continued to consult her, despite the prince's objections.

From approximately 1956 on, the faith healer's position assumed political implications. Rumors circulated that there might be an abdication in favor of the heiress-apparent Beatrix, which was quickly denied, that the prince had accepted her magical aid in selecting the winner of a race, and other such royally unsettling suggestions. Miss Hoffmans always denied she had anything to do with them. Still, by June, the reigning family had authorized a commission to investigate "the publication abroad of our private life," and before the year was out it was announced that "the queen has decided to entertain no more relations direct or indirect with Miss Hoffmans." The faith healer died in relative obscurity a dozen years later, in November 1968.

It need hardly be emphasized that mystic healing has appeared and flourished throughout all of recorded history and in nearly every culture in the world.

In the Union of Soviet Socialist Republics mystical healing appears in a wide variety of forms, from Siberian crones who claim the gift, through Colonel Alexei Krivorotov, who worked with his son, an orthodox physician, for about eight years, gaining considerable recognition and success. While not instantaneous his cures have been investigated by scientists and, at least tentatively, accepted as valid.

In the tradition of Russia's most revered mystic healer, Karl Ottovich Zeeling, murdered in a 1937 Stalinist purge, is a psychic named Rozova. He is supposed to be able to diagnose infectious microbes clairvoyantly.

In parts of Ceylon, the treatment of disorders by mystical healers is quite organized. Among the specialists in that Asian country are the *ganitaya* (astrologer), *sāstra-kariya* (soothsayer), *ānjanan-kariya* (clairvoyant), *edura* (exorcist), *bandhanaya* (devil-charmer), and *kapua* (people's priest).

"Medical science" in Ceylon is perhaps as "sophisticated" as that of the Western world. The areas of knowledge include: 1. *Saliya*, which relates to the use of surgical tools; 2. *Salakiya*, covering any injections; 3. *Kaya-jigisha*, which deals with internal ailments and problems of the nervous system; 4. *Bhūta-viya*, by which is diagnosed and treated possession by ghosts, demons, or victims of the "evil eye" or "bad mouthing" 5. *Kaumāra*, the study of the sicknesses of children and infants; 6. *Agada tantra*, which devotes itself to poisoning by plant, animal, and contaminated or spoiled food; 7. *Vadi-karana*, the resolver of sexual problems; and 8. *Rasāyana*, which dedicates itself to chronic or incurable diseases, e.g., cancer, beriberi, and leprosy.

When one falls victim to any of the foregoing, the *vedārala*, or local general practitioner, is called in to diagnose the situation, and he determines what the problem is and which "specialist" should be consulted. The patient is then subjected to the problematical surgery, or potions, little different from that to which the "civilized" world is subject to.

Twenty-five degrees east and about ten north, Eleuterio Terte of San Fabian, Pangasinan, the Philippines, has practiced "psychic surgery" for some years, during which time he submitted his "operations" to still and cinematic photography and the observations of many believers and skeptics. None of the films has clearly revealed exactly what was occurring and few of the observers have been convincing in their arguments, whether pro or con.

The legends concerning the tall, spare farmer are many and complex, and his converts or ex-patients include physicians, attorneys, professors, or members of their families, as well as countless less-educated persons. Among the various operations accredited to Terte are the removal of appendixes, kidney stones, fatty tissue lodged near the heart, stomach tumors, and cataracts. He also plucks infected teeth from their sockets, leaving an almost instantly healed gum. The diseased elements, which he apparently severs from the interior of his patients' bodies by thrusting his fingers directly into their flesh without opening it, are swiftly dropped into a jar and whisked away from any subsequent observations. Terte also usually performs his mystical procedures in shadow or limited light. His advocates acclaim the efficacy of his ministrations, and those who should be more demanding in their control conditions, such as newsmen, magicians, photographers, seem bewildered, if not convinced.

At the height of his career the San Fabian psychic surgeon was said to be the local leader of the island's congregation of Union Espiritista Cristiana de Filipinas, a spiritualistic group of an alleged 3,000,000 membership, with nearly 150 parishes, which follows the teachings of French mystic Allan Kardec. Having discovered his power in a vision received in 1950, within less than a decade Terte was attracting several hundred persons to his services, most of whom had come for a cure from one affliction or another. Not unexpectedly, when he attempted to extend his practice to Quezon, capital of the Philippines, on the island of Luzon, the health officer of the period, Dr. Petronio Monsod, dismissed the healing farmer's claims, convincing most people the healer was in fact a hoax and charlatan.

More famous among the growing promotion-minded Philippine *Espiritista* cult of about three dozen healers is Anthony

Agpaoa. While some versions of his career describe him as a former protégé of Terte, most do not, preferring the recollections of his childhood wherein his "Protector" came to him like the traditional sandman, lulled him to sleep, leaving him to awaken at the top of a tree with a glass of water in each hand. Even "Dr. Tony" makes no attempt to interpret the symbolism, if any, of the tale.

One report on his career relates that his healing gifts were considerably greater at an earlier period—he cured simply by looking hard at the patient. Unfortunately, he was taken with a touch of a common human disease himself, greed, and attempted to employ his gift to dowse some buried treasure, causing his Protector to suspend this aspect of his gift, although the promise was made that it would be reinstated in 1973. On the other hand, one report recounting the foregoing explains that the regrettable episode occurred in 1950, and very shortly afterwards remarks that Agpaoa's power will peak in 1978 when the psychic surgeon will be thirty-nine years old. If this is true, the account is all the more astonishing because the subject of it would have been but eleven years old when he found his charismatic talent tempted by avarice, and perhaps even younger when it became functional. In any event, since then he has been reduced to manual medical labor.

The general contention of believers—whether from what they have supposedly seen personally or on cinematic film—is that Agpaoa cleaves the flesh apart, his hand enters through the incision, he executes the virtually bloodless operative procedure (although occasionally the wound is said to erupt in a crimson and unnerving geyser of gore), withdraws from the cavity, and the tissue springs together again, leaving little or no scar. These exercises are preceded by no antiseptic or anesthetic, nor followed by any infection or pain, although, from time to time, a splash of alcohol is poured into the wound, presumably during the surgical activity.

The impression left by this account is that the healing is so rapid as to allow the mystic doctor only a few seconds to remove his hand or be faced with the problem of having to open the patient again to extract it! Of course, there has been a precedent. Consider the number of sponges, sutural scraps, and even occasional instruments left inside patients under orthodox care in some of the foremost hospitals in the Western world!

Agpaoa has been investigated by William Henry Belk, a long-time sympathetic inquirer into things psychic, with conflicting conclusions. Professional ESP proponent Harold Sherman has mostly defended the claims made for the Filipino, while New York surgeon Dr. Seymour Wanderman is reported to reject him entirely, as do several magicians who have observed him on motion pictures taken of his alleged operations. In addition, George Bishop notes in his book that Carl George, American Broadcasting Company newscaster responsible for editing hundreds of feet daily for the network's Los Angeles outlet, has said, with respect to the cinematic evidence offered by Mr. Sherman: "Six or seven cuts [i.e., editing], at least. The film simply did not show what it purported to show." [1]

In October 1967, a tour-pilgrimage was assembled by a Wyandotte, Michigan, steelworker who thought that a previous visit to the healer had benefited a back problem from which he suffered. More than a hundred physically afflicted people residing in the Detroit area were transported to the islands to be treated by Anthony Agpaoa. Shortly after their return it was revealed that the spiritual doctor had collected around $72,000 from the supplicants. As the program had been initiated in his jurisdiction, United States Attorney Robert Grace of Detroit issued a complaint—reflecting the reactions of the vast majority of persons who had taken the trip—charging fraud and obtaining money thereby. Still, as long as the slight, offhand surgeon remained at home he was safe from prosecution, as no extradition treaty existed between this country and the Philippines.

But for some reason, never quite made clear, Agpaoa traveled to San Francisco on November 9, was arrested, charged before a United States commissioner, and, after posting $25,000 bail and promising to appear in federal court in Detroit, was released. If

[1] George Bishop, *Faith Healing: God or Fraud?* p. 190.

convicted, the charges against him would have called for a $10,000 fine and up to ten years' imprisonment. He lost little time in boarding a Manila-bound jet plane and forfeiting the bond.

In addition to the original charges, a fugitive warrant has been issued for Agpaoa, but there seems little chance he will ever return to this country to "prove" the validity of his medical technique, as he once asserted he wished to do. It seems likely that he has satisfied himself with a smaller, more parochial clientele, with an occasional patient from the Western world or Far East dropping by.

As far as North American researchers are concerned, in Brazil lives psychic healing's José Arigo, of Congonhas de Campo, Minas Gerais. Since beginning his practice about twenty years ago the unsophisticated Roman Catholic healer is reputed to have attended more than 2,000,000 patients, which is made possible by his contention that he sees about a patient a minute when he is working—or about 275 every day of the year since 1953.

According to one of the more popular accounts, Arigo was born exactly one year after the death of a "Dr. Fritz," who, through the agency of Arigo and with occasional consultations with mystical medicos Dr. Gilbert, a French ophthalmologist, and a Japanese, Dr. Takahashi, who specializes in tumors, actually directs most of the psychic's medical practice. The matter is made even more complicated because José—in the great tradition of mystic therapists throughout the world—eschews all credit for the results of his activities, describing himself as a mere channel for the healing powers of Christ and his etheric assistants, some dozen entities banded together in the beyond to aid the infirm on earth.

Historically speaking, he first recognized his miraculous gift upon becoming aware that he was a telekinetic, i.e., he could move objects without touching them. His initiation in medicine occurred when he cured a senator of cancer on the night preceding the politician's flight to the United States for an operation to eliminate the affliction.

The father of five children, Arigo works in the civil service during the afternoon and at a spiritual clinic during the evening. He abstains from drink and tobacco, works in a light trance state, and issues his diagnoses and comments during surgery in German, which, naturally, he does not know in his waking state.

Whereas most "psychic" surgeons concentrate on "operations," Arigo treats the great majority of his patients with prescriptions, many of which—in a style very reminiscent of Edgar Cayce—are old remedies which have long since been abandoned or products so new as not to have reached the local pharmacy. In addition, when he does "operate," his fingers do not serve as scalpels; instead he uses any blade at hand, frequently a penknife borrowed from a member of his audience. Yet he does follow the Filipino tradition of renouncing anesthesia and the need for aseptic conditions or instruments. Dr. Ary Lex, former president of the Academy of Medicine, in São Paulo, Dr. José Hortencio de Mediros Sobrinho, of the State Institute of Cardiology, William Henry Belk, sometime apologist for psychic practitioners, and the noted parapsychologist Dr. Andrija Puharich endorse many of the claims made for and by the Brazilian.

Unlike most investigators, Dr. Puharich has two qualifications to recommend him as an "expert" witness: first, he is an internationally known researcher in the fields of the outré; second, he underwent the "surgery" of the healer in question personally. Arriving in Arigo's quarters, with a small growth on his arm, diagnosed by his own American specialists as being benign, he submitted himself to the Brazilian's knife, because he feared the corruption might impair the movement of his fingers. According to reports, the psychic made a tiny incision, no more than a centimeter long, without actually touching the tumor, pressed his thumb and forefinger on either side of the growth and expelled it from the arm, causing it to drop to the floor. The account specifies the length of the entire procedure as approximately fifteen seconds and the almost total disappearance of the scar in two days.

The number of diseases susceptible to the wizardry of the primative curers are usually unlimited, and Arigo lists among them assisting the recovery from a colostomy operation which appeared to have failed as the patient had lost one-half of her weight; blindness, cysts, and lipoma of the arm. His "operations" have been filmed several times, but since such cinematography is very easily edited the results have convinced few spectators many thousands of miles removed from the actual happenings. Certainly, there is nothing the psychic operators do, whether their incisions are digital or effected by cold steel, that cannot be reproduced by any run-of-the-mill illusionist. Yet, that realization proves nothing. The artificiality of all of the science-fiction motion pictures of the 1920s, 1930s, 1940s, and 1950s can in no way prove that men have not walked upon the moon. On the other hand—viewed from an absolutely objective position—nothing the public has read in the newspapers and magazines, heard on the radio, or seen on the television really proves that they have!

In studying the reports of establishment or psychic science, there is little opportunity to draw empirical conclusions. Very frequently even that which we think we perceive is illusion. By their nature, such phenomena occur more readily within a group framework, for among their most fundamental characteristics is contagion. Many examples can be found of what amounts to the programing of the audience attending the healing service as, for example, in the case of the Union Espiritista Cristiana de Filipinas.

XVIII
The Mind Sciences and
L. Ron Hubbard

Leaders of what can be roughly described as "mind science" groups disdain the use of any instrument or medication to effect healing changes in their patients in favor of mental programming. Most of these groups, whose theories are usually derived from theses of suggestion psychological theories, such as psychoanalysis and Couéism, (see Glossary), claim to achieve both prevention and cure of various psychological, emotional, or spiritual problems. Many bodies preach rather simplistic tenets; these offer prophylactic programs consisting of avoiding outright self-destructiveness and being optimistic, and recovery schedules chiefly devoted to encouraging the subject to be optimistic and to avoid outright self-destructiveness.

An early example, around 1950, of a "mind science" was created by Thurman Fleet and called "Concept Therapy." Originally this school of health concentrated on the retention or re-establishment of "philosophic" well-being, but soon it began to include nutrition, social behavior, and almost any other aspect of daily existence which readily comes to mind. It developed a definite chiropractic cast. Fleet issued slender books of the "laws" of Concept Therapy, which covered diet, movement, restoration of health, and hygienic maxims. Essentially, all of his "laws" merely directed one to discover the cause of one's disturbance, accept it, dissipate it, and get well.

Fleet was very successful for some time. He established a school at his $500,000 headquarters near San Antonio, Texas, where he turned out "doctors." (If the trip was impractical for one who could pay the required tuition, the course could easily be arranged by mail.)

Eventually the founder decided that the vastness of his beneficence could no longer be encompassed by the foundations laid for mere Concept Therapy, and that "philosophy" evolved into Conceptology. This entire program was soon to find the ultimate admirer, imitator, and elaborator, Lafayette Ronald Hubbard.

The sciences of "elevated thought" intended for the acquisition and maintenance of "total" health were numerous, although very similar in most respects. "Humanetics," the "philosophy" of Richard W. Wetherill, also released unknown abilities and expanded the range of the normal brain, which, naturally, cured a variety of illnesses. The prophet explains that the overwhelming majority of mental and physical problems are the result of "wrong thinking." This condition permits the mind to be subjected to "illogical commands," the unrelieved repetition of which causes them to become fixed. Obviously, "negative" mental processes ensue and the patient is in serious difficulty. "Humanetics" channels one into an awareness of these "illogical commands" and swiftly aids in their dispersal.

It is apparent that the mainstream of "mind science" flows from the "scientification" of mysticism by Paracelsus, Mesmer, Puységur, Braid, Charcot, Ellis, Freud, Jung, et al.; nonetheless, a few splintered off in an attempt to reclaim some of the more charismatic aspects of heterodox healing. "Nexology," conceived by a Reverend James W. Welgos of Alabama, is an example. He claimed that his discipline was the gateway to countless psychic powers, e.g., clairvoyance, psychokinesis, astral projection, and weather control. By combining it with more directly religious promises, Welgos created "Human Engineering." He also employed the theory of "command" phrases, projected in terms of implanted affirmations—his own style of positive thinking.

The pharmacist Eli Greifer invented "fried-potato-therapy,"

"ego-magnification-therapy," and an anthology of poem-specifics for particular ailments.[1]

One of the most successful and dangerous of all the examples of the "mind sciences" began as "Dianetics," the product of the fertile memory, collation, and imagination of pulp-magazine writer L. Ron Hubbard. The alleged origins of both the find and the founder have become increasingly more extravagant in the biographies by his disciples. Within a decade of his messianic emergence, one of his representatives spoke glowingly of his early interest in people, "from the time he was first able to walk." As an adolescent he is reported treking across the Gobi Desert with a military officer, who had trained under Freud, from whom he learned a "tremendous" amount about the human mind. At the same time as this pilgrimage, he allegedly became quite proficient in "some of the Oriental languages, studied their philosophies, and found the basic truth that truth is truth . . ." [2]

According to spokesmen for the new "guru," he then returned to the United States where he finished his formal education. He studied engineering, and dabbled with thoughts parallel to Einstein's theory of relativity (whether the general or the special is never clarified). From this study he deduced that since the brain was an organism encompassing both energy and mass, there must be an applicable thesis concerning their relation in terms of human behavior.

During the Second World War Hubbard is described as having been an American naval officer.[3] He is reported to have been blinded by an explosion and discharged "totally disabled." Subsequent medical examinations revealed no physical cause for

[1] While referring to several sources for information on the preceding "psychic science" cults, including personal interviews, I wish to accord special credit for refreshing my mind on several points to The Way-Out World by Long John Nebel. (Englewood Cliffs, New Jersey: Prentice-Hall, 1961).

[2] A quote from John MacMasters, Director of the Scientology Foundation of New York. c. 1967. Also see "All About Scientology," a pamphlet by and about L. Ron Hubbard, printed by the Scientology Foundation, New York, 1966, which features a brief biographical sketch of him. It credits Hubbard with no academic degrees, merely noting that he attended one or more classes in various subjects at two colleges. "Scientology Revisited," an article by William S. Burroughs, dismisses Hubbard's education, "degrees and credentials [as] hardly relevant."

[3] Hubbard, "All About Scientology", p. 8.

the loss of his sight and it was diagnosed as psychogenic. While in this state he began to devise the thesis upon which his initial project, "Dianetics," was based. In the words of John MacMasters, director of the Scientology Foundation in New York, Hubbard began to ask, "When a man thinks, what happens? Thinking generates energy, energy has something to do with mass, therefore there must be some sort of mental mass that has never been taken into account . . ." which led him to re-examine what the conditions had been of his accident and what attitudes he had derived from the experience. By means of this examination he regained his sight, and wrote a good deal for pulp magazines.

Dianetics was unveiled in the early 1950s, a pseudopsychological discipline drawing, in various measures, from psychoanalytic schools and several aspects of mysticism, with particular emphasis on "clearing" the mind of "engrams," which were experiences "containing pain, real or fancied." They are supposedly not really available to the possessor's awareness and their content has "command value at the reactive level." Dianetics was dismissed by orthodox medicine as simplistic—in concept, if not explanation—and quite possibly hazardous, especially to those who were not entirely stable.

Hubbard overcame the looming tax, medical, and legal difficulties by reclassifying it into an "applied religion" and renaming it "Scientology." According to *Time* magazine, what was being taught was a "sort of religion of religions" consisting of fragments of Hinduism, the Bible, Taoism, Buddhism, and a miscellany of bits from the philosophies of a few Greeks, a couple of Germans, an Englishman, a Dutchman, a Roman, and Sigmund Freud. Yet serious philosophy or theology are not important ingredients of the cult's catechism.

Material from the master of the movement, circa August 1960, contained some notable observations. For example, a new definition of psychosis:

> The person who raves and screams at the very thought
> of receiving an order is, of course, completely insane. The
> person who fights an organization that gives him clean

instructions to help him is, of course, insane. A psychotic is that person who cannot receive orders of any kind, who sits unmoving and goes berserk at the thought of doing anything told him by another determination. Want to know if they are crazy? Give them a simple order.[4]

Confronted with this excerpt from the revised medical dictionary of Scientology, by interviewer John Nebel a half-dozen years after its publication, Mr. MacMasters, defending the cult, responded, "Well, don't you think he [Hubbard] might have changed his considerations too?" After equivocating as deftly as he could manage in defense of his mentor, the scientologist changed the subject. Nonetheless, there is a danger in an organization which insists that mental health—"being a clear"—derives from slavish obedience, and any deviation indicates insanity. According to such standards a refusal to stand up or weep, laugh or lie, rape or kill on command would make one certifiable.

Mr. MacMasters then explained that "anybody that doesn't reject that sort of order, to guard and slaughter a lot of people, like Hitler treated the Jews—this is, carrying out an insane order is the reverse—"

"They [the Nazis] did not regard such orders as insane," I pointed out. A physician present at the interview pertinently noted: "Now, you are saying the organization might give an insane order."

"If you carry out an insane order you are also insane, because you have become part of insanity," conceded the Scientologist.

The discussion had reached a point where the subject might be regarded as insane for not following an order, whether innocuous or lethal, or might be judged insane for carrying out an insane order, i.e., insane for not behaving insanely within the framework of the first definition. Furthermore, the organization might be giving insane orders and, therefore, be collectively insane, only its leaders would insist that it was not, that only

4 This passage, as well as several other quotes found in this chapter on Scientology is drawn from *The Long John Nebel Show*, repeated August 11, 1968, on WNBC, New York, through the courtesy of *The Long John Nebel-Candy Jones Show*, WMCA, New York.

those people who refused to follow its instructions were demented.

The defenders of the faith had in fact fallen back on the position that insane movements issue insane directions and holy ones issue holy laws. Their movement included the superior percentage of the world's population—since they were the teachers, the possessors of the special earth-saving knowledge and program—therefore what they demanded was good, that is, sane. Again it should be noted, that suggests that anyone who fails to follow the cult's orders is insane.

Although there have been some modifications in technique, from time to time, the basic contention of Scientology's purported therapists, or "auditors," is that the scientifically un-iso-latable "engram," which is permeated by the pain or problem-making factor of some incident, can be deactivated by a mental and verbal repetition of the experience. Analyzed a sufficient number of times, the "auditor" assists the "pre-clear," i.e., the subject submitting to the treatment, until memory is "flat," i.e., the "engram" is neutralized.

To aid in this process, Hubbard at one point introduced the "E-meter" (the Hubbard Electrometer), an electrical device consisting of two simple cans, held by the patient, which are wired to a gauge, the reaction of which to given responses from the subject, indicate the progress being made in the "clearing" process.

Yet the recollections of Scientology itself is not without "engrams." In 1963, the United States Food and Drug Administration descended upon the Washington church and seized its stock of E-meters, claiming that the sect untruthfully assured its members and potential acolytes cures of neurotic, psychotic, and, broadly speaking, almost all psychosomatic disorders. Two years later, a governmental committee in Australia described the body's precepts and promises as "evil, fantastic and impossible," and its principles "perverted and ill-founded." [5]

[5] *Time,* August 23, 1968.

Along with other trials, these rejections were followed, in 1968, by the British Home Office's denying entry to almost 1,000 Scientologists who had intended to hold an international meeting in England. The exclusion was not a personal or capricious decision by one anonymous staff member; the move represented the general position of the government. The House of Commons was informed by the Hon. Kenneth Robinson, Health Minister, that the pseudoreligion was "a potential menace to the personality" and "a serious danger to health." [6]

Basically, the Scientologists argue that "life," the subject matter of the entire thesis, is a channel, vessel, or catalyst by which various activities of energy and mass manifest themselves, but is not *of* the physical universe itself. It directs energy and wave-lengths, mass and matter, but is, in itself, none of these. It functions in the cosmos and records the persistence of awareness, while not being *in* space or subject to time. To designate this condition, life, they have instituted the use of the word "theta," the eighth letter of the Greek alphabet, akin to the Hebrew "teth," for whatever symbolic or arbitrary reasons, and pronounced that all is physical except Theta, i.e., life. As with many, and more lavishly than most, Scientology has developed its own special jargon: "organism"—a physical aspect of the universe subject to the influence of Theta; "brain"—an organic entity through which "Mind" works, but not to be confused with "mind"; "mind"—the channel or device via which Theta exercises its power; "facsimile"—retained experiences; "self-determination"—freedom of choice and from control; "sanity"—free will as graphed from nil, or death, to "levels of causation higher than man has ever reached"; [7] "aberration"—deviations from "self-determination"; and "release"—an adept whose progress toward Scientological goals is measurable. There are many more terms employed by the cult: all groups that promise ultimate truths and revelations require a private code. The public cannot tolerate religions, philosophies, and the like, which speak in

6 Ibid.
7 Hubbard, ibid p. 3.

languages readily understood. That is why the abandonment of Latin in favor of the vernacular mass was one of the Roman Catholic Church's most self-destructive moves in the past hundred years.

During a conversation some years ago with John MacMasters and Robert Thomas, the Director of Scientology in New York and the Executive Secretary of the Scientology church respectively, I posited that Scientology was intended to improve people's spiritual, mental, and emotional existence, and they agreed with the premise. They added that the organization tended to feel the responsibility, of "possession," with respect to the earth, reminiscent of Ayn Rand. I asked what supported the sect's thesis that it could do what no other philosophy, religion, ethic, or what-have-you could accomplish; what distinguished it from other life- and mind-saving disciplines. They replied that the human race was in such a rapidly deteriorating state it was necessary to employ their more advanced and effective techniques to save as many worthwhile individuals as possible, particularly as it was capable of achieving the desired ends with greater speed than other methods such as assorted religions or psychotherapies. Furthermore, as time was ever more a fundamental consideration, it was the pragmatic approach of Scientologists to proselytize among the most receptive prospects available, as they would "respond" swiftly and achieve the movement's alleged ends of saving mankind, rather than deal with persons whose problems were deep enough to require much more attention.

"Its entire purpose is to help mankind to know mankind," summarized MacMasters.

"Or we might even say Mr. Hubbard's purpose is to save the world," I continued.

"Yes, call it that, if you will," he granted.

"Does he have a white horse?" I inquired.

"No. You see, I thought you were working up to something just like that, but I don't think—"

"Well," I immediately countered, "it is hardly unfair. When a man comes out and tells me that he is going to save the world, I would like to know whom he is going to save it for—me or himself."

"For everyone," assured the Scientologist.

Accepting this as being an accurate reflection of Hubbard's goal, I inquired: "What makes you think that the world that Mr. Hubbard would save would be one that I would accept as the *true* world [which is postulated as the universal human condition once the cult has cured mankind's difficulties], and, secondly, why he would be able to preserve a race that, perhaps, a great many people don't want saved at all?"

"Do you think that any sane person really wants to see this planet blown up?" asked Mr. MacMasters incredulously.

"I think the totally sane person realizes that it doesn't matter. If we are immortal, certainly the Grand Preserver is going to insure our salvation from whatever annihilation occurs to this mere matter upon which we exist, and if we are not immortal, then we matter no more than the matter."

"I don't think that any Great Preserver is going to reach out and help anybody who's that irresponsible as to be constantly destroying what has been created," replied MacMasters, in a typical Scientological retort, namely, attempting to dramatically emphasize a rebuttal to a point wholly unrelated and irrelevant to the one made by his interviewer.

Upon being asked whether he, and his faith, believed in free will, he asked, "What is freedom?"

I noted I had not inquired about freedom, and he then pursued his fresh tangent by demanding to know what I meant by "free."

"I am certain that you know perfectly well the psychological, theological, or philosophical meaning of the phrase 'free will' in a discussion of this order," I countered in all sincerity, but he merely reiterated, "What is 'free will'?"

Regrettably, after several minutes I became convinced that he was quite unfamiliar with the term or even its superficial implications and offered him an explanation. Mr. MacMasters finally acknowledged that they accepted the thesis of what I had described as "free will," but added, "We accept it with this proviso, and that is that there is no such thing as *freedom* [in one sentence 'free will' had slipped away from us again] until one knows truth." It was very clear the group's proponents wanted no part of "free will."

In all expositions of Scientology, independence of the individual is never mentioned, despite the attempt to make its programs appear as if they encouraged personal initiative. As with all "priesthoods," the maxim, before all others, is: *Give me them while they are weak in body and spirit and I will have them for the rest of their lives.*

Less than a decade and a half following the formulation of the sect of Scientology it had established its headquarters in England, and claimed offices in more than a score of countries, with about a dozen "churches" in the United States. Yet, as Scientology grew, L. Ron Hubbard retreated further and further from the fray, and in 1966 retired from active service, contributing the use and good will of his name to the organization for approximately $250,000. He had never been easy to contact personally as he reigned in Great Britain, but after becoming a sort of naval Buddha, sailing about the Mediterranean on a 3,000-ton yacht, with an entourage of several hundred persons, he achieved almost complete inaccessibility.

In 1969, Scientology "cleared" one of its legal "engrams" when the United States Court of Appeals, in Washington, D.C., reversed the six-year-old decision regarding E-meters and written material relating to the cult's practices. The decision was handed down by Judge J. Skelly Wright. He compared the "auditing process," for which the group claimed the instruments were essential, to the confession of the Catholic Church, since the process was asserted to be intended for the restoration of spiritual, not physical, health. The ruling reflected an unfortunate lack of understanding of the Scientologists, and their contention that certain severe physical disorders are "psychogenic" and, therefore, curable through the therapy of Scientology. After the fashion of the early years of Christian Science, Scientology uses the aura of religion to practice medicine without being required to have a medical training or license.

Two years later two more tons of similar material were ordered returned by a United States District Court, but with the stipulation that the E-meter must carry the specific warning that it "has no proven usefulness in the diagnosis, treatment, or prevention of any disease, nor is it medically or scientifically capable of improving any bodily function."

XIX
Communal Camps and Concentration Cures

Today Scientology continues to grow, although at a slower pace, and its influence on other movements, particularly those which may be catalogued as "collective therapies," has been considerable. In recent years, the "tribal dance" has assumed several generic names, but the phrase "group therapy" has come to represent the genre. Vulgarizing it emotionally, it becomes "encounter groups."

In virtually every case, from the investigative speculation of the nineteenth century through Reichian or transactional psychology, ritual and sex are critical elements in group therapy. Many encounter groups are composed of strangers. Thrust together for hours or days, the participants undergo a trial by any standard, especially combat, which differs little in basic concept and intent from the mystical initiation of a voodoo cult, despite the contention that the experience improves emotional health and opens the mind to new enlightenment.

The Esalen Institute has become notorious as the center for many varieties of group therapy. While on the whole employing reputable practitioners, the Institute has had many less professional imitators, who have wreaked much psychic damage. One study [1] of the phenomena of encounter groups describes the deterioration of a once successful young man who joined a California organization modeled after Esalen, was quickly engulfed by it, becoming a section leader. He also began taking acid, and

[1] Bruce Maliver, *The Encounter Game*

shortly thereafter blew out his brains with a .357 Magnum pistol on the grounds of the Esalen Institute. The same researcher remarks on a half-dozen other suicides encountered in his investigations relating to groups asserting similar claims of psychic healing. There is little doubt that even an apparently healthy personality may find his character deteriorating when faced with the effects of such Esalen-type "therapy." The neurotic individual—let alone those suffering more serious psychic debilitation—puts his sanity and, perhaps, his life on the line. These "covens" of our day are as blasphemous with illogicality and degenerated sexuality as any bizarre cult of the past.

Obviously such enterprises are intended to help mental and emotional problems, despite the fact that most of these groups are directed by persons who lack any psychiatric credentials, or therapy training. Still, if they have "presence" or a Machiavellian mind, they may "succeed" more frequently than many of the more schooled therapists who do not possess these characteristics to the same degree.

Participants are urged to scream themselves into hysteria, then to touch, grope, or grab the individual next to him or everyone in sight. Anybody unstable enough to indulge in this rite is engaged in what one investigator called "psychological karate." The American Group Psychotherapy Association observed that "a much lower incidence of adverse side effects produced by a drug would cause its immediate withdrawal from the marketplace by federal authorities." [2]

Emerging from the "mind sciences," developed through the fifteen years following the Second World War, Esalen was founded in the late 1950s by Michael Murphy, a student of psychology and philosophy, in the Big Sur on the Pacific coast. Within a decade it claimed at least 25,000 adherents. Soon the physical techniques were assuming an increasingly greater emphasis, led by Dr. William Schutz, who had borrowed ideas from

[2] Reprinted in *Time*, April 30, 1973. "Mental health" has been sold "over the counter" for years. A recent example is William Penn Patrick's *Holiday Magic, Inc.*, whose victims are reduced to scatological and quasi-necrophilic behavior, akin to madness, which is often the only permanent result. (See Gene Church and Conrad D. Carnes, *The Pit: A Group Encounter Defiled.*)

Wilhelm Reich, Moreno's psychodrama, Fritz Perls' ("Lose your mind and come to your senses") Gestalt therapy, and the "somatopsychic" thesis of Alexander Lowen.

While nudism had already been introduced to the more "advanced" cells of the movement, it was structured into the "ritual" of encounter groups by psychologist Paul Brindrin in 1967; he eased his subjects out of their clothes and inhibitions by immersing them in water of body temperature where "you don't know where the water really ends and the body begins." He also concentrated on marathon sessions which tended to erase the psychological line between fancy and reality, exhaustion and abandon, enervation and acceptance.

In other instances, the group technique is used to effect specific results which they regarded as essential to their parochial concept of mental health, e.g., the black-white "hate" sessions conducted by Dr. Price M. Cobbs, where the participants try to use race differences and hostilities (rather than nudity) to catalyze a less-corrupted line of communication between individuals.[3]

Other examples of group therapies include the late Fritz Perls' Gestalt therapy, Transactional Analysis, and numerous descendants of Britain's post-World War Two "milieu therapy," e.g., Dr. Thomas Detre's "Tompkins 1" program, inaugurated at the Yale-New Haven Hospital in 1963, "sensitivity training," the "Chicago oasis" experiment, the Orizon Institute of Washington.

It should be clearly understood that many of these last mentioned are operated by members of the medical or sociomedical establishment, psychiatrists, psychologists, and sociologists, and, while not happily embraced by the traditionalists, are recognized elements of semistandard medicine. Still, their origins, programs, and techniques place them in the category of charismatic healing.

This kind of cultism has thoroughly permeated the upper tiers of industry, and company officers are ever more frequently

[3] William H. Grier and Price M. Cobbs, *Black Rage.*

found in "encounter" centers, exemplified by the Executive De-velopment Laboratory, one of several such groups directed by National Training Laboratories, and the American Behavioral Science Training Laboratories based in Detroit, where Warren Avis is still trying to motivate people to try harder if they want to get ahead. Another example is the Human Development Insti-tute in Atlanta, a Bell & Howell subsidary, which teaches the ambitious junior executive how to get moving into the big-busi-ness picture, using the experience gained from encounter groups.

The spectrum of mystical healing has become progressively sophisticated, although no subtler, over the years. Throughout most of its history it was founded on the most appealing of all propositions, i.e. that the patient was going to get some-thing—the maintenance, restoration, or creation of physical, mental, or spiritual well-being—for nothing, except the cheapest of all commodities, faith. Today we have "progressed" to a stage of cultural neurosis and social cynicism where we reject hetero-dox healing unless it causes us pain, and, generally speaking, a good deal of money. The medicine will not help unless it tastes revolting; if most doctors were not anxious to perform unneces-sary operations the matrons of America would have to invent surgical mechanics to do them; without subconscious sadomaso-chism half of the parasitic industries of the nation—most special-izations of medicine, almost all pharmaceutical manufacturers, terminal charities, and the like—would be reduced to doing something beneficial for the population. Altruism (except in the hands of the most skilled) rarely yields a profit.

Practically all of the "mental health" enterprises mentioned can guarantee you both pain and expense, even if they produce no therapeutic results.

Group Therapy or "coven-curing" has descended to alleged entertainment. Games, e.g., "Group Therapy," "Sensitivity," and "Insight," have been devised and marketed which constitute mini-encounter sessions and bear to their source the relationship the ouija board does to spiritualism, despite the obvious risk to insecure or disturbed players. They are reminiscent of that venomous old parlor pastime "Truth," which was no more than an inquisitional or tribal ritual demonstrably dangerous to fragile egos and quite capable of destroying friendships and dissolving marriages.

In the spring of 1973, a new vernal vitalism appeared with the opening of the Esalen Sports Center, in San Francisco. Several hundred persons—physical education instructors, coaches, athletes, and the curious—arrived for the occasion. It featured a well-known quarterback and a linebacker, a yoga tennis clinic, and the notion that sports "can even serve as a powerful metaphor for man's spiritual quest."

Despite many thousands of years of mystical medicine's manipulation of the mental processes, it was not until the late nineteenth century that the "scientification" of "mind techniques" began to be systematized. Mesmer, Braid, Charcot, et al., and the later, but hardly less heterodox, speculations of Ellis, Freud, and the various schools of psychology, psychoanalysis, and psychiatry evolving from their efforts, were part of this new "scientific" exploration.

In the twenties, Coué and other "superficialists" proposed autosuggestive devices via one obvious cliché after another, with or without religious embroidery, e.g., Norman Vincent Peale's "power of positive thinking" or Maltz's "psycho-cybernetics."

For the most part, the health cults which prospered up until a few years after the Second World War were relatively harmless in their vacuity. A few may even have effected some occasional, minor psychological improvement, especially in the socially insecure. But then came the torrent of authoritarian and hysteria-inducing "mind sciences" which peaked in power in the fundamentally one-to-one approach of Scientology and like sects and in the psychic orgy techniques of the encounter movement. The impact of the former increased steadily until about 1960 and has fluctuated in force since then; the latter flourished uncontrollably from early in the following decade, but began to level off, and even decline, during the last couple of years. Still, it is possible that, while the two coasts and a handful of major cities have noticeably exhausted their enthusiasm for the socio-psy-cho-sexual possibilities of "group therapy," the less urban areas of the rest of the country have yet to revel in this newest commu-nity-participation sport.

There is little doubt that millions of people in this country have been involved in one or another kind of encounter exercise. It is very likely that—given enough "faith" in this latest "human potential" mysticism—some persons have been benefited, but it is even more certain that inexperienced, unstable, avaricious, or sadomasochistic individuals have appointed themselves "leaders" and done incalculable and irreversible psychic and physical damage to many "patients," unto insanity and death.

The psychologist Carl Rogers, an early exponent of en-counter approaches to mental health and disorders, has been quoted as defining the movement as "the most rapidly spreading social invention of the century and probably the most potent" (which doubtlessly could have been said of witchcraft during several centuries). Professor Sigmund Koch of Boston views the activity more as "a convenient psychic whorehouse for the pur-chase of a gamut of well-advertised existential 'goodies' . . . one enters for . . . liberating consummation but settles for [a] psychic striptease."

By the first months of 1974 statistical data were emerging from a $1,250,000-dollar inquiry conducted by the liberal-dominated National Institute of Mental Health. It drew on a sampling of 1,500 subjects who participated in about 150 groups at the Berke-ley, California, campus YMCA. It contended that "encounter" can work because it frequently improves self-image and self-confidence, relaxes one sexually, and decreases loneliness, but conceded that groups have no statistically relevant effect on attitude, ability, or results with respect to personal, educational, or professional endeavor.[4]

Stanford University, in another study,[5] concentrated not on random participants but on the leaders who had directed sessions

[4] Study by National Institute of Mental Health, under the direction of Dr. James Bebout of the Wright Institute, Berkeley, California, 1973.

[5] Morton A. Lieberman, Irvin D. Yalom, and Matthew B. Miles, *Encounter Groups: First Facts.*

of over 200 students in almost a score of different expressions of the movement, including basic encounter, Gestalt and transactional analysis, and marathon. It was even less enthusiastic in its conclusions. It indicated that one-third of the subjects received some benefit and two-thirds abandoned the project or had been the victims of negative results—a ratio that suffers severely by comparison with most "orthodox" programs for restoring mental health. The "casualty" rate was notably but not surprisingly high—at least 10 per cent; the term "casualty" designates participants whose psychological state had deteriorated by maladaption or an increased anxiety factor.[5]

It concluded, "Encounter groups present a clear and evident danger if they are used for radical [psychic] surgery in which the product will be a new man."

Our survey of the Mystic Healers should end where it began, with a declaration of "faith." Faith is, and always has been, the foundation of the healing arts, mystical or mundane. A "new man" is forever the objective. Restored flesh, or bone, or nerve, revitalized emotion, mental, or spiritual health, all are meant to lead to this end. Faith and a new well-being is the hook and clasp of all healing, with everything between mere beads of ritual.

If we look back along the path of mystic healing that we have traveled, it may appear to have been populated by a strange variety of flora (formulae) and fauna (physicians). But, in truth, the journey has kept closely to the main trail. Limits of time and space have precluded excursions along the thousands of half-hidden byways of wondrous cures. Even the primary path has been traversed hurriedly, with names quickly noted, methods briefly mentioned, and mysteries but fleetingly revealed. Because most people really believe them to be "scientific" many of the modern mystic healers have not been discussed at all!

A final word of caution: the vast majority of "magic" potions and practitioners to be found in 1974, like those proclaimed throughout all history, will most likely not improve your health. Remember: If you would know the value of an elixir, ask the one for whom it did not work; if you would know the power of a healer, ask the patient whom he cannot cure.

Glossary

The following are clarifications of words and phrases either generally unfamiliar or peculiar to mystical healing or its practitioners. Italics indicate the word, or a form of it, will be found defined further elsewhere in the Glossary.

A

Absent diagnosing: a practitioner's spiritual or psychic evaluation of a subject's condition without him being physically present.

Alchemy (-ist, -ical): a form of philosophical and magical chemistry, often pictured as having as its ultimate goal the transmutation of base metals to precious ones and the discovery of the legendary *philosopher's stone* by which such feats were thought to be accomplished.

Alien consciousness: the personality of a dead human being or a non-human entity—usually one which has invaded an individual's psychic character; see *invasion, possession,* etc.

Animal magnetism; mesmerism: See magnetism.

Anthropomorphism: attributing human form or nature to gods, animals, or inanimate objects.

Aphonia: loss of voice due to physical or hysterical paralysis of the vocal cords.

Armageddon: In the Bible the final battle of Good and Evil, preceding Judgment Day.

Astral projection: the alleged ability of certain mystics to transmit the invisible or spiritual aspect of their living personalities, in a phantasmal or seemingly real apparition, to another location in space.

Astral self: the alleged psychic or spirit (not to be confused with soul) aspect of a human personality subject to the directions of an adept's mind; the *etheric* self. Not to be equated to a *Doppelgänger,* which is a separate entity.

Attunement (to the source of healing): heightened spiritual awareness of the origin and process of the power of divine curing.

Aura: an alleged emission of *etheric* energy exuding from the human (or other) body, varying in strength according to the body's physical and psychical condition.

Auric rupture: a break or violation of the *aura* which allows corruption, foreign influences, or non-human entities access to an individual's body and spirit.

B

Block: psychological barrier, usually self-imposed; common Freudian concept, now absorbed by many therapies, cults, etc.

Book of the Dead: usually either the Egyptian or Tibetan mystical writings relating to the ancient religions of those cultures.

C

Cabalistic (cabala): relating to an occult *theosophy* or system devoted to metaphysical interpretations of Scriptures and other writings by certain rabbis and Christian mystics.

Call: see *gift.*

Camp meetings: evangelical services, usually featuring a specialist or noted preacher in *fundamentalist* sermons, or, occasionally, *faith healers;* predecessor to the modern, more sophisticated *crusade.*

Canvas cathedrals: evangelists' tents.

Charged water: a solution allegedly infused with an unknown, but therapeutic, natural element or quality.

Chemotherapeutic: describing medical techniques employing chemicals.

Chirothesy: the healing by the "laying-on-of-hands."

Circuit rider: an itinerant minister, found today only in more inaccessible regions of the South.

Clairaudience: a sense which permits one to hear beyond the range of, or under conditions impossible for, normal audibility.

Clairvoyance: a perception beyond the range of, or under conditions impossible for, normal vision. Inaccurately, often used to collectively describe "extrasensory perception."

Cloning: the creation of exact copies of individuals by cultivating cells from their bodies.

Couéism: the doctrine of Emile Coué (1857-1926), a fashionable French psychotherapist of the 1920s who advocated a cheery optimism as a means of regaining health.

Conceptology: see concept therapy.

Concept therapy: a "philosophic" cult of alleged self-help, founded by Thurman Fleet, which employs *Couéistic* pseudo-psychoanalytic and sometimes chiropractic programs to correct most physical and nonphysical problems. Evolved into *Conceptology.*

Controlled hysteria: the skill of raising the emotional state of an individual, or crowd, to an abnormal, but directable, intensity.

Controls: spiritualistic *guides,* helpers. See *mediumism.*

Convulsionists: a group of religious fanatics who excite themselves into uncontrollable physical and psychological spasms.

Cosmic electricity: see mesmerism, gravitas universales, effluvium, etc.

Cosmic spiritual harmony: an alleged mystical, theosophical, or religious state where one is "in tune" with universal well-being.

Crusades: a series of *evangelical* services, often held in a number of different cities, frequently in rapid succession; sometimes several days of gospel meetings in one community.

D

Deliverance: a term used by some groups, e.g., certain Assemblies of God churches, to indicate being "saved," "coming to Christ," etc.; often also indicating a "cure" of an infirmity.

Devices: instruments or designs; occasionally plans.

Diaduction: modern term for *gravitas universales, ether, effluvium,* etc.

Doppelgänger: the *"etheric"* double of a living person; some religions and cults believe that all individuals have such a terrestrial twin in the form of another human being or a bodiless spirit which under particular circumstances may usurp from physical beings their natural habitation; rarely, an allusion to a non-human entity assuming the appearance of a given individual for the purpose of permanently displacing or destroying him.

E

Effluvium: an alleged extrasensory element which permeates man, according to some, and fills the universe, in the cosmology of others; it is capable of restoring health. See *ether, magnetism.*

Elixirs: potions, medicines.

Ether (ic, -icism): a variation of the ineffable energy postulated by *magnetism;* the invisible "fifth" element of the universe which, when attracted to the human body, could relieve it of all its ills. See *gravitas universales.*

Etheric body: an *astral self;* a *Doppelgänger.*

Etheric disease: illness of the spirit; disorder of the psychic self.

Evangelism (ist, -ical): preaching of the gospel; applied to certain Protestant denominations, e.g., Baptist, Methodist, who profess that salvation is achieved by a submission to, and a unity with Jesus, rather than through the sacraments and good works; especially used to designate the more zealous gospel preachers and crusading revivalists.

Exorcism: the practice of exorcism is prehistoric, and has always been primarily religious in nature—in contradistinction to spiritualistic or para-psychological, for example. Explicitly it connotes the temporary subjugation or influencing of devils or other evil spirits to the human will by oaths and rituals. On occasion it has questionably been applied to conjuration, but in more modern times, it has alluded to the specific expelling of diabolical *entities* and *forces,* from individuals whose minds or personalities have been invaded.

A highly specialized activity in Judaic Law and in formal Christian churches, including the Greek, Old Catholic, and Roman. It is the province of one of the minor orders of each of the last three, but requires the approval of the regional bishop for its practice, which, in true and proper cases, is quite rare.

In black magic, and other occult arts, forms of exorcism exist. However, they are different in nature and practice from those described above, and even less frequently encountered.

F

Fundamentalism (-ist, -istic): a set of religious beliefs founded on a literal interpretation of the Bible, particularly with respect to the gospels and charismatic acts; characteristic of certain Protestant sects.

G

Gift: an alleged para-normal ability to do what appears impossible, e.g., healing the sick, foretelling the future.

Gift of knowledge: allegedly divinely inspired clairvoyance or prophecy. See *gift, call,* etc.

Glossalalia: hysteric or ecstatic utterances of unintelligible sounds, regarded by Pentecostal and other sects as divinely inspired, and even having some profound indecipherable meaning; in *parapsychology,* sometimes the speaking of a language, while in a trance state, not known to the subject when in a normal, waking condition; known also as "speaking in tongues."

Gravitas universales: cosmic influences; see *mesmerism.*

Guides: a term often used by mediums to describe those spirits of dead persons who "speak" to them.

H

Healing: restoring or establishing health by heterodox or thaumaturgic medicine.

Healing, Absent: a practitioner's alleged spiritual or psychic curing of a patient without the patient's being physically present.

Healing, Animal: a practitioner's alleged curing of animals, usually pets; far more common in England than the United States.

Healing, Charismatic: allegedly the restoration of health by means of divinely inspired *gifts; laying-on-of-hands.*

Healing, Faith: alleged curing of ills by psychic or spiritual means, or divine intercession; term used mostly in the United States.

Healing intelligences: allegedly divine, possibly angelic, representatives of God, who act for Him through living human beings to accomplish miraculous cures.

Healing, Machine: alleged therapy employing functioning instruments or stabile devices, rather than mere chemicals, charms, or purely *thaumaturgic* forces.

Healing, Mind science: a "school" of alleged psychic therapists, usually expressing the meditative or psychoanalytic approach; often featuring mystic, religious, or theosophical elaborations.

Healing pool: an alleged convergence of therapeutic spirituality; see also *hydrotherapy.*

Healing, Psychic: alleged curing of ills by means of parapsychological, occasionally spiritual, *gifts;* usually claiming extranormality rather than religiosity.

Healing, Psychological: alleged non-physical curing of mental disorders, not necessarily spiritual or religious in nature or technique; physical therapy achieved through influencing the thought processes.

Healing, Scriptural: according to Kathryn Kuhlman, truly divinely inspired curing, replicating the Biblical miracles, in contradistinction to psychic or contemporary *faith healing.*

Helper: see *guides.*

Holy rock: music applying a rock-and-roll style to gospel tunes.

Holy rollery: derived from a fundamentalist sect (Holy Rollers) which worships by shouting and physical agitation, even flailing about on the ground.

Holy stones: pebbles allegedly imbued with magical properties.

Homeopathy: system of medical treatment based on the theory certain diseases can be cured by giving very small doses of drugs which in a healthy person and in large doses would produce symptoms like those of the disease; colloquially, the use of herbs and other botanical products for medical purposes.

Humanetics: a "philosophic" cult of alleged self-help, founded by Richard W. Wetherill, which claims "wrong thinking" is the basis of most physical and non-physical problems.

I

Incantation: chanting of any sequence of words or mystical sounds in worship or to evoke a magical result.

Indian guide: see *medium.*

Invasion: allegedly the initial infringement of a foreign personality on an individual's psyche; the successful completion of which constitutes *possession.*

L

Laying on of hands: a phrase describing the Biblical, and comparable *thaumaturgic,* technique of spiritual medicine where the practitioner places his fingers or palms on the

patient's head or the afflicted portion of his body to
effect restoration of health.

License of validation: a recognition of an individual's ordination
by a religious organization.

Limbo: an hypothesized indeterminate state between the world
of life and whatever evolutionary stage may be the
natural successor to death; a condition of being caught
above one plane of existence and below another; halfway to the astral level.

Logos: in Greek philosophy (viz., the word) reason, regarded as
the controlling principle of this universe; the crux of
early Christian theological argument, particularly in
Hellenic metaphysics.

Lost souls: those whom an individual preacher or an entire religion regard as not having achieved salvation, i.e., unity
with Jesus, an ordained place in a heaven, eternal life.

M

Medium: a spiritualistic practitioner; one who claims the ability
to establish contact with the personalities of persons
who have died, or with non-human entities who exist
on other "planes." Until recently common procedure
had such communication achieved via a *guide,* or *control,* i.e., an advocate (very frequently the spirit of an
American Indian) who could function between life and
death; today the tendency has been for mediums to
assert their contacts are direct, or, at least, are imple-
mented by less exotic *helpers* (perhaps a Scottish physician, a New England ship captain, or other like individuals who died in the late 17th or early 18th century).
There are a number of different categories of mediums,
and their prestige often is based upon the degree and
kind of power they allegedly possess, e.g., clairvoyant
medium (as distinguished from a non-mediumistic
clairvoyant), voice medium, physical medium.

Mentalist(s): properly a theatrical performer who simulates telepathy; colloquially, telepathists, clairvoyants, etc.; occasionally *hypnotists*.

Mesmerism: the thesis and practice of Franz Anton Mesmer (1734-1815) that there exists a universal element or quality necessary to human health, the lack of which causes illness, which can only be alleviated by the restoration of this essence, bringing the subject into cosmic harmony again.

Metaphysical: to traditionalists in the *occult,* almost anything purportedly magical.

Metaphysical minister: any practitioner of various "churches" which often incline more toward being societies of "ethics"; see *Theosophy.*

Mystical fluid: see *gravitas universales, effluvium, mesmerism.*

N

Natural anointment: see *the gift.*

Necromancy (-er): by the use of human or animal corpses, or parts thereof, to allegedly communicate with personalities who have died.

O

Occult: what is covered or concealed; to be revealed only to adepts of magical arts and practices; colloquially, a collective term used to designate various types of *"metaphysical"* schools, e.g., *alchemy,* true astrology (not to be confused with the vast majority of what is merchandised in the United States); improperly applied to 1. pseudo-arcane crafts such as graphology, the commonly encountered palmistry and tea-leaf reading, 2. *extrasensory perception* or *parapsychology.*

Occult reading: any number of evaluations, anticipations, analyses, or advice, the base of which is one of the mystic arts, e.g., certain techniques of divination, *tarot* interpretation, and non-parapsychological clairvoyance.

Oracle: a purported channel through which divine beings convey information, or their wishes, to human beings; a seer or prophet.

Orgone box: a specially constructed cabinet (usually of wood and lamb's wool) designed to capture orgone energy, in which the subject sits to be "recharged."

Orgone energy: a universal element postulated by Wilhelm Reich (1897-1957), the lack of which contributes to physical and mental ills. A modern version of *gravitas universales, ether,* and *effluvium.*

Osteopathy: a theory that most, or all, illness is the result of the displacement of bones, causing pressure on nerves and/or blood vessels, which skeletal manipulation will cure; forerunner to contemporary chiropractic.

Outré medicine: eccentric therapy; heterodox healing.

P

Pantheism: the thesis that God is not an individual but the composite of all the natural laws of the universe; or the recognition of the worship of gods of all religions, sects, and cults.

Parapsychology: the study of "psychic phenomena," or effects inexplicable by traditional concepts of "natural law."

Pentecostal: A description of Protestant (and some segments of the Roman Catholic and Eastern Orthodox) *fundamentalist* churches which adopt a literal interpretation of the Bible and emphasize direct inspiration from the *Holy Spirit,* often practicing in the regular course of their worship *glossalalia,* prophecy, and *healing.*

Philosopher's stone: a legendary *alchemical* catalyst by which base metals could be transmuted into precious ones.

Physical mediumship: a form of *spiritualism* or *psychic phenomena* which allegedly produces physical manifestations of the absent party, e.g., levitation, materialization, etc.

Placebo: a harmless, unmedicated concoction given to a patient to humor him psychologically; original Latin: "I shall please." Found in Catholic vespers service for the dead.

Planted patient: "shills" or pretenders placed in an audience by alleged *healers* to proclaim that their ills have been cured.

Poltergeist: a destructive energy force projected, often involuntarily, from a human being (usually a minor); a mildly malevolent entity devoted to incidental mischief; occasionally, and questionably, a prankish ghost. Almost always occurring in whatever purported form where children around the age of puberty are to be found.

Possession: the alleged usurpation of a body, or the subjugation of a spirit (brain), by a human personality who has died, by a non-human entity, or by devils, as agents of Lucifer, or Satan himself. Religionists contend that it must be cured by *exorcism.*

Post-hypnotic suggestion: the introduction of a direction while a subject is in a hypnotic condition, to be acted upon after he "awakes."

Potions: elixirs, medicines.

Poultice: a medicated bandage applied to a sore or infection; originally cloth soaked in the liquefactions or salves of herbs.

Proxy patient: a "stand-in" for, or representative of, the actual subject, used in some of the mechanical charlatanry of the 1920s in the United States.

Psychic phenomena: occurrences, mental or physical, which appear to have no present scientific explanation, but may have a logical rather than a "mystical" one. Any of the alleged "extrasensory perceptions," e.g., *clairvoyance,* psychometry, precognition.

Psychodrama: a *group therapy* technique, made popular by Jacob L. Moreno, which employs the dramatizing, or acting out, of an individual's problems, usually with counter participation or subsequent criticism.

Psychokinesis (-etic): the moving of matter by means of alleged "mental energy," without any physical contact between subject and object.

R

Radiant emission: unidentifiable energy allegedly exuded from an individual; *astral* or *etheric* force generated by the human body.

Recidivistic cure: an apparent further *healing* where the affliction reappears and the subject becomes again diseased, crippled, or otherwise infirm.

Rhinoplasty: operation for the purpose of reconstructing or altering the configuration of the human nose.

Rhythmist(s): an individual allegedly in harmony with the natural state of the universe.

S

Sacrarium: shrine, sanctuary; a basin, usually with a drain, used for religious purposes, such as baptism.

Sadomasochism (-ist, -istic): from Comte Donatien Alphonse François de Sade (1740-1814) and Leopold von Sacher-Masoch (1836-1895); coexistence of sadism and masochism in a single individual; describing a relationship between a sadist and a masochist; socially, the interplay physically, psychologically, emotionally (often in charade) of a voluntary (usually disguised as involuntary) pain exchange between two, or more, persons.

Sawdust trail (occasionally, path): a term alluding to the aisle(s) leading to the salvation platform and the *evangelist* in revival *crusades,* so called because of the sawdust liberally spread on the earth floor, especially in wet weather, beneath old-style *camp-meeting* tents.

Science of mind: name and phrase used by different groups generally propounding an "ethical religion," often with modified *theosophical* embellishments.

Seed faith: the promulgation of spiritual conviction and prayer which will allegedly be rewarded by a manifold response to one's own needs and petitions. A term and thesis of Oral Roberts.

Sensitive(s): a general term indicating any practitioner of alleged mediumship, psychic abilities, etc.

Sexual cures: any of the therapies which recommend or demand sex as a technique for restoration of mental health, i.e., in practice, often with the practitioner or other patients, rather than in understanding or phantasizing (Freudianism). Numerous contemporary therapies, especially of the group type, prescribe such programs, although most deny this publicly.

Shaman (-ism): a priest or medicine man of tribes in Northeast Asia who allegedly can influence good and evil spirits; also applied to like mystics among Eskimos and Indians of Canada and the United States.

Speaking in tongues: see *glossalalia*.

Spirit guide(s): see *guides, medium*.

Spiritism, spiritualism: allegedly the practice of communicating with personalities who have died; also, occassionally, with non-human entities who purportedly exist on other "planes." See *medium*.

Spiritportation: a religious version for *teleportation*.

Spiritual proxy: see *healing, absent*.

Spontaneous remission: the reversal of a (usually progressive) disease's development or the degeneration of some aspect of health, often suddenly, for which no scientific explanation is available.

Stigmatist (-ta, -tism): one who inexplicably, suddenly or gradually, becomes the vehicle of the crucifixion wounds of Christ, sometimes periodically, sometimes persistently. Theologically, occasionally regarded as of divine origin, although (e.g., in Roman Catholicism) increasingly less frequently. Medically, usually viewed as a manifestation of a highly particularized religious hysteria functioning psychosomatically.

Suggestive hypnotism: see *post-hypnotic* suggestion.

Supernormal: exceptional; beyond the norm, but within natural laws.

Syllogistic: describing a reasoning process where a conclusion is drawn from a major and a minor premise, e.g., all cats are feline (major); the Countess Marya Zaleska is a cat (minor); therefore, the Countess Marya Zaleska is feline (conclusion).

T

Tarot cards: any of a number of packs of cards, with various series of numeric and pictorial depictions, each subject to dissimilar interpretations, primarily used for allegedly revealing the past, evaluating the present, and predicting the future.

Telekinesis (-etic): the alleged moving of matter from a distance, precluding any physical contact between subject and object, purportedly by mental or psychic energy. See *psychokinesis.*

Telepathy (ic): the alleged communication of thought directly from brain to brain without regard for distance, intervening matter, or the employing of any recognized sensorial techniques, i.e. speech, gesture, etc; inaccurately "mental telegraphy."

Teleportation: the alleged transference of an object or person from one point to another by seemingly non-physical means, without regard for intervening matter. The process is usually, but not necessarily, instantaneous, and most frequently over a considerable distance. Not to be confused with *astral projection,* a purported phenomenon restricted to the *etheric* self.

Testifier: an allegedly cured individual who gives an account of his *healing,* or a witness for any religious experience.

Testimony (-ies, -ials): declarations affirming the improvement or cure of a disease or affliction by the intervention of, or petition to, a divine source; like assertions respecting psychic (not necessarily religious) alleged therapies.

Thaumaturgy (-ic, -ist): magic; the purported performance of miracles.

Theosophy (-ist, -ical): any of several semi-religious systems which propose cosmic unity or absorption by meditation; specifically a cult begun by Maria Petrovna Blavatsky, and developed by Annie Besant and C. W.

Leadbeater, consisting of an amalgam of numerous Eastern and Western philosophies and religions.

Time gap: the period from the initiation of the curing process to its total fulfillment.

Trance diagnosis and healing: alleged spiritual or psychic evaluation of a patient's condition while the practitioner is in a self-, or otherwise, induced hypnotic state; famous for its employment by Edgar Cayce.

Trance (state): an induced altered consciousness in a variety of intensities of the hypnotic condition, e.g., "light," "somnambulistic," etc.

Transference: in psychotherapy, specifically Freudianism, the redirection, by the patient, of an emotional emphasis from one person, usually a parent, to the practitioner.

U

Unfoldment: spiritual evolution, in this life.

W

Way-showers: guides (in the usual, not mediumistic or spiritualistic, sense).

Selected Bibliography

There are literally hundreds of volumes dealing with the general field of mystic healing. Those listed are among the works consulted for this book and will furnish a broad picture of this bizarre and curious world. An asterisk (*) following the title of any work indicates that it is an autobiography, or an "official" biography, and therefore may be regarded as essentially propagandistic. Of course, some of the "critical" works may also be biased—in the other direction.

Binet, Alfred, and Férè. *Le magnetisme animal.* Paris: Alcan Company, 1887.

Bishop, George. *Faith Healing: God or Fraud?* Los Angeles: Sherbourne Press, 1967.

Carson, Gerald. *The Roguish World of Dr. Brinkley.* New York: Holt, Rinehart & Winston, 1960.

Caustic, Christopher (pseud. of T. G. Fessenden). *Terrible Tractoration!! A Poetical Petition Against Galvanising Trumpery, and the Perkinistic Institution.* New York: Samuel Stansbury, 1904.

Church, Gene, and Carnes, Conrad D. *The Pit: A Group Encounter Defiled.* New York: Outerbridge and Lazard, 1973.

Eddy, Mary Baker. *The People's Idea of God: Its Effect on Health and Christianity.** 6th ed. Cambridge, Massachusetts: J. Wilson and Son, 1895.

Eddy, Mary Baker. *Science and Health.** 1st ed. Boston: Christian Science Publishing Company, 1875.

Eddy, Mary Baker. *Science and Health.* Vol. II (actually 2nd ed., not second volume).* Lynn, Massachusetts: Dr. A. G. Eddy, 1878.

Eddy, Mary Baker. *Science and Health.** 3rd ed. Lynn, Massachusetts: Dr. Asa G. Eddy, 1882.

Eddy, Mary Baker. *Science and Health.** 19th rev. ed. Boston: First Church of Christian Science, 1886.

Eddy, Mary Baker. *Science of Man by which the Sick are Healed, or, Questions and Answers in Moral Science.** Lynn, Massachusetts: T. P. Nichols, 1876.

Edwards, Harry. *The Healing Intelligence.** Burrows Lea, Shere, Guildford, Surrey, England: The Healer Publishing Company, Ltd., 1965.

Edwards, Harry. *Spirit Healing.** Burrows Lea, Shere, Guildford, Surrey, England: The Healer Publishing Company, Ltd., 1960.

Gilson, Etienne. *History of Christian Philosophy in the Middle Ages.* New York: Random House, 1955.

Grier, William H., and Cobbs, Price M. *Black Rage.** New York: Basic Books, 1968.

Hall, Manly Palmer. *The Story of Healing: The Divine Art.** New York: Citadel Press, 1958.

Holbrook, Stewart H. *The Golden Age of Quackery.* New York: The Macmillan Company, 1959.

Hudson, Thomas J. *The Law of Psychic Phenomena.* Chicago: A. C. McClurg and Company, 1897.

Humbard, Rex. *Miracles in My Life.** New York: New American Library, 1972. (paperback)

John of the Cross, St. *Ascent of Mount Carmel* (trans. E. Allison Peers). Garden City, New York: Doubleday and Company, 1958. (paperback)

Kallet, Arthur. *100,000,000 Guinea Pigs.* New York: F. J. Schlink, 1933.

Leadbeater, C. W. *The Science of the Sacraments.* Madras, India: The Theosophical Publishing House, 1957.

Leuret, François, and Bon, Henri. *Modern Miraculous Cures** (trans. A. T. Macqueen and John C. Barry). New York: Farrar, Straus and Cudahy, 1957.

Lieberman, Morton, Yalom, Irvin D., and Miles, Matthew B.

Encounter Groups: First Facts. New York: Basic Books, 1973.

Maliver, Bruce. *The Encounter Game.* New York: Stein and Day, 1973.

Millard, Joseph. *Edgar Cayce: Mystery Man of Miracles.** rev. ed. Greenwich, Connecticut: Fawcett Publications, 1967. (paperback)

Maltz, Maxwell. *Psycho-cybernetics:** *A New Way to Get More Living Out of Life.* Englewood Cliffs, New Jersey: Prentice-Hall, 1960.

Moreno, Jacob L. *Psychodrama.** New York: Beacon House, 1946.

Mumford, James Gregory. *A Narrative of Medicine in America.* Philadelphia: J. B. Lippincott, 1903.

Ostrander, Sheila, and Schroeder, Lynn. *Psychic Discoveries Behind the Iron Curtain.* Englewood Cliffs, New Jersey: Prentice-Hall, 1970.

Peale, Norman Vincent. *The Power of Positive Thinking.** Englewood Cliffs, New Jersey: Prentice-Hall, 1952.

Phillips, Jeane. *Mary Baker Eddy Early Writings Compared with the Quimby Manuscripts.* Pasadena, California: Toujour Publishing Company, 1931.

Quimby, Phineas. "The Quimby Manuscripts," unpublished papers in the Library of Congress, Washington, D.C. Copy made by E. E. Collis also available at the 42nd Street Branch of the New York Public Library. Reproduced in 1939.

Roberts, Oral. *The Call.** Garden City, New York: Doubleday and Company, 1972.

Roberts, Oral. *Deliverance from Fear and Sickness.** Tulsa, Oklahoma: Privately printed, 1954, rev. ed. 1967. (paperback)

Roberts, Oral. *If You Need Healing Do These Things.** Tulsa, Oklahoma: Privately printed, 1947, 3rd rev. ed. 1965. (paperback)

Roberts, Oral. *Miracle of Seed-Faith.* Tulsa, Oklahoma: Privately printed, 1970; 16th printing, 1972.

Roberts, Oral. *The Miracle Book.* Tulsa, Oklahoma: Pinoak Publications, 1972.

Schutz, William C. *Joy: Expanding Human Awareness.** New York: Grove Press, 1968.

Smith, Joseph T. *An Historical Sketch of Dr. Elisha Perkins, Inventor of the Metallic Retractors.* Baltimore: Privately printed, 1910.

Spence, Lewis. *An Encyclopaedia of Occultism.* Hyde Park, New York: University Books, 1960.

Stearn, Jess. *Edgar Cayce: The Sleeping Prophet.** Garden City, New York: Doubleday and Company, 1967.

Stewart, Don, with Wagner, Walter. *The Man from Miracle Valley.** Long Beach, California: Great Horizons, 1971. (paperback)

Street, Noel. *Pathway to Spiritual Healing.** London: Regency Press, 1965.

Sudre, René. *Parapsychology.* New York: Citadel Press, 1960.

Sugrue, Thomas. *There Is a River.* New York: Holt, Rinehart & Winston, 1942.

Thornton, Francis Beauchesne. *The Catholic Shrines in the United States and Canada.** New York: Wilfred Funk, Inc., 1954.

Wagner, Karl. *Report on Father Pio.** Ebreichsdorf, Austria: J. Probst, 1967. (paperback)

Wirz, Paul. *Exorcism and the Art of Healing in Ceylon.* Leyden, Holland: Brill Company, 1954.

Young, James Harvey. *The Medical Messiahs.* Princeton, New Jersey: Princeton University Press, 1967.

Young, James Harvey. *The Toadstool Millionaires: A Social History of Health Quackery in Twentieth-Century America.* Princeton, New Jersey: Princeton University Press, 1961.

Zweig, Stefan. *Mental Healers.* (trans. Edward Cedar Paul). Garden City, New York: Garden City Publishing Company, 1934.

Index

A. A. Allen Revivals, Inc., 79, 85, 88–89
Abrams, Dr. Albert, 51–53
Absent healing, 152–153, 166–167
Abundant Life, publication of Oral Roberts's Evangelistic Association, 76–77
Academy of Science, Paris, 26
Ada, Oklahoma, 70–71
Agpaoa, Anthony, 136, 204–207
Akron, Ohio, 94
Allen, Asa Alonso, 69, 77–81, 84–90, 100–101, 105–107, 109
American Cancer Society, 54
American Medical Association, 49
Animal magnetism, 24, 27, 29, 46
Arigo, José, 207–209
Assembly of God, religious sect, 83, 194
Association for Research and Enlightenment, 67. *See also* Cayce, Edgar
Association of Unity Churches, 132
Auditor, 213, 215. *See also* Scientology
Augsburg Academy, Germany, 23
Aura, 171

Balfour, Sir James, on Charles I, 18
Barbanell, Maurice, 150
Bastien and Bastienne, by Mozart, 22
Bateman's Pectoral Drops, 48
Baughman, Dr. John Lee, 100, 132–149, 194

Bavarian Academy of the Sciences, 23
Beethoven, as friend of Mesmer, 22
Belk, William Henry, 206, 208
Bennett Medical College, 55
Bernadette of Lourdes (Bernadette Soubirous), 183–184. *See also* Lourdes Shrine
Bernard, Saint, 17
Bernard, Dr. Robert, 19
Bernhard of the Netherlands, Prince, 202
Biery, Dr. Martin, 124
Billy-des-Fontaines Shrine, 19
Bishop, George, 102–103
Bludenz, Austria, 21
Book of the Dead, The, 16
Boone, Nicholas, 47. *See also* Perkins, Elisha
Boone, Pat, 76, 97
Braid, 13, 29, 211
Brindrin, Dr. Paul, 223
Brinkley, John R., 55–61
Brinkley, Minnie T., 57–58
Brinkley Operation, The, by John R. Brinkley, 59
British Medical Association, 161
British Medical Council, 161
British Weekly, 48
Brockton Hospital, London, 152
Burris, Jackie, 92, 96
Butler, Pennsylvania, 122–123

Cabrini, Mother Frances Xavier, 188–189